STOCK MARKET INVESTING

Guided by

RISK MANAGEMENT

100% data-driven methodology
with risk management guiding tactical decisions

- 1st Edition -

Sidney Shauy, MBA

Rodrigo B. Shauy

PALLAS VESTA
PUBLISHING CO. LLC

Published by Pallas Vesta Publishing Company LLC, New Jersey, USA

PALLAS VESTA
PUBLISHING CO. LLC

Pallas Vesta Publishing Company LLC
New Jersey, NJ – United States of America

Discounts for bulk sales are available. Please contact us by email below.

ISBN: 978-1-960691-09-5 (eBook)
ISBN: 978-1-960691-10-1 (Paperback)
ISBN: 978-1-960691-11-8 (Hardcover)

First Edition: August 2024

www.Engineering-Finance.com   www.RISP500.com

Printed in the United States of America. Reviewed by Rodrigo B. Shauy. Cover design by Microsoft CoPilot AI. Less than 2% of content assisted by ChatGPT.

SPECIAL THANKS

To my family, for their unconditional love and support, always

To my parents and grandparents, my eternal gratitude

To my mentors, for their wisdom and inspiration

GENERAL DISCLAIMER

While a great deal of care has been taken to provide accurate, informative, and helpful material on the subjects addressed in the book, neither the publisher nor the author is responsible for any errors and omissions, or the results obtained from the use of this information. The book contains ideas and opinions of the author. The strategies outlined in the book may not be suitable for every person under any circumstances, and they are not warranted or guaranteed to produce any particular results. The book is intended to provide general information for educational purposes only.

The book is sold with the understanding that neither the author nor the publisher is engaged in providing legal, business, financial, investment, tax, accounting, securities or any other professional advice. The author is not a licensed advisor. The reader should always consult with their own trusted and licensed professional advisors before adopting any of the suggested strategies in the book or drawing inferences from them. The contents of this book are provided "as is," without guarantees of accuracy, completeness, or timeliness regarding the results obtained from their use. The reader assumes full responsibility for the use of this information and uses it at their own risk. Neither the author nor the publisher will be liable for any direct, indirect, special, incidental, consequential, or punitive damages of any nature. In no event, whatsoever, will the author, Sidney Shauy, nor the publisher, Pallas Vesta Publishing Company LLC, their related companies, partners, agents, employees, associates, service providers, or their employees, be liable to readers or anyone for any decision or action taken in reliance on the contents of this book and its consequences. The information and all figures in this book that were accurate at the time of the writing may become inaccurate or outdated with the passage of time and by changes in the economy and markets. New laws and taxes may be enacted. Figures, including prices and rates, and assumptions are not guaranteed and are subject to change at any time. Any slights against individuals, groups, organizations, or companies are unintentional. Models used in the book are based on assumptions, which may or may not apply to everyone, and are subject to errors, omissions, and change. All models are simplifications of reality and must be understood as such. As in all models, assumptions, and numerical examples in the book, it has been stressed multiple times that individual results vary based on a wide range of factors related to each person's unique set of circumstances, needs, goals, quality of execution of strategies, in addition to uncontrollable factors, such as the moment and status of the economy and markets.

Clarification about references to S&P 500® :

S&P 500® is a trademark of S&P Global. It has nothing to do with the RISP 500™, which is a stock market risk metric developed by the authors based on data related to the S&P 500®, through a proprietary algorithm owned by Risk Scientific LLC.

About the Author

Sidney Shauy is an analytics-driven investor/trader using quantitative methods and risk management. The author has over 30 years of combined experience with world financial markets in leading global banks - Citigroup, Morgan Stanley, Lloyds Bank, ABN Amro, Bilbao Vizcaya, in New York, Hong Kong, and Sao Paulo - and real estate syndication investing and insurance structuring. In about 20 years, the author worked in all key functions in the trading floor: trading, portfolio management, structuring, and risk management. The author has managed multi-billion dollar portfolios for his employers successfully during multiple financial crises since the 1990s. In recent years, he worked with high net worth clients helping them strategize and structure investment portfolios and served as *subject matter expert* to prominent global strategy consulting firms on select projects. Expert in financial derivatives on multiple asset classes – stocks, currency, interest rates, commodities - including hybrid and exotic derivatives, he is constantly testing market data to develop new algorithms.

Automation engineer by training and quadrilingual, Sidney Shauy earned an MBA degree from the Wharton School at the University of Pennsylvania.

Site: www.Engineering-Finance.com

Blog: engineering-finance.medium.com

Site: www.risp500.com/

SIDNEY SHAUY

ENGINEERING FINANCE

Building Futures Together

Table of Contents

Preamble

Imagine for a minute a world in which you could know ahead of time, and especially ahead of others, where the market is going to go next, or what the next price about to be printed on the tape is going to be. This would not only solve all problems we face as investors and traders, but would also give us an edge over the rest of the playing field. We could avert every market crash. We could also fully exploit bull market rallies. We would time the market to perfection! Even if there is just a tiny time advantage letting us know this information slightly earlier than others, it would already give us a gigantic investor outperformance, would it not?

Back to reality now. Even though a "crystal ball" letting us see the future with certainty doesn't exist, what is the next best alternative to guide us in a world with so much uncertainty? It's a dangerous world where one single bad trade or a sudden market crash coming from nowhere could so easily erase the performance we tirelessly built in a year or more without mercy. Ask yourself these questions right now: Am I using the BEST tools to manage my investments? Are these tools efficiently protecting my P/L during market downturns <u>and</u> helping me profit during market rallies? And last but not least, am I being properly rewarded for the risks I'm taking?

When you hear the words "risk management", what exactly comes to mind? Perhaps words like VAR (Value at Risk), stop loss, hedging, diversification, beta, Sharpe ratio, Monte Carlo simulation, volatility, correlation, etc. etc., right? While this is all good stuff and widely used as risk management metrics and methods, they do only exactly what they were designed to do: help you manage investment risks. That's all. They help you control your risks by covering or adjusting your positions but they don't help you avert losses by avoiding risk altogether when it knocks the door. Remember, if you had a crystal ball, you wouldn't even need risk management because you wouldn't be a sitting duck exposed to extreme risky situations; rather, you would have already been completely out of the market in safety positions early on. You would not be hit by the downturn. But a crystal ball doesn't exist. So, what now?

We believe in **Stock Market Investing Guided by Risk Management (SMIGRM)**, in which risk management takes a more central role helping investors and traders make decisions by **exploiting risks instead of being pushed around by them**. Remember the very reason you make a profit in the stock market is that you took risks for it in the first place, isn't it? If you did, are risks front and center in your decision-making process? If not, it's not your fault: you never had the tools. Risk management may have served you well as a secondary tool but it's about time that it evolved to take a more proactive and central role.

In the book, we are going to show you how SMIGRM and the RISP 500™ Project is taking risk management to become the **next best alternative to a crystal ball**. Far-fetched? Impossible? We believe you will be pleasantly surprised!

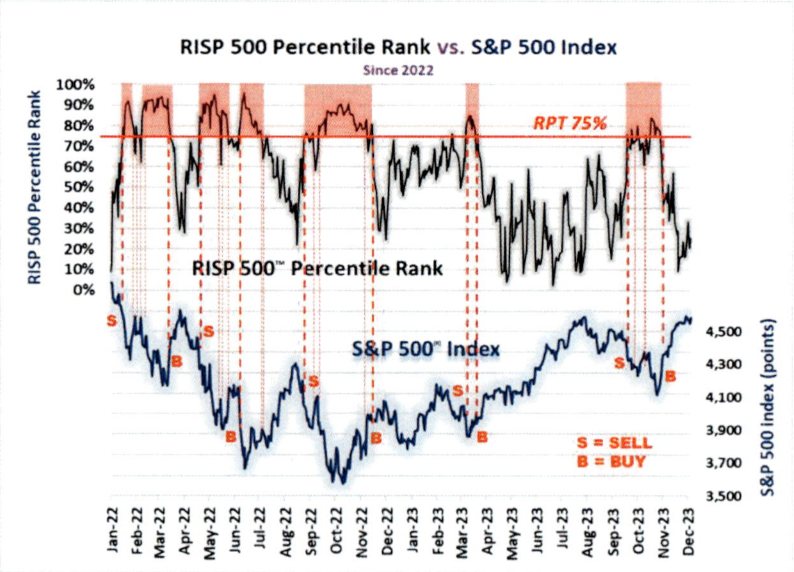

STOCK MARKET INVESTING
Guided by
RISK MANAGEMENT

CHAPTER 1

1. Designing a Roadmap to Investment Success

Stock Market Investing Guided by Risk Management (SMIGRM) may be a novel concept for you but you will quickly grasp the concept and the method because we will guide you step by step following a logical train of thought. For this introduction, let's discuss its 5 main pillars:

- The Risk vs. Return Duality
- Static vs. Dynamic Asset Allocation
- Asset Performance vs. Risk Environment
- Deterministic vs. Probabilistic World
- The Secret to Success: Statistical Edge + Asymmetrical Payoff + Law of Large Numbers

These concepts are foundational to the method, which is the reason they are presented here before you read the core of the book. Hope you will enjoy the journey! More importantly, I hope it will open your mind to a new world of possibilities for you and help you achieve much better results as an investor or a professional wealth manager.

Investor Preferences Are Evolving

Before we delve into the core concepts listed above, let's just take a quick step back and discuss two current developments as we move on to complete the first quarter of the 21st century. One interesting movement is the exponential adoption of index funds. First introduced in the early 1990s as an alternative to mutual funds, ETFs tracking the most popular stock market indexes, e.g., S&P 500®, Nasdaq 100, etc., gained increasing popularity over the years. The second interesting development that has been slowly gaining traction over the years is the emergence of the DIY Investor (Do It Yourself). More people are gradually trying to manage their own investments. For a variety of reasons, right or wrong, the fact is that this crowd is taking financial matters in their own hands. Technology has obviously helped fuel this trend. In a way, this phenomenon is not limited only to personal finance; people are increasingly searching for answers online and seeking education in all fields and aspects of life. The medical doctor is no longer the only source of trusted information. Nor are attorneys, mechanics, and others considered sole authorities in their respective fields. Information technology, and now artificial intelligence, are changing people's attitudes. Advisors and wealth managers need to be one step ahead and deliver above average results to really distinguish themselves. With this in mind, let's discuss how these major trends impact investment performance for investors.

Is Passive Investing the Final Answer?

Last decade, billionaire investor Warren Buffett famously bet a million dollars with the investment management industry that over a period of 10 years, actively managed funds would not beat the S&P 500® index. Although he was widely recognized as one of the best stock pickers of all time, Warren Buffett was well aware of how hard it is to generate the elusive alpha by beating the S&P 500® index picking the right winning stocks and doing so consistently, year after year. The result: Warren Buffett has categorically won the bet. At the same time, over the last 10 years, we have witnessed an explosive growth in popularity of passive investing and massive amounts of investments flowing to index funds at the expense of actively managed funds. Index funds' assets under management (AUM) have grown about 12-fold from 2000 to 2022 (according to Statista) while actively managed funds doubled in the same period. A growing number of investors think that inexpensive passive index investing can get them better results than paying for the skill of fund managers to actively pick the right winning stocks. They have essentially given up on alpha. Right or wrong, only time will tell but it's a fact that investor attitudes have been changing over time. Fund managers may need to reinvent themselves, perhaps with the help of SMIGRM to be super-competitive, but what about investors? Is passive investing really the final answer?

Well, let's turn our attention to the most popular index funds which are those tracking the S&P 500® index. Numerous articles have been written in prominent news outlets discussing passive investing, sometimes referring to it as the "lazy investor" approach or the "Buy & Hold for the Long Run" approach. But could simply holding an investment passively in a S&P 500® index fund or ETF (e.g., SPY, IVV, etc.) for years be the best we can do to achieve long-term investing success? Well, this assertion only works if stocks always go up in the long run. But do they? Not really…

Actually, we don't even need to go too far to debunk the myth. We can use simple logic and some facts. A great number of people believe in a myth that is repeated so many times, especially by the mass media, that it became widely accepted as truth. If that statement were true, then passive investment must be the answer because all you have to do is absolutely nothing, even when the market is in meltdown mode, because you just have to have the patience to hold it long enough. That could be only in theory, because in reality, most investors will not have the stomach to keep holding a losing position in a crash beyond their tolerance level and will pull the plug at some point, eat an indigestible loss, and throw their plans out the window.

There are, of course, many reasons for stocks to go up most of the time, but there is not a single reason ***why*** stocks must ***always*** go up even *in the long run*. All there is to back this up is anecdotal evidence from the last 70-80 years of an impressive bull market run (marked by impressive crashes as well but essentially still a long bull market) for the U.S. stock market after World War II, when the U.S. dethroned the U.K. to become the world superpower. The U.S. dominated the world economy, led in technological innovation, and especially, had its own currency, the mighty U.S. dollar become the world's reserve currency. This gave the U.S. the unparalleled superpower at the world stage. After Nixon took the U.S. dollar out of the gold standard, the U.S. could now print as many dollars as it wished. Unlike any other country in the world, the U.S. could easily export its own woes, inflation, and financial crises to the rest of the world because they adopted it as their reserve currency. Yes, no country has ever had that kind of power and this was also one of the main pillars of the country's economic success in the last century. This obviously reflected on the S&P 500® during the same period. So, looking back, it gives you the impression that the argument is true: stocks do seem to always go up. But if you look at the charts of stock markets in other countries around the world, you will see that such an argument is much weaker. Now, back here in the U.S., the most important question we must ask ourselves is whether this bull market will continue well into the future. Will the U.S. still dominate the 21st century as it did the 20th century? And when we refer to "long run", how long is long enough?

Passive investing may certainly be a fantastic option if an eternal bull market could be guaranteed. But it can't. In addition, even if it could, every investor will still experience different outcomes depending on their particular entry and exit points to/from the market. You really don't have much control over the results. For these reasons, we believe passive investing is a good halfway solution at best. It could beat active investing (picking stocks) but it's still far from being the final answer, in our opinion.

The Risk vs. Return Duality

Is 10% a good rate of return for you? How about 20%? Well, it really depends on the amount of risk you took to earn such a return, doesn't it? As you know, there is a price to pay for the privilege to earn a return on an investment (ROI) — any type of investment for that matter. For example, 10% per year may be considered too good (even to be believable) for a 3-month T-bill backed by the full faith of the U.S. government but the same 10% is probably not be an attractive rate of return for a venture capital investment in an early-stage biotech startup betting on an unproven drug therapy. As the saying goes, there is no free lunch. The price to pay is called RISK. In fact, risk and return are an inseparable pair like the two sides of a coin: If you want to earn a higher rate of return, you must be willing to accept a higher amount of risk. Unfortunately, for marketing purposes in the investment management industry, the spotlight is always focused on returns. Risk is mentioned, of course, but rarely given the same attention and its due importance.

Now let's examine some facts. What is the long-term average return of the S&P 500®? Well, depending on the period in consideration, it typically varies from 8 to 12% a year on average. Is this a decent return? As you know, the market never moves in a straight line, so you will always have fantastic years, horrible years, boring years, crazy years, and everything in between. How about the risks investors must have taken to earn such a return? There are a dozen ways to measure risk, but in practice, one of the most useful metrics for investment risk is what is called a "drawdown." Simply put, if you aren't familiar with it, a drawdown is how much an investment is down from its most recent peak before it recovers back to the same peak. For example, during the 2008 financial crisis, the S&P 500® dropped 56.8% from October 2007 to March 2009, recovering all such losses only by March 2013. In other words, it took about 6 years just to undo the damage of the crash. Those holding the Nasdaq index experienced an even worse outcome. The Nasdaq 100 regained the previous peak only on April 23, 2015 following the 2000s internet bubble bust - it took 15 years just to break-even.

Now, let's go back to our initial question. Suppose you are buying and holding the S&P 500® in an index fund for the long run. How attractive would an investment be for you to expect to earn 8-12% per year on average, knowing that you could lose as much as 56.8% at any time? I don't know about you but I find such a prospect dreadful, to say the least. But that kind of risk is exactly what Buy & Holders for the Long Run are exposed to, most often without even realizing the danger. If it has already happened once; there is no reason why it couldn't happen again. And the longer they hold the position, the more likely they will experience another market crash. Note that we are not criticizing passive S&P 500® index investing because if you were holding individual stocks or a poorly-diversified portfolio of stocks, your drawdowns might and would invariably be even worse!

In other words, what has been sold as the safest way to invest may not be as safe as most people thought. The prospect of making 8-12% per year on average over a long period of time with the possibility of losing 50% or more from a single drawdown would no longer look as attractive after knowing this information. What we need is investing for a much better RoMaD (Return over Maximum Drawdown). The ratio must be attractive and sustain the test of time over a very long period. We will discuss RoMaD more in this book. It may hold the key to decide between investing in different assets and between different investing methods. We should always take the risk-return pair together into account when making investment decisions, never the expected return alone.

The most consequential aspect of the risk-return duality is that if you eliminate risk totally, return is also gone. That's why very low risk instruments like savings accounts pay ridiculous returns. As we will soon discuss the probabilistic world we live in, the goal is never to eliminate 100% of risks; the best we can and should do to succeed as investors is maximize the return-risk ratio (RoMaD), or maximize returns for the risks we take.

Buy & Hold for the Long Run is the ultimate static strategy. Its asset allocation is designed never to change over a very long period of time, rain or shine. But professional wealth managers do change asset allocations from time to time, for many reasons. It could be that they changed their view on the market or on a specific stock. It could be that they found a better opportunity. It could be that they got stopped out of a losing position. They may be just reacting to new pieces of information. Or it could also be that risks have risen too much. This is all good. But are they allocating the best possible assets in terms of performance in each risk scenario?

Static vs. Dynamic Asset Allocation

Ask yourself first: how dependent are your current investments on the stock market to be continuously on a bull market? If the stock market enters a bear market (e.g., 2022) or just moves sideways for long periods of time, what happens to your investments? Would they suffer as a result? We learned from history that bear markets may last weeks, months, and even years – what are you going to do during bear markets if you only have a strategy that works during bull markets?

Investors need strategies that perform well making money for them even when the stock market is down or going nowhere. When investors have strategies that are highly dependent only on the stock market having a shiny day, it is certainly a recipe for long-term underperformance. This explains why a great number of mutual funds and also hedge funds don't have stellar performance numbers, especially when the stock market refuses to cooperate. Everybody is a genius during bull markets. Many people blame the industry's fees but we believe the problem is deeper than that. We believe Stock Market Guided by Risk Management (SMIGRM) can solve these problems for both investors and wealth managers and we will show you how in this book.

The most common solution employed by the investment management industry to weather market downturns is asset allocation. They will trade to hedge or execute stops derisking portfolios when the situation turns bad, naturally, but asset allocation is the key and it will be maintained, fixed and balanced as much as possible. The most popular example is the mixed allocation with stocks and bonds. This is based on the belief that the correlation between returns of stocks and bonds are low, if not negative, which is to say that they tend to move in opposite directions. So, theoretically, assuming this is true, gains from bonds would compensate for at least some losses from stocks when the stock market faces headwinds. In fact, so strong is this belief that the industry created standard recommendations for people to use at any age. For younger folks, the recommendation is a higher allocation to stocks vs. bonds, e.g. 80% stocks vs. 20% bonds, and as they go up the age groups, the recommended allocation calls for less allocation to stocks and more to bonds. The reason is simple:

youngsters will have a much longer investment time horizon than older folks and such a balanced portfolio would be better able to weather market corrections and crashes encountered along the way. Older folks and pre-retirees just don't have enough time to recover from large dips and therefore they should allocate more bonds than stocks, the recommendation goes. The industry has even created and launched funds with target retirement dates planned for investors to conveniently place in their retirement money.

Unfortunately, however, we don't think the strategy is resting on a solid foundation. History tells us a different story about the correlation between stocks and bonds. The relationship between the duo is complex and a convoluted one, at best. Research shows that the correlation depends on the level of inflation, interest rates, expected growth rates for the economy, and even the stock market's volatility! If you recall, 2002 provides the best recent example. In that year, the S&P 500® lost 18.6%. Have bonds hedged the loss? Nope, bonds had their worst year in 97 years! According to the Vanguard Total Bond Index, bonds lost 13.7%. In other words, both went down, so no matter if you held a 60/40 or a 40/60 portfolio, you lost money anyway.

But even if the correlation assumption were true and bonds did hedge against stock losses, still the strategy isn't the smartest one. Why? Because you are always sacrificing returns in exchange for safety. You can say it's a cost for hedging, but it will dampen the return on the investment. Here's an example. The VBIAX is a good Vanguard's 60/40 balanced fund, which has a target allocation of 60% stocks and 40% bonds at all times with a low expense ratio. Since its inception on November 13th, 2000 until the time of this writing, the VBIAX has earned an annualized return of 6.70%. As you can see, some of the return earned in good times was sacrificed to hedge against potential losses during bad times.

See the problem? You could now be asking: why not allocate 100% to stocks in good times and rotate to 100% bonds in bad times instead of rigidly allocating 60% to stocks and 40% to bonds in a fixed allocation at all times? If you asked this question, you are on the right track to one of the fundamental pillars of SMIGRM. This is what we call a context-dependent dynamic allocation. In other words, instead of holding a fixed allocation that is suboptimal in all scenarios, why not match the assets that perform best in each scenario and rotate them according to each scenario? This means becoming optimized all the time from being suboptimal all the time.

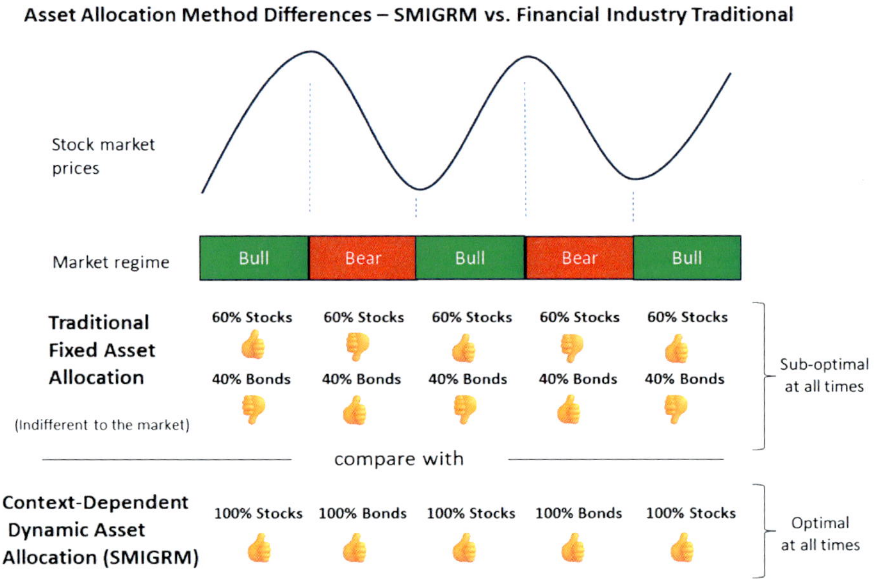

How do we define scenarios or context? SMIGRM defines them as the corresponding risk environment. The reason will become clear as you read the rest of this book, but in a nutshell, risky assets (e.g., stocks) tend to perform best under low and moderate risk environments. In contrast, safe assets (e.g., T-Bills, gold, etc.) tend to perform best under high risk environments. We mean relatively to other assets, of course. This happens because of investor risk aversion.

Everyone has a different risk tolerance but everyone has one. As risk or uncertainty increases, investors tend to move away from risky assets pushing their prices down. Therefore, SMIGRM calls for a continuous measurement of risk in the market (this is mission of RISP 500™: Risk Index for the S&P 500®) to orchestrate the rotation between risky and safe assets. This is why we call the process Risk-Dependent Dynamic Asset Allocation.

Finally, after discussing Static vs. Dynamic Allocation, the last point we want to make is the fixed belief problem. Have you seen pundits predicting doomsday for the stock market lately? I'm sure you know quite a few of them already. Especially when the stock market is doing really well, these people seem to cry wolf louder. They assume that everything that goes up must come down. They seem to be always the same ones, the *permabears*. Do you find this kind of advice helpful at all? The U.S. stock market has had an impressive run since the end of World War II. There have been crashes, of course, some of which even spectacular ones, but for the most part, it has been a persistent, long bull market. Either these gurus never give you a specific timeframe for their predicted crashes or their timeframes are proven wrong over and over. Permanent doomsday prophets really help no one. It can scare beginner investors, but most people just ignore them after a while. On the flip side, there are *permabulls* as well. These are usually on the sell side of the industry. The myth that "stocks always go up in the long run" was probably also originated by them.

Nonetheless, neither *permabears* nor *permabulls* are helpful — for anybody. They add no value to your investing methods and results, but may destabilize them by taking you off course for no real reason from time to time. Their advice would be valuable only if they could also pinpoint the exact (or even an approximate) time of a crash. Everybody already knows crashes happened many times in the past and will continue coming in the future. Without the critical timing information, honestly, just crying wolf helps no one.

How About Matching Assets to Risk Environments?

The solution really starts with the realization that each type of asset behaves differently in response to different external contextual conditions. Under the right conditions, stocks will experience their best or worst days. So will any other type of asset, e.g. bonds, real estate, gold, etc. This is obvious, but few have actually created methods or investment decision models to explore them because the number of factors to be considered is humongous and have co-dependencies among them, making it a very complicated undertaking. In our quest for solutions, we faced the same obstacles. However, we looked into a smaller but crucial set of variables to simplify this enormous problem and focused our efforts on the stock market alone (since most other assets have relatively high correlations with it). This book will give you more details on how we came up with this solution (we were not the only ones) but I can anticipate it for you here: we zeroed in on RISK. There are two most obvious reasons for this:

Investor Risk-Aversion Principle: when risks and uncertainty go up, investors seek safety by selling risky assets, which in turn push their prices down, and vice-versa. So, there is more than correlation here, but there is causality, which is a much stronger inverse relationship than just correlation between risk and the probability for the market to trend up or down.

Returns are produced by risk taking activity: as discussed previously, you get the privilege to earn a return for the amount of risk you have taken. There is also a strong cause and effect relationship here: no risk, no reward; higher risk, higher probabilities of earning a higher return.

By categorizing several levels of risk in the stock market, the solution calls for investing only in the best-performing assets for each risk level. This is matching the right assets with each contextual risk environment for maximum return potential. This is also exploiting risks to maximize investment performance in lieu of being pushed around by them. We believe that risk management must be more active than reactive. For example, when risks are high, rotate to safer assets such as T-Bills, money market funds, gold, or even cash. But when risks are low, invest in stocks, index funds, and even leveraged funds.

Now, contrast this dynamic context-dependent asset allocation approach with the static asset allocation approach adopted by most of the investment management industry or even with the perma-static buy & hold approach. Which do you think should logically outperform? Think about it. How many portfolios, carefully and expertly planned, thrived or actually survived the onslaught of the market crashes of 2000, 2008, or 2020? It doesn't matter what allocation percentages are made to stocks, bonds, commodities, real estate, etc. — it's just a matter of which allocation lost more or less money, because they all lost or haven't made the money they could have made if they had adopted a dynamic context-dependent allocation strategy to fit changing market conditions in a timely manner. Feel the difference? In the book, you will find out why this is the first stepping stone toward a robust Stock Market Investing Guided by Risk Management (SMIGRM) method.

There’s No Such Thing As Bad Weather; Only Bad Clothing

As you can see, the same happens with stock investing: there’s no such thing as a bad market; just wrong assets invested at the wrong times, under unfavorable circumstances.

Now you may ask, how about the so-called "all weather" portfolio? Would such a portfolio, specially designed to stand against all types of weather in the markets, solve the problem? Well, let's examine how these portfolios were constructed. If you read the prospectus or the fund's brochure, you will easily find out that it is still a static portfolio. It is just more diversified than most funds out there with other asset classes included in it, such as stocks, bonds, gold, commodities, and cash. Surely it may stand bad weather (market crashes) better than stock-only and stock-bond portfolios, but again, for fixing the allocation making it largely unresponsive to changing market conditions as it goes through market cycles, it seriously sacrifices gains during stock market booms.

Now consider this: wouldn't it be smarter to match the best performing-asset to hold specifically for and in response to each different external context or scenario that comes our way?

You see, there is really no way around this problem resulting from fixed and static portfolio allocations. You may argue that since everybody in the entire investment management industry does things in some way, it must be the right way or what is called best practices, right? Yes, but only until someone starts finding better ways to do the same things: it's called progress. It's called evolution. It's about time the investment management industry should rethink old, traditional ways to start evolving again.

Still not convinced? Let me offer you a simple analogy just to show you the absurdity of the situation. Suppose you are building yourself or investing in a professionally-managed all-weather portfolio with the following (very typical) asset allocation:

- 40% Stocks
- 40% Bonds

- 10% Commodities
- 10% Gold

… and you hold this allocation to face bull markets, bear markets, economic booms, recessions, high and low inflation and interest rates, etc. What will happen? Simple: at every moment in time with a different external context (or "weather"), part of your portfolio will do really well while the rest of it will do really poorly. As a whole, you will do just "fine", with a below-potential return, but "fine". After all, the portfolio was designed to work exactly like that. As an obvious result, it will probably never perform very well on average or as a whole in the long run.

Now, let me present the analogy: You are about to go out on an exciting and adventurous long trip. Say you are trekking and hiking the Appalachian trail. Since you know you are possibly going to encounter different types of weather (hot, cold, rainy, snowy, windy, etc.), you must be prepared. So, before you step out of your house, you will put on:

- 40% T-shirts
- 40% Raincoat
- 10% Winter Jacket
- 10% Windbreaker

Would you actually put on all these patches of clothes at the same time (and keep them on for the entire trip) as prescribed? Or would you rather simply wear only what is appropriate for the moment and take the rest in your backpack? If you answered "yes" to either, why would you do the same thing to your investment portfolio? It becomes so obvious when we pause to think about it logically.

Therefore, in our view, optimally, portfolios must be actively managed by dynamically changing the allocation in response to changing market conditions. We mean rotating assets immediately as the situation unfolds through different weather conditions. But then the next question is how it can be accomplished?

We believe the best common denominator that consolidates information from each of the contextual scenarios is RISK. This is because, besides the two main reasons presented earlier, risk consolidates all the concerns, uncertainties, and fears in the market in a single, measurable number at any given time. By measuring the risk in the system at each moment in time, we can get a pretty good picture of the changing "weather" in the market and respond appropriately.

This is exactly why this book is titled Stock Market Investing *Guided by* Risk Management. We started the first chapter demystifying the existence of a crystal ball for future stock prices (side note: it's incredible but there are still people who believe in its existence claiming they have it in some shape or form) and quickly moved to explain why this might even become a "revolution" in the way Risk Management is used today. Instead of a control function limited to calculating potential losses and recommending proper actions to reduce positions or engage in hedging activities, Risk Management can and should be used proactively (instead of reactively) and take the central role of guiding investment decisions. As we will show in this book, risk has a direct relationship with probabilities for the stock market to go up or down (remember that this is due to the risk-aversion principle). After all, since stock market investing is a risky business and you can expect to earn a return only if you take up risks, shouldn't it be natural to use the risk information to guide investment decisions?

Often, it's in the simple things in life where we can find most wisdom. Filter out all the noise, confusion, and complexities of modern life. Go back to the basics and think things over. Sometimes the answer may be found in the unpredictability of life itself or in common sense things as simple as wearing the right clothes appropriate for different weather conditions.

The Secret to Investment Success in an Uncertain World

With every passing day of my life, I'm more and more convinced of one thing: the secret to success is everywhere in the universe, hiding in plain sight. As humans, we are always trying to fit everything into a mental model linking cause and effect in a direct relationship. For example, if you don't study hard for exams, you'll get poor grades and may fail. If you work hard on a project, you will earn the fruits of your labor. If you take this medication, you will get better and be cured. If you invest in these assets with these principles, you will make money. If you pray hard enough, your wishes will be granted. But we all know that life is more complicated than that. For each of the above examples and so many more you can think of that resulted in a successful outcome, you can also find countless counter-examples resulting in failures. Why does this happen?

In our millions of years of evolution, the ability to make cause-effect associations quickly enabled the survival of the species. We like things that are deterministic: it gives us a sense of security and inner peace. We love deterministic formulas. Newton's law of gravity is a prominent example. If you let an apple fall from a certain height, you can determine precisely the exact time, location and speed second by second throughout its trip to the ground. It's great when we feel we have the process under control, because there won't be any surprises. By contrast, we don't like random processes we can't control. We don't feel safe and in control. Even Einstein balked at the randomness of the quantum world — he once famously said that "God doesn't play dice with the universe." As humans, we really dislike nondeterministic relationships. But they are everywhere in nature. The entire universe is nondeterministic. And so is the outcome of everything we do.

In the investment world, many of us work models and methods that implicitly assume a high degree of determinism. We love formulas that can deterministically assure us of the outcomes. However, nowhere can nondeterminism be more prevalent than the investment world. The word RISK is so predominant in the investment world precisely for that reason. But still, many investors believe that stock selection ability alone can determine successful outcomes over time with a very high degree of confidence. You expertly allocate assets in a strategically designed portfolio and hope it will outperform the market. The allocation may be reevaluated and changed perhaps once a year or more or less frequently. Isn't this what is most typically done? If this is the right formula, why do some investors succeed and others don't? And why winners of today are turning out to be the losers of tomorrow? Why is it so hard to win consistently? The answer is that these investment methods, which are the most common and even taught in business schools, assume that the world is more or less deterministic, and that we humans have more control over outcomes than we actually do. Unfortunately, the real world isn't anything but. Any asset that looks undervalued or overvalued today will most likely not look the same tomorrow because the environment is constantly changing. It's a moving target and can't be precisely determined because the underlying context is also always changing. We will discuss this in the book but this is why static, passive investment methods (buy & hold for the long-term because "*stocks always go up in the long run*") and methods that don't take the context (external risk environment) into account will likely fail in the long run. They will invariably fall victim to the misguided belief or assumption of a determinism that is just not there.

So, what's the solution? It is everywhere actually, hiding in plain sight. The universe is random. Everything that happens in life is nondeterministic. We live in a probabilistic world. Sorry, Professor Einstein, but God does in fact play dice with the universe. Have you heard the expression "numbers game?" In business, everything is a numbers game. For sales and marketing, for example, there is no single ad message or marketing method that will resonate with everyone resulting in 100% success. There will be better and worse messages but it will still be a numbers game. So, here's where the solution starts: Probability and Statistics. For those who skipped Probability & Statistics in school, we suggest doing a basic review of one the most useful subjects you can ever learn in life. If you have learned the principles of Risk Management, you know that it is totally based on the principles of Probability & Statistics.

In the investment world, nowhere are these principles more evident than in one of the riskiest businesses in that world: early-stage venture capital investing in brand new start-ups. According to a Correlation Ventures' study about the distribution of realized returns of U.S. ventures over the past decade (2009-2018), 64% of these investments failed to even return the invested capital back. Here is the breakdown of the results found:

Returns less than 1x	**64%**
Returns between 1x and 3x	18%
Returns between 3x and 5x	6%
Returns between 5x and 10x	7%
Returns between 10x and 20x	3%
Returns greater than 20x	**2%**

In other words, to find two 20x unicorns in a sample of 100 startups that all looked highly promising on paper, venture capital firms must lose 100% of their capital invested in 64 of them that will completely fail the expectations. Given the extremely unfavorable odds, the very survival of venture capital firms depends on finding enough 5x-10x returns or higher to keep them alive in the game (not greed, just survival!). Can venture capital firms improve their odds? They certainly can by doing a finer job with due diligence and leveraging on lessons learned but there is no escape to the reality that this is still a numbers game, a very tough numbers game! Venture capitalists must improve their chances by investing in a very large number of companies. No wonder they like to co-invest with other venture capital firms in the same companies, diversifying and spreading out the risk. We brought up this example to show you that even in a business that is generally riskier than stock market investing, the numbers game is at the core of the strategy to win.

Now, we wonder why virtually no one in the investment business or academia ever discusses Probability & Statistics with investors or students. Have you ever heard the investment industry, TV market pundits, internet gurus, or even business school professors talk much about Probability & Statistics when discussing investments with you? The focus is always on asset returns, their merits (fundamentals, etc.), allocation & diversification, etc. Even the word "risk" is often mentioned a few times but not a word about Probability & Statistics or win rates of the presented investment strategies (odds of winning and failing). They are pretty darn important to know for your investment decision making, don't you think? Not a criticism, we just wonder why.

We Live in a Probabilistic World

In a probabilistic world, nothing is certain but there is a probability associated with every possible outcome. It's just like the venture capital firm return table shown above. Should we panic or feel insecure? Not at all. Luckily for us, some very smart people have already formulated Probability & Statistics. The best way to deal with a probabilistic world is to make it "more deterministic" in favor of our desired outcome. To do this, we can use the "Law of Large Numbers", which we will explain in just a minute. But first, let me offer you an analogy.

I grew up watching Formula One car racing in Brazil, where my compatriot, the legendary Ayrton Senna, was the best of his time. I wondered how racers could still maintain a relatively high speed around corners. I learned that the most efficient way to slow down the least around corners and curves was to drive in the most straight-line trajectory possible through the curve. Drivers' ability to slow down the least around corners will be best positioned to win the races. The reason we brought this example up is to show that the best solution to problems is often the simplest and the most logical after you learned it, which will be useful for us in this discussion.

To take advantage of the Law of Large Numbers works in a similar way. According to Wikipedia, the Law of Large Numbers states that "*the average of the results obtained from a large number of independent and identical random samples converges to the true value, if it exists*". Wikipedia offers an example: "*While a casino may lose money in a single spin of the roulette wheel, its earnings will tend towards a predictable percentage over a large number of spins*". Let's take another example. Imagine a life insurance company. If it had only one client, who would pay premiums for a much larger death benefit, the insurance company would almost certainly lose money and go bankrupt. But if the company covers a sufficiently large number of individuals, it's fair to assume that not everyone will die at the same time and too early (a small probability outcome). Therefore, such an insurance company will have a much better chance of surviving and be profitable. The same logic with large numbers applies to venture capital firms. And the same principle should equally apply to stock market investors too (we will show you how in this book). You get the point.

Some investments will turn successful; others won't. Traders see it clearly because they typically place multiple trades over time. In our view, being best positioned for long term success is implementing the trio Statistical Edge, Asymmetrical Payoff, and Law of Large Numbers.

The Formula to Success: Statistical Edge + Asymmetrical Payoff + Law of Large Numbers

In a probabilistic world (e.g., outcomes of games or stock market returns), where results aren't guaranteed nor can they be forecasted with certainty, you can't use analytical tools that treat them as deterministic. That is why price forecasting and valuation models applied to stock prices rarely work more than 50% of the time. In contrast, in general physics as an example, which is an exact science, you have laws and principles that are deterministic, such as Newton's law of gravity. Aside from quantum physics, of course, you can always calculate the outcome of a physical experiment with certainty and precision. That's how we predict the exact trajectory of celestial bodies and can send men to the moon, for example. But deterministic formulas and models won't work so well to predict the outcome of games and stock prices. If you use mainstream analytical tools to make investment decisions in the stock market, well, think about how good they really have been in your own experience.

To successfully navigate in a probabilistic world like the stock market and to make sure you have the best chances to win the game (note that we used the word "chances", which is probabilistic), you must use statistics-based tools and strategies that turn probabilities in your favor. Let me start with an example you are most likely already familiar with – casino gambling – and then turn the discussion to the stock market so that you will easily understand the concept. Do you know why the house (the casino) always wins? The casino may and will lose some games, of course, but in the long run, it will always be net positive. Guaranteed. Why? The answer is simple. The casino rigged the game in its favor, giving the house a small statistical edge. For example, if the casino had a probability of winning 51% of the time vs. 49% for the players, this slight 1% net advantage would snowball in the long run, making sure the house would win. Imagine playing this setup over hundreds and thousands of trials. Some players will have a net win and some players will have a net loss, but the house will make sure to end up with a net win, especially after a sufficiently large number of trials. That is exactly why and how the house always wins, as it's widely known. It's the Law of Large Numbers in action!

So, how can we adopt the same strategy casinos do to ensure our long-term success? Well, it's certainly not by buying and holding stocks blindly for the long-term hoping with the "*stocks always go up in the long run*" mentality (which is a myth as there is not a single rule or finance principle that guarantees it as a fact). Casinos don't operate based on hope or beliefs and neither should we. They are a serious business and so should be our investments. Casinos will set up the game rigged in their favor. As stock investors, we can apply the same principles rigging the system in our favor too. The strategy is based on 3 fundamental pillars:

- Statistical Edge
- Asymmetrical Payoff
- Law of Large Numbers

Let's examine each one of them in detail below and offer ways we can replicate them too as stock investors.

1. Statistical Edge

Since the only certainty in stock market investing is that there is no certainty of outcomes, at every moment you are making a decision to buy, sell, or hold, you must be judging probabilities. You must ask yourself (or your analytical tools) what the probability the stock price is going up, down, or staying the same is. If you don't have the exact probability number, a proxy with a direct relationship is sufficient. But if your tools don't give you that information, you need a new tool that does. That is because you would only take the action for which odds are favorable. When odds aren't favorable, just don't play (stay out of the market) and wait for the odds to turn favorable again before placing another bet. If you do this, you will be emulating the casino's strategy. The best tool to accomplish this feat that we know of is the very essence of this book: Stock Market Investing Guided by Risk Management (SMIGRM), which you are about to find out.

2. Asymmetrical Payoff

Stock market investing is a risky business. When you risk \$1, you should not expect to win \$1, but more. Say, you want to make \$2 or \$3 or more for each dollar you risk. This is the kind of asymmetrical payoff you should be aiming for when you invest in any game with uncertain outcomes, such as the stock market. As a parallel, remember we said venture capital funds need at least a few 5x-10x returns or higher for every 100 startups they invested on just to survive in the game? They typically target 10x potential startups. For earlier stage startups, investors target even 30x! This is necessary to assure that the few profit "home runs" properly compensate for the losses incurred from the majority of losing bets placed in such a risky business. You see, the lower the odds of success (or the higher the amount of risk involved) of an undertaking - any undertaking - the stronger should be the required target asymmetrical payoff. Of course, stock market investing is generally a lot less risky than venture capital investing (just an extreme example to illustrate the point) but it's the exact same logic.

Just like the casino rigging the game in its favor, how can you implement an asymmetrical payoff in your own stock market investing strategy? Simple. Just make sure you cut your losses quickly and let your profits run. Unfortunately, most people do the exact opposite. When they are losing, they are so discouraged at realizing the loss by selling the stock that they keep holding it longer in the hope the market will soon turn around. Then the market moves further down and by the time they throw in the towel it's often too late with a much larger loss. But when the market goes up, they are quick to sell and pocket the profit for fear of losing it, just to see the stock move even higher. Sounds familiar? Yes, it happens to everyone. That is emotions taking over what should be driven by rational decisions only. This is also asymmetrical payoff but working against you. You want the exact opposite: an asymmetrical payoff in your favor.

Lastly, a simple and good old stop loss should be your best friend. For example, if the stock is currently trading at $10 and you are confidently expecting (based on solid research, not a hunch or a guess) the stock to reach $16, you may want to set the stop loss at $8. This way you are risking $2 to make $6, or a 3-to-1 payoff. You get the idea.

3. Law of Large Numbers

Statistics is the ultimate numbers game. Once you have set up a strategy with a Statistical Edge and an Asymmetrical Payoff, all you need to do is to repeat this setup over and over many times over a long period of time. Just like rolling the dice or tossing a coin, after a sufficiently large number of trials, outcomes will converge to the expected values. Or, just like a casino, you should start to see net profits pile up over time. Of course, you will experience losses along the way, but also wins. You must also always remember to cut losses early and let profits run.

By doing these 3 things in conjunction, over time the gods of statistics should favor you and reward you for your discipline.

There is one last concept we want to discuss because it's really important and will help you grasp the ideas and principles discussed in the book.

Putting It Altogether: Risk Calculation to Lead the Way

Before discussing the last key concept, let's sum up with a quick recap of the concepts discussed so far to come up with a comprehensive solution:

Risk vs. Return Duality: we have discussed the importance of using RoMaD (Return over Maximum Drawdowns) as a metric to decide between investment/method alternatives. We want to maximize return potential at the lowest risk or potential losses possible. In other words, we want to maximize long-term RoMaD.

Static vs. Risk Context-Dependent Dynamic Asset Allocation: we discussed why matching the best performing asset to its corresponding risk environment makes the investment activity per se a lot more logical, reducing the inefficiencies of static asset allocation models. As a result, it significantly increases RoMaD. This will be proven in the latter part of the book with actual numbers.

Deterministic vs. Probabilistic World: by recognizing the probabilistic nature of stock market investing, we explained why we must always use concepts of probability and statistics in our investment activity. Any investment method that doesn't take them into account front and center is incomplete, at best.

The Formula to Success: Statistical Edge + Asymmetrical Payoff + Law of Large Numbers: finally, we showed how casinos, insurance companies, and venture capital firms dealing with high risk make sure they are profitable over the long run operating in a highly probabilistic environment. Stock market investing is similarly probabilistic. We simply can't determine outcomes; there is always a probability associated with events and outcomes - and that is what we call RISK. The triad of the formula is there to help us exploit risk in our favor as investors or money managers instead of being pushed around by it. The formula calls for a small statistical edge in our favor, which repeated over a large number of trials will definitely tilt the results in our favor and in a big way. Just like casinos and venture capital funds do to make sure they make money in the long run ensuring survival and profitability as a business, we can also use their methods as investors in the probabilistic world of the stock market. To amplify this effect, we must also implement an asymmetrical payoff feature to our investing activity by limiting losses while they are still small and letting profits run with no limits on the upside.

All these concepts put together results in the Stock Market Investing Guided by Risk Management (SMIGRM) Method. We will discuss the method at length and offer a contrast with existing, traditional, and popular methods so you can make your own mind what method is best for you.

The only concept that is still missing from this discussion up to this moment is the RISP 500™. It is the maestro that conducts the entire orchestra. The RISP 500™ is a proprietary model with the primary goal to measure the risk embedded in the S&P 500® at every moment in time. The percentile rank of each measurement in reference to itself measured over a long period of time in history will give us the best determination as to which kind of risk environment we find ourselves in at every moment. We can also see this information as a proxy for probability (not certainty, remember) for the market's direction.

SMIGRM is a different way of guiding oneself navigating in the troubled waters of the stock market. It's based on all the principles and concepts discussed above. It has nothing to do with fundamental or technical analysis people are so accustomed to. No price targets, no pundit opinions, no valuation, no dissecting financials, no market assumptions, no fancy charts, no forecasting, no futurology, no asset allocation pie charts, no static "balanced portfolios", no guesswork, no BS; just a very principled, science-backed method and hard, cold data. That's it. We believe it is based on a much stronger foundation, more logical (just remember the right clothing for the weather analogy), and the results should prove it.

In this book, we will discuss the science behind the algorithm that powers the RISP 500™ algorithm. We will discuss the main variables that are measured and their importance as pieces of a puzzle to provide us the guidance we need to navigate this risky, probability-governed world of stock market investing.

All the best arguments in the world would be incomplete without solid proof. We will show and discuss the results of back-testing (13 years) plus 2 ½ years (and counting) of live trading 8 strategies. The RISP 500™ project is actually a much-improved version of earlier projects, which already gave us excellent results. We are constantly testing and improving the tool because the market is not static. Those who study volatility and correlation, for example, know very well how these variables are not constant over time. All models must be recalibrated from time to time. What used to work yesterday is not guaranteed to work tomorrow if you are not always paying attention, recalibrating parameters, and testing, testing, testing.

In the following chapters, we will introduce you to the RISP 500™ properly. As we said, the RISP 500™ is the maestro of the entire orchestra. It will provide the "guide" in Stock Market Investing Guided by Risk Management.

Roger Federer, during the commencement speech to the Dartmouth College Class of 2024 revealed that despite winning almost 80% of all singles tennis matches in his entire career, on a point-by-point basis, his point-win rate was only 54%. It's almost a 1:1 win-loss ratio but Roger had a ***small edge of 4%****, which was all he needed to become one of the greatest of all time.*

CHAPTER 2

2. Can Risk Management Guide Investing?

Why the RISP 500™ was created

As professional traders with decades of experience in the world's largest banks, we found that the existing methods everybody uses, centered around variations of the fundamental and technical analysis, though improving over the years, haven't fundamentally changed the way investors make decisions. Both study the past and try to make inferences about the future. Fundamental analysis, mostly used for stock selection, dissects financials of corporations and studies their competitive strength in their respective markets and industries. With this information, fundamental analysts will typically perform a valuation of the company and its stock price, and based on a number of assumptions, forecast price targets for the stock price over a few time horizons. Technical analysis, mostly used for market timing purposes (seeking best entry/exit points), are based on past history of the stock price behavior and indicators derived from such behavior to predict its next big move. Both tools have guided investors for generations since the 18th century and results are mixed. Some people made fortunes, some lost fortunes, and everyone else lies in between. Like any tool, they have pluses and minuses. Since conclusions are made based on making future predictions, like forecasting stock prices or price targets, these methods must make many assumptions about the future, such as projecting future sales, expenses, competition, trends, etc. As you know, assumptions may be highly subject to estimation errors. The conclusions of the analyses are also highly dependent on the analyst. Two different people looking at the exact same set of data and charts will invariably see different things and arrive at different conclusions.

We started to question whether we were really using the BEST tools available to navigate the markets. If we weren't, then new tools must be developed. We have seen colleagues in the industry and investors struggle with these common problems (you may easily relate if you have experienced them too):

- The stock market is getting more volatile and more unpredictable. It's becoming harder to navigate the markets or read the signals from whatever method people use and deliver the same performance they used to do in the past. But there are indeed long-term tectonic shifts at a fundamental level gradually changing the paradigm of the post-war world order. Market volatility has generally increased after 2018. Corrections and crashes may become more frequent than before and to many of us, existing tools seem not very adequate to deal with the challenges of the new reality.

- There is an overload of news, conflicting opinions, and unfounded analyses in the era of social media and fake overnight gurus. In other words, there is more confusion today than ever.

- Some **Hard to Decide Situations** are getting harder for everyone to navigate markets with confidence. With more volatility in the markets, it has become harder to determine the best timing for executing entries to and exits from the market. Investors are easily caught in these situations but again, it's not their fault if they don't have the proper tools to deal with these situations.

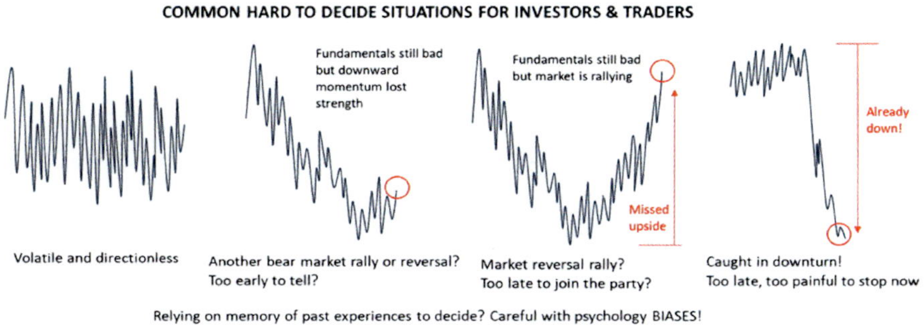

Let's examine some real cases that occurred in recent years.

NEWS HEADLINES (OCTOBER 15 – OCTOBER 30, 2022)

❶ "This is where we feel more worried, and next earnings season is going to be really critical." (OCT 3)

❷ A high-stakes earnings season likely to be wrought by slashed forecasts and worsening fundamentals tied to inflation and rising interest rates (OCT 3)

❸ The Fed's reverse repo use just hit a fresh record of $2.4 trillion — why that's one of the clearest 'bad signs' for the market. (OCT 5)

❹ 200-Week Moving Average Shows It's Time to Buy the Dip! (OCT 17)

❺ No doubt about it: Bloomberg economists now see a 100% chance of a recession within 1 year — here are 3 simple ways to prep for this 'guaranteed' decline. (OCT 19)

❻ Markets face another sizable increase to the U.S. central bank's benchmark interest rate, with officials expected to deliver a fourth-straight 75-basis-point hike. (OCT 30)

In a situation like this, what would you do? This occurred during the 2022 bear market. Fundamentals were still bad at the time, the media were painting a dubious picture, but the market was showing signs of an emerging rally. Would you jump right in or wait?

NEWS HEADLINES (JUNE 15 – JULY 15, 2022)

❶ So, What's the Consensus On How Long This Bear Market Will Last? (JUNE 15)

❷ Despite last week's rally, we're in a clear downtrend ... how low might the S&P fall? (JUNE 27)

❸ 'There are some similarities to the dot-com bust in 2001'. (JUNE 30)

❹ Why the latest round of tech layoffs feels a bit different. (JUNE 30)

❺ Tech stocks are having their worst year ever. (JUNE 30)

❻ Tech stocks 'could drop another 15% to 20% at least': Strategist (JULY 1)

❼ The National Association of Realtors reported that existing home sales declined for the fourth straight month (JULY 15)

❽ Oil Prices Go Up On High Demand And Tight Supply (JULY 15)

How about the above scenario that also occurred during that same bear market? Fundamentals were also quite bad as you can see from the headlines at the time. But the market has rallied quite a bit, erasing all the earlier loss of the S&P 500 index. What would you do if you were still on the sidelines? Wouldn't it be too late to join the party now?

NEWS HEADLINES (JANUARY – MARCH 25, 2020)

1 Twitter bans Zero Hedge after it posts coronavirus conspiracy theory (FEB 3)

2 10 coronavirus cases confirmed from cruise ship quarantined in Japan (FEB 5)

3 First U.S. Coronavirus Patient Released From Hospital (FEB 5)

4 What is the coronavirus from China and what are the symptoms? (FEB 10)

5 Coronavirus: First death confirmed in Europe (FEB 15)

6 Iran reports 2 novel coronavirus deaths, the country's 1st cases (FEB 19)

7 Coronavirus cases on Japan cruise ship rise to 634 (FEB 20)

What if you were caught off guard by a surprise downturn coming from nowhere like the 2020 Coronavirus Crash? Initially pretty contained in the epicenter, the outbreak quickly turned into a global pandemic. When you took stock of the situation, you had already lost by a lot in the stock market. What would you do then? Buy the dip? Look for safety?

All these situations make investors confused about how to respond. It's no wonder many investors and even professional portfolio managers dislike trading! Making decisions under so much uncertainty and so much pressure requiring quick decisions in tough market situations is not for everybody. We believe people shouldn't be making decisions in a hurry under pressure because that is how mistakes and misjudgments happen! What they need is a proper objective tool.

- Traditional risk management tools are limited to controlling risks. They weren't designed to guide major decisions or actively give you an edge to improve your returns. They are designed to make sure you don't lose (beyond your set limits); not to help you profit from taking calculated risks. No wonder risk managers are mostly in support functions inside banks and investment firms (in middle and even back-offices!).

- Mainstream popular practices, rules of thumb, and beliefs may easily lead to underperformance, at best, or disaster, at worst.

    - "**Buy the dips, sell the rips**": it's an immediate urge to buy every time a stock goes down or sell when it goes up as if stock prices must always self-correct back toward an imaginary "mean" they are destined to revert to. Contrary to this popular belief, stock prices don't have "mean-reversion" features. There is simply no mean to revert to; for proof, just look at the chart of the S&P 500® over a long period of time. Can you spot a mean it's been reverting to? In trending markets (consistent bull or bear), this practice may help you make some money but as soon as the market regime turns and you're caught off guard, it can backfire big time.

    - "**Buy under-valued stocks, sell over-valued stocks**": it's so obvious but it's easier said than done. That's because valuation is highly subjective. What is under-valued for some is often over-valued for others, and that is why a market exists. Per se, this principle is quite useless but many people use it to make (or justify) investment decisions.

    - "**Stocks always go up in the long run**": this is a very common myth. There is no evidence for such a claim, but many people still believe it. The same is often said of home prices, equally without any solid irrefutable proof. Take a look at the chart showing 150 years of history of the S&P 500® index representing the U.S. stock market. As you can see, the U.S. stock market really took off after World War II. Note that the growth is actually even more dramatic than depicted on the chart because it's on a logarithmic scale. What explains this impressive and explosive growth?

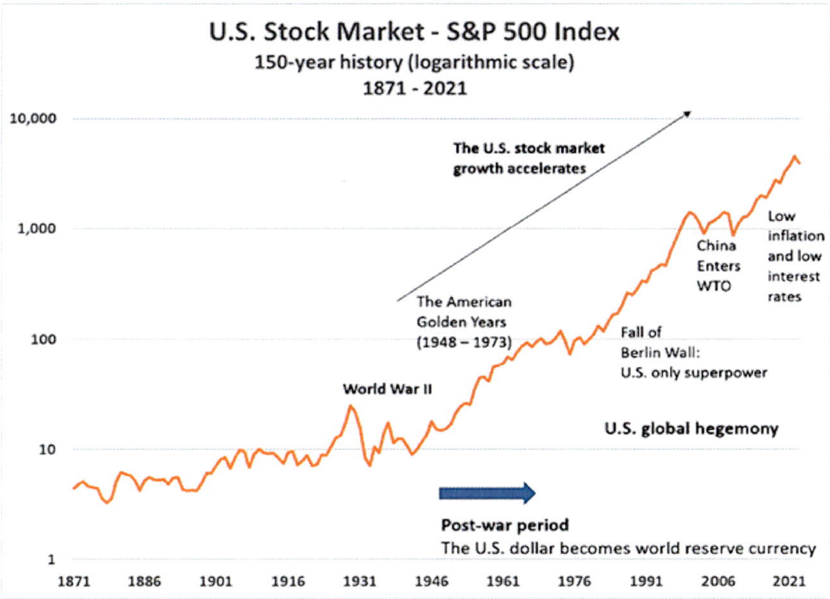

After World War II, the U.S. emerged as the greatest victor in all senses of the word. The U.S. became the greatest world economic engine, the U.S. dollar became the world's reserve currency, Americans created all the major international institutions (World Bank, IMF, etc.), American corporations dominated the world, and the American world order was established. Invariably, as a result, the U.S. stock market reflected the last 80 years of economic growth and abundance, giving the impression stocks always go up in the long run. If you look at the charts of other stock markets around the world, you won't see such a nice, pretty picture. A notable counter-example is the Japanese Nikkei 225. This is evidence stocks don't always go up in the long run. And how long is long enough for you? How about 30 years? The Nikkei 225 hasn't recovered its peak even after 30 years! It finally did in February 2024, which is about 40 years later!

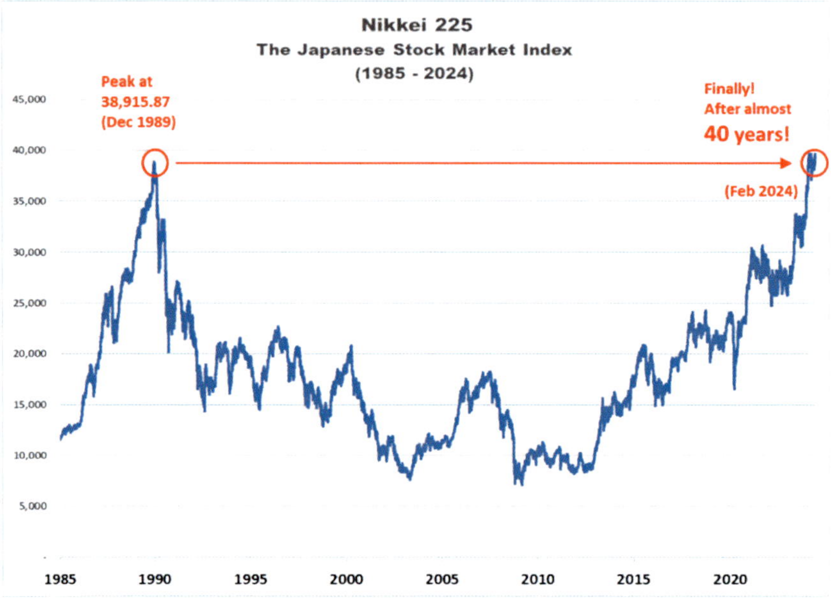

TIP ☞ But now, consider this. Times are changing. The entire G-7 club of the 7 richest nations in the world, which includes the United States, no longer represent more than half of the world economy as they once did. It declined to less than 30%. That is why the G-20 was introduced. The G-20 now accounts for 80% of the world's GDP. By 2023, the 5 BRICS countries (Brazil, Russia, India, China, South Africa) alone have already surpassed the G-7 (USA, UK, Germany, France, Italy, Canada, Japan). The mighty U.S. dollar is for the first time in history being seriously challenged as the world's reserve currency. Though still small, the de-dollarization trend is real as a growing number of countries started reducing their dependence on the greenback for trade and reserves. This is slowly and gradually weakening the U.S. world economic power. This trend is projected to continue by the IMF and world economists. At the same time, U.S. national debt is reaching unprecedented levels ($33 trillion at the time of this writing). The speed is also staggering: the debt grows by $1 trillion just every 3 months. Large central banks around the world have been reducing their holdings of U.S. treasury bonds over the years. China is now seriously competing with the U.S. in the high-end industries of today and in the most promising industries of tomorrow (AI, quantum computing, new materials, etc.) and winning the race in many fields such as EVs, green energy, etc. Another indication of this trend can be seen from the number of patents countries are filing every year: in 2019 alone, China filed 2x the number of patents the U.S. did and about 44% of the entire world. Most importantly is that another pillar of the dynamism of the U.S. economy is also being gradually eroded: income and wealth inequalities are reaching all-time highs. See charts.

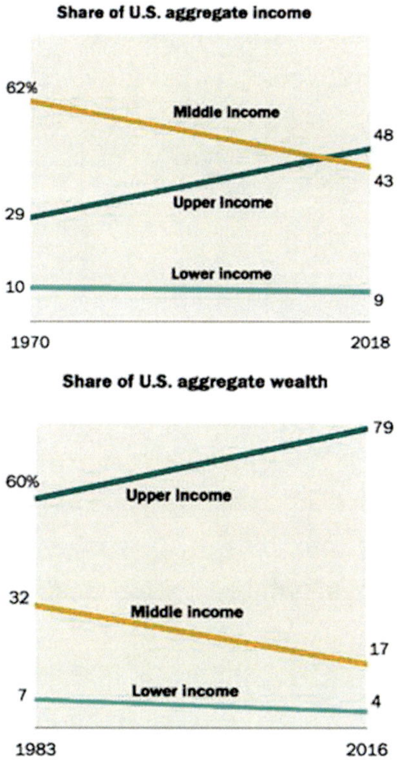

Source: PEW RESEARCH CENTER

The force that once powered the spectacular performance of the S&P 500®, though still potent, is gradually losing strength. It might not be visible solely looking at the S&P 500® yet, which at the time of this writing, is still breaking records. There are more reasons behind this strength such as the immense liquidity available in the markets - especially after a decade of quantitative easing, low inflation, near zero interest rates, and the pandemic era's gigantic stimulus money flooding the markets. Some of this excess liquidity already brought back inflation and higher interest rates. But the foundations that propelled the exponential growth of the U.S. economy post-World War II are gradually weakening. Don't be fooled by the apparent strength of the S&P 500®. There is a lot of liquidity (money) in the hands of wealthy people supporting the stock market. But the world is indeed changing. Don't assume everything lasts forever. Even risks of a new world war have been on the rise as global power struggles intensify. We have already seen the increase of the volatility of the stock market since 2018. Sure, the S&P 500® is not anywhere near what the Nikkei 225 was, but don't just assume it will always be that way and that stocks will always go up in the long run. To navigate this brave new world, the need to manage risks proactively and take early action against adverse market movements is greater now than ever.

TIP ☞ Long-term buy & hold investors, passive investors: beware and be careful!

- **"Double down your bet if you're losing"**: some investors take aggressive actions because they can't tolerate losses (it sounds so contradictory, it's preposterous). It's irrational to try to save a defeat under so much uncertainty. Based on what evidence will the market revert at the time of your own choosing? In psychology, this behavior is called the "regret aversion bias." Throwing good money after bad to save a defeat may inevitably lead to financial ruin.
- **"Guess, wish, and pray"**: This is most common for individual retail investors but it does affect all of us because we are humans. There is a high degree of subjectivity in stock investing and as a result, human biases abound and can easily lead to poor results. Neuroscience has discovered how humans make purchase

decisions. According to research conducted by Harvard Business School professor emeritus Gerald Zaltman, 95% of our decisions are directed by subconscious mental processes. We want to believe that we superior human beings make our decisions based on reason and logic, but in reality, according to neuroscientists, our decisions are based on our mental subconscious emotions and then justified by reason. In other words, we find reasons to justify decisions already made emotionally, often without us being aware. Here is where the danger lies. Often, investors get so enamored with an idea or a stock that they would go to great lengths to justify holding it even if it's already losing money. This is a problem all of us face as humans, so we need objective tools to help protect us from ourselves! We need a tool based on hard, cold data, free of biases or wishful thinking. The RISP 500™ was also designed with this in mind. It is entirely based on hard data, collected, filtered, processed, and its meaning is properly interpreted. Actions can be taken quickly, even automated, taken in response to data.

Data-Driven Decisions vs. Dangers from Investor Psychology

As discussed before, human psychology can really create problems for investors that result in poor long-term performance. The human mind, as powerful as it is, does have shortcomings when it comes to decision making and are subject to be clouded by multiple behavior biases. We have already discussed a few. One that is very common in our field is the **self-attribution bias**. In layman's terms, it is a bias in which we tend to over-attribute to ourselves the merits of a successful investment while tending to blame others or reasons out of our control when investments go bad. This bias can easily lead to overconfidence (not supported by real evidence) and excessive risk taking. Who hasn't heard people bragging they made a killing investing in such and such stocks, while implicitly or explicitly attributing the success to their own personal skills? Everyone can be a genius in a consistent bull market. But wait until the market turns bear or becomes volatile or confusing.

Another common bias is the **negativity bias**. This must have originated with our evolution in a world full of dangers to help protect ourselves and ensure our survivability as a species. This bias makes us put more weight on negative experiences than positive or neutral ones, affecting our judgment and behavior. Think about your own behavior during the 2020 Coronavirus Crash that sent the S&P 500® down 34% lasting just a little over a month from February 20th to April 7th, 2020. What followed was an impressive rally that went on from the rest of the year 2020 right through the entire year of 2021. If you sold your stock positions, how soon have you returned to the market? Incredibly a very large number of people, including seasoned investors, were so scared of what they've seen that they haven't returned to the market even many months after the crash was over. This episode made too many people miss what could have been a great ride for them. The mind attached so much weight to the negative side of the crash that it let investors miss the positive side of it.

But the point I want to make here is that if we depend solely on our own judgment as investors, we can easily become overconfident or underconfident at the wrong times, whereas hard data will tell us the truth about the real risks in the market, guiding us to make rational decisions based on data only.

These and other problems plagued the industry for years. The result is a massive industry-wide underperformance by investors and investment managers, who could be otherwise making excellent returns had they only had more appropriate tools to make their most important decisions. Do you remember Warren Buffett's 2008 public challenge betting $1 million that actively managed fund managers would not beat a passive S&P 500® index fund over a 10-year-period, which he won?

It is really not supposed to be like that. Something is certainly very wrong. Clearly, we were also not happy with the existing tools, methods, so we put our minds to finding solutions. We tested many models trying very hard but we weren't able to make significant breakthroughs in this quest for years… until the 2008 Global Financial Crisis in the U.S. broke the Pandora's box wide open for us!

Blood in the Streets and Pain in American Households

Needless to say, the 2008 GFC hit both large and small investors alike, and everyone else in between. Few were spared the massacre. The first, most obvious question is how did this happen? How come our best models forecasting future stock prices didn't see anything big like this quick enough to free us from harm? Missing the first wave of the downturn is excusable for most investors, but why didn't they exit the market before the worst part of the downfall took place? After all, looking back, there was enough time.

Was it the "Boiling Frog Syndrome"? Or too many false reversals? Ambiguous or conflicting signs? Misleading news? Bad advice? Perhaps all of the above? In fact, investors did have months to jump ship but the majority never did. But why? Stories abound from people who lost big during the crisis. The sad part is that horror stories like these are bound to repeat at every new crisis every few years.

How about you? What has been your experience investing in the stock market in the last 15 years?

How often have you had really hard moments to make key and crucial decisions? Would an early warning system have helped you outperform?

My Own Journey

You may be wondering who I am, how I learned so much in my career, and how we developed the RISP 500™ algorithm, the pumping heart of the SMIGRM Method. Recently speaking to an audience of accomplished investors, I received praise for my ability to navigate turbulent markets, but I can assure you it wasn't always like that. My own journey has been a difficult one with many ups and downs, to say the least.

Humble beginnings

I was born in Taiwan and my family emigrated to Brazil when I was only 5 years old in the 1970s. My family struggled like so many middle-class families, especially because of the decades of hyperinflation. To give you an idea how bad it was, in March 1990, inflation reached 3% per day.

That's right, I did write *per day* and not per year as we commonly express the inflation rate. In the 1990s, the annualized inflation rate registered 150,496%! You may be wondering how people got by in such an extreme situation. The answer is that people adapt and find solutions. I remember my dad sent me to the bank every single day with a bag of cash to invest in the overnight deposit instrument (which was basically a 'reverse repo' on a basket of Brazilian Treasury bills. For those who don't know, an overnight reverse repo is just a purchase to sell back the next day). My dad had a small business (difficult to manage in such an environment!) and every day we needed to rush to get the cash received from customers invested immediately in the overnight facility or the money would lose 3% of its value right away.

The overnight facility covered at least some of the losses to inflation, so it was better than nothing. That was one of my first money lessons in life. Later, after I started my banking career, I learned a lot more, especially from the numerous financial crises I experienced firsthand and from the perspective of someone managing risks in an emerging market (Brazil) during such times, where volatility was truly extreme.

Sharpened by successive financial crises from the 1990s to 2020s

In about 30 years, after facing challenges from so many financial crises around the world, you've got to learn something. For me, it started with the Mexican currency crisis of 1994. I felt firsthand its contagion effects in the Brazilian markets. I had graduated from college just a few years earlier (1991) as an electrical engineer with a specialization in automation, though I never really worked as an engineer. I was hired right upon graduation to Lloyds Bank in Brazil to start as a junior systems analyst (IT) for the traders. It was my first glance at a trading floor. Marveled by what I've seen, I knew right there it was where I wanted to be. I wanted to be a derivatives trader because I knew I was a nerd and loved numbers and complicated formulas. The more complex, the better - I thought - because it's where competition was going to be lighter. To improve my chances, I got myself attending the same post-grad program (IBMEC) where traders were receiving training to prove I could be as good as they were. I ended up with higher grades than senior traders at Lloyds! But without proper connections (which unfortunately mattered more than skills), Lloyds still refused to let me become a trader, not even a junior assistant trainee. Undeterred, I looked outside the firm, and I was hired by ABN Amro Bank for their trading desk. I started trading swaps, forwards, and options on interest rates and FX (BRL/USD currency trading). In time, I noticed client demand for hedge against both interest rates and currency at the same time, so I developed a new product for the bank, naming it "Bi-indexed", the first of its kind in the market. It was my first creation ever and over time, new products were also created. Then came year 1997 and we were hit by the Asian Crisis contagion right into our markets. In 1998, we were hit by the aftermath of the Russian Debt and Currency Crisis. In 1999, Brazil itself was at the center of the turmoil. In those years, I was already managing billions of dollars for my new employer, Citibank Brazil, as a risk manager.

What's more, on my personal side, I was saving money for my future business school in the United States. I was saving U.S. dollars for 2 years of tuition and living expenses of a top MBA program, which was one of the most expensive. Thus, a maxi-devaluation of the Brazilian currency couldn't have come at the worst possible time for me! It could completely derail my saving efforts and send my educational plans right out of the window. I acted super-fast. I bought as many dollars as I could on the very first day of the devaluation. The teller said he had no more dollar bills, but he could sell me travelers checks. I bought them all too, and I bought the rest the next day. Not only did I save my business school plans, but I was also able to successfully manage the bank's risk portfolios. The lessons here were: be watchful and mindful of risks, especially if you have much to lose; be mentally strong with focus to think clearly and strategically, and act swiftly and decidedly. The next year, 2000, I embarked on a two-year educational journey with the MBA program at the Wharton School at the University of Pennsylvania.

Later, as a trader and risk manager in the U.S., I continued to be tested over and over again by successive global financial crises beyond emerging markets. The most notable ones include the Dot Com Bubble Burst of 2000-2001, the Great Financial and Subprime Housing Crisis of 2008-2010, the Volmageddon of 2018, the Coronavirus Crash of 2020, and the Everything Bubble of 2022. In each crisis, I learned more and more because none of them were exactly identical, though they shared many similarities. After each one of them, new lessons were learned but new questions arose too. It's a sign of progress, I guess.

Why am I highlighting my experience with financial crises? It's during hard times that we build the most wisdom and character. People who have never lived through hyperinflation will have a hard time imagining it because certain things happen during a hyperinflationary period that would not otherwise happen in normal times. The same goes with each different financial crisis. With social media, we see new market experts popping up every day on YouTube and selling courses for thousands of dollars claiming expert status. But were any of them actually tested enough during harsh times? Do they have proper educational credentials? What has been their track record during times of distress? Everybody is a genius in bull markets and everybody has a few good stories to tell. But it is during unusual and challenging times that problems appear and expose the true nature of how things work. For example, neuroscience researchers learn the most about the brain through mental illnesses. In the aviation industry, aircraft safety engineering and design are improved every time a plane crashes and the NTSB investigates the causes of accidents. And we learn how things work in our daily lives when they break or stop working, forcing us to learn how to fix them to get them working again. Peaks of learning do tend to occur during challenging times. We learn the most about the inner nature of things not during normal times but when they break down.

CHAPTER 3

3. Turning Pain into Gain: Building a Reliable Early Warning System

How the RISP 500™ Solution was Created

The key question we started asking ourselves was: could the 2008 GFC crash be averted? The answer is not simple by any means, but we did find an answer to this crucial question. While nobody, I mean absolutely nobody, has a crystal ball to predict future events, let alone external shocks like the COVID-19 pandemic coming out from nowhere, we started asking ourselves whether there would be early signs that could offer us clues and help us estimate probabilities of potential next moves for the market and gauge its seriousness. One thing we knew: price forecasting models would hardly give us signs for early warning. The best shot for our quest for an early warning system had to come from signs that can be read and interpreted from the present; not in the past and certainly not from the future.

The Ace in the Hole: Risk Can Be Translated into Win-Loss Probabilities

The a-ha moment came when we realized that while future price action may or may not repeat past behaviors because it depended on the entire macro-context at every point in time, reaction to risk tends to be more constant over time. Risk rising above certain thresholds trigger selloffs in the stock market as flight to safety takes place and intensifies with rising price volatility. If we could accurately measure risk, match it with corresponding market reaction, we could build a database to which we can compare present measurements. What makes SMIGRM work is the direct relationship between risk, win-loss probabilities, and market reaction. Thus, even if risk rises too quickly, you may have a better chance to exit the market for safety before the crowd. For example, if you measured the risk today and it turned out to be in the same order of magnitude to that of the day the S&P 500® tumbled at the wake of the 2020 Coronavirus Crash, what are you going to do with your stocks?

But what if you were already caught in a downturn? Should you exit immediately with a loss or wait for the market to revert? We know how hard it is to make a decision under such circumstances. We've been there too; in fact, all the time! But knowing the risks can give us clues about win-loss odds to help us make more informed decisions.

Level of Risk		Investor Reaction		Win-Loss Odds		Market Direction (Prices)
LOW	→	Risk-seeking behavior	→	Favorable to Investor	→	Probability (UP) > Probability (DOWN)
HIGH	→	Risk-averse behavior	→	Unfavorable to Investor	→	Probability (DOWN) > Probability (UP)

The First Risk-Guided Trading System (Not Ours!)

The very first working and successful prototype we have ever seen wasn't created by us. One fellow trader was first to achieve success with a viable algorithm prototype a few years ahead of us. We must guard his name because we're not authorized to make it public. He is a brilliant trader, one of the most disciplined I have ever known during my years in trading floors with several large global banks. The algorithm he had developed had achieved incredible success, but had also had a few hiccups along the way. Here is the performance his fund delivered to his clients from 2014 to 2018 using this newly created

Year	S&P 500	Fund
2014	11%	25%
2015	-1%	14%
2016	10%	15%
2017	19%	52%
2018	-6%	3%

system. Compare it with the S&P 500® for the same period and see it for yourself.

We were very impressed. We knew that beating the S&P 500® was extremely difficult. And to do so over multiple years consistently (during both good and bad years) was pretty much unheard of. We have learned a great deal from these novel ideas and decided to develop our own system. We burnt the midnight oil dissecting incredible research papers and developing our own methodology, putting it to the test of the markets and fine-tuning it to create a brand-new system.

More Than a Solution: A New Philosophy Was Emerging

We enthusiastically applauded his achievement but we actually took a few steps farther. We started to question: could the risk metric be more than just an early warning or a trading signal? Could the role of traditional risk management be upgraded to do more than just help you control risks by adjusting the size of your positions or hedging when market risks rise and fall? Can risk actually guide decision-making?

Based on these new ideas, the RISP 500™ Project was born. Our goal was actually much more ambitious. Instead of just creating a trading signal for a few pre-selected strategies, we wanted to create a general risk management tool that any investor could use – professional wealth managers and the public alike – for any strategy. Since investors have different goals and risk tolerance levels, we wanted a tool that they could easily customize for their own unique needs and goals. In addition, investors have their own preferences as to which strategies and assets they want to invest in. For investors who already have their own strategies and investment style, active or passive, they should be equally able to use the RISP 500™ just as easily.

It took us a lot of efforts and a long time to develop the entire model, filter and select the most relevant variables, calibrate them, build the database, test, fix errors, refine, test again, refine again, and periodically recalibrate variables and fine-tune the model to adjust to a constantly evolving market, improving its performance to finally have our own viable model algorithm. An earlier version called Outperform delivered incredible results as a trading signal project and it was discontinued in mid-2023. We decided to make a serious improvement and make it the tool we had envisioned: we wanted a risk management tool and not a trading signal project only because it would benefit more investors, including professional wealth/fund/investment managers and advisors, who already have their own preferred strategies. We could finally proudly complete the construction phase of the RISP 500™ Project and hope it will help you too with a new powerful weapon in your investor toolbox or arsenal. Instead of a trading signal or warning signal, our proprietary RISP 500™ risk metric is much more because it can help anyone make decisions according to their own risk tolerance levels and their own preferred asset choices and strategies. We believe it translates best the meaning of Stock Market Investing Guided by Risk Management.

What is the Logic Behind the RISP 500™?

In a nutshell, the RISP 500™ Project is based on a piece of very simple logic:

"The probability for the stock market to go up or down at any given moment is intimately connected to the level of uncertainty or perception of risk in the minds of investors at a collective level."

Since no one has a crystal ball to predict the future with certainty, we can only work with probabilities. The argument is based on the historically observed fact that when risks in the market are high, the odds for the market to respond negatively is greater than the odds for it to respond positively, and vice-versa. Does it mean that every time risks increase, the S&P 500® will go down? No. But it's more likely it will than not. This logic is similarly used in gambling and Game Theory. Take poker players, for example. Like stock investors or traders, poker players also operate under an environment of risk, uncertainty and must deal with probabilities. They must be calculating and reassessing their win-loss odds at every turn. When the odds favor them, they can play more aggressively. When the odds don't favor them, they are more likely to play more conservatively or even pass, depending on their personal risk tolerance and goals. Intelligently responding to odds after calculating them at every moment will ensure that players are making optimal decisions in a probabilistic world. This is exactly our goal.

We do this by executing a simple daily workflow: Measure → Calculate → Take Action:

You may simply adopt 2 levels of risk (LOW and HIGH) like in the example above, if you like, and establish an Action to Take such as a simple Risk ON / Risk OFF. But you may always add more levels, like the example below, with 4 levels of risk (Extremely Low, Moderately Low, Moderately High, Extremely High):

THE RISP 500™ ASSET-RISK STRATEGY MATRIX

	Level of Risk	Directional Asset	Leverage	Volatility
	EXTREMELY HIGH	CASH	NO	VXIM (LONG VOL)
RISP 500™ ▶	MODERATELY HIGH	IEF, IYR (BONDS, RE)	NO	NO
	MODERATELY LOW	SPY (S&P 500)	SSO (S&P x2)	NO
	EXTREMELY LOW	QQQ (NASDAQ 100)	QLD (NASDAQ x2)	SVXY (SHORT VOL)

Conservative Investor

Moderate Investor

Aggressive Investor

NOTE: This asset selection is only an **example**. Asset selection must be customized for each investor according to risk-return profile, risk tolerance, and goals.

TIP ☞ Every risk level can actually be explored with different assets by smart investors. Most investors today, including investment managers, are so used to focusing on a single strategy with only one or two asset types that they miss a fantastic opportunity to boost their returns. For example, long-only equities, long/short, growth/value, sector, etc. and stocks-only or stocks/bonds. If investment managers just added one new dimension (a risk dimension) to their existing strategies, a new world of untapped profitable opportunities will open up by selecting and timing different assets to explore different risk levels. In each level of risk, you can invest in assets that tend to perform best for that risk level. You can actively switch between them, under the guidance of a risk measure like the RISP 500™. This is risk management on a whole new level, taking a proactive and active role to help you outperform your own results standing you out from the crowd playing the same old game.

CHAPTER 4

4. Stock Market Investing Guided by Risk Management: A New Paradigm

And we venture to speculate that it may be revolutionary to the way investors currently make investment decisions. But it hasn't started that way. From our studies, we found out that the best early indicators of risk and potential trouble in the stock market came from the equity derivatives markets (or the so-called VIX world). In fact, it wasn't only us, because several other researchers and practitioners were already also working in the same direction.

Why equity derivatives (VIX world)? It actually makes perfect sense why the equity derivatives market is a rich source for early signs of trouble. Without being too technical, I offer an analogy to help explain the concept. Imagine you are a car insurance company selling policies to protect customers from auto theft and collision. Since you are selling protection from adverse events to customers, for a premium, you are essentially absorbing their risks upon yourself. To survive with all these risks and still thrive in the insurance business, you must know all about theft and collision probabilities much better than your customers and you must be able to price them accurately and still make a profit. You must also be extremely sensitive (way more than anyone else) to any change in the market's stats and collective perception of risks. Make sense? Back in the stock market, the risk "insurers" are the sellers of put options and other derivatives structured to protect large, institutional investors (such as pension funds, etc.) from the downside risks of their stock portfolios. For a premium, risks get transferred to them in the derivatives market, and that's why they always have to be one step ahead of everyone else. They must be extremely sensitive to the miniscule change in the market's collective perception of risk. All we needed to do was to read the data from this market, filter out the noise, and extract useful and valuable early signals for our early risk warning system. We will discuss the mechanics and details of how this is done later in The Science Behind the RISP 500™ Methodology.

What's More Reliable: Your View, My View, or the Market's Collective View?

What is more reliable: a forecast (future) or data you can measure right now (present)? I'm sure you would answer that data measured at the present is much more reliable than a projection based on subjective assumptions. As we discussed, most methods people use to navigate the markets (fundamental, technical analysis, or a combination of both) involve some degree of a projection or forecast about the future. Well, an educated guess is still that: a guess. But you may argue, "What about the information you extract from the VIX markets? Aren't VIX indicators, such as VIX Futures, forecasts about future volatility, too?" Yes, the data we measure from the VIX Futures market is about the risk collectively forecasted in the market at the present moment.

Here is the catch that must be noted and understood. First, VIX Futures data reflects the market at the present moment. Second, VIX Futures is a market and thus its traded prices reflect a collective consensus on future values of the VIX index. People are betting real money on it. It is not my forecast, your forecast, or a forecast of some research analyst or investment professional; it's the market's collective view. For these reasons, we trust this data much more than personal opinions and their forecasts, which may be much more prone to errors and human biases.

In fact, the evolution of asset prices in any market is always the net and final result of the entire collective action of market participants at each given moment in time. Isn't it, after all? The collective perception of risk, measured or not, ends up defining market behavior and the supply-demand dynamics for stocks or other risky assets. Such information may be collected from the markets themselves. As discussed, one such market is the equity derivatives market. That is where most of the information used as input in risk management-guided systems are collected, filtered, and analyzed, but we look at many other sources as well.

The Gain-Loss Asymmetry

What is the "secret" to long-term survival in the game and outperformance? It starts with your defense. Why? **Pullbacks** (price drops of 5-10%) are relatively easy to recover from and we do this often without much pain, perhaps in a few weeks or months. **Corrections** (price drops of 10-20%) are harder to swallow and take longer to recover. But still, we may recover within a semester to a year or so. **Crashes** (price drops of more than 20%) are dangerous and may take years to recover, depending on their severity. This is in part due to the gain-loss asymmetry.

The gain-loss asymmetry: A loss costs more to recover than a gain of the same percentage change. In other words, if you lose **48%** of your stock position (such as what happened to the S&P 500® during the 2000s internet bubble crash), you will need the market to go up by a whopping **108%** just to get back to your original position (only to break even). It took the S&P 500® almost 7 years to recover.

Loss Percentage (Drawdown)	Subsequent return required to break-even
-20%	+25%
-30%	+43%
-40%	+67%
-50%	+100%
-60%	+150%

That's why a few large losses are so costly for most people and may take years to make whole again, just to undo the damage suffered. Such drawdowns may cause irreparable damage to "buy & hold" investors, both active and passive, soon-to-be retirees, and may even mean game over for small money traders and aggressive traders. Always remember:

The best way to avoid having to dig out of a hole is by not falling in it in the first place!

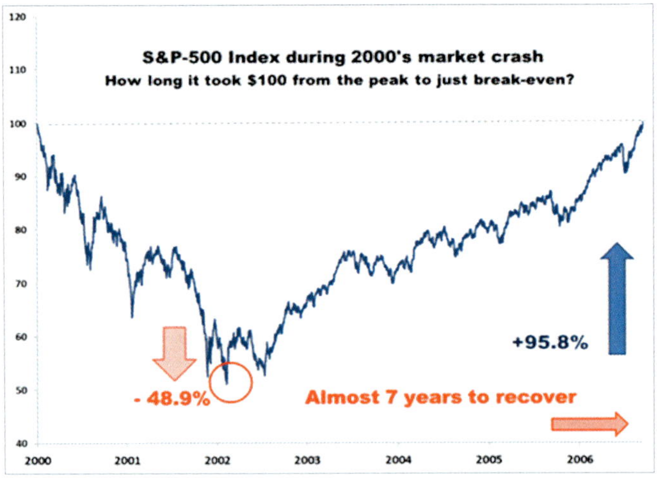

Now, picture this: **you don't have to fall into these traps!** If you diligently measure the risks in the market on a daily basis, with the help of RISP 500™, you will be warned early to avoid the riskier moments of the market awaiting in safety positions before returning when the market becomes safer again to **profit from the recovery stage of the crash**.

Check the section titled "See It in Action: How RISP 500™ Protects Investors from Market Crashes" later in the book to see how the worst of the 2008 Global Financial Crisis and the 2020 Coronavirus Crash were averted by the RISP 500™.

How the RISP 500™ Is Determined

Now that you have learned how the RISP 500™ Project came about and why Risk Management is so important for all stock investors, let's discuss how the RISP 500™ is determined.

The RISP 500™ is a measurement of risk present at the stock market. It is the end result of a large number of computations on variables carefully selected from various markets (not only the stock market itself) to detect early minute changes in the markets that have the potential to escalate quickly and create a dangerous money-losing drawdown. The algorithm or model that performs the number crunching and produces the daily RISP 500™ is proprietary and was developed over many attempts and much improved over the years. It's not a static formula but it learns from the markets as they evolve over time. Parameters are recalibrated as necessary and new relevant variables may be added while variables that lost relevance may be dropped. This is an important feature because regimes do change over time in the markets and we must be vigilant and adapt the model as changes occur and everything evolves.

The RISP 500™ algorithm takes in data from multiple markets because they are all interconnected and the inter-market relationships, although not always constant over time, can be exploited. See diagram. Price action in the stock market is ultimately the net result of the collective supply and demand for stocks, which in turn are influenced by a much larger number of variables.

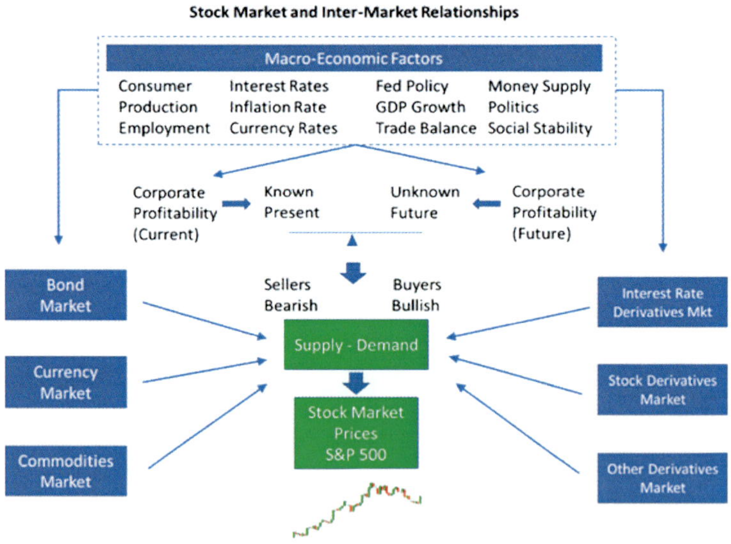

For example, do interest rates affect this delicate balance of forces of supply (sellers) and demand (buyers) in the stock market? Sure!

What about the value of the U.S. dollar? That too! Where do you get the freshest information about interest and currency rates? The bond market and currency (FX) market, respectively. From their respective derivatives markets, you can even get their volatility expectations. By the way, the VIX-equivalent indicator in the bond market is the MOVE (Merrill Lynch Volatility Estimate) and in the currency market, it is the JP Morgan FX Volatility Index. All these markets are interconnected and subject to the same macro-economic factors in the U.S. economy and world economy as well. But not all factors or variables have equal weight in determining stock prices. Variables directly extracted from the stock market itself and the equity derivatives markets (VIX world) are naturally given greater importance in the model because they already incorporate information from variables further upstream. Plus, we trust raw market data more than economic data (coming from formulas, etc.), projections, and surveys. Read The Science Behind the RISP 500™ Methodology to learn more details.

The RISP 500™ Percentile Rank

The RISP 500™ is a calculated number that summarizes the risk information extracted from all the variables the algorithm collects and measures. Currently, it is working with more than 15 relevant variables that give us the best picture of the current risk in the market consolidated in a single number. To be considered good, it must give us an accurate picture both in terms of magnitude and timing. It must be sensitive enough to detect minute changes in sentiment but also have a fast reaction time. These are all necessary requirements if we want an early risk warning system.

However, the calculated values of the RISP 500™ are not normalized or standardized. In other words, they don't have an upper or lower limit. The best way to use the RISP 500™ is by its **Percentile Rank**.

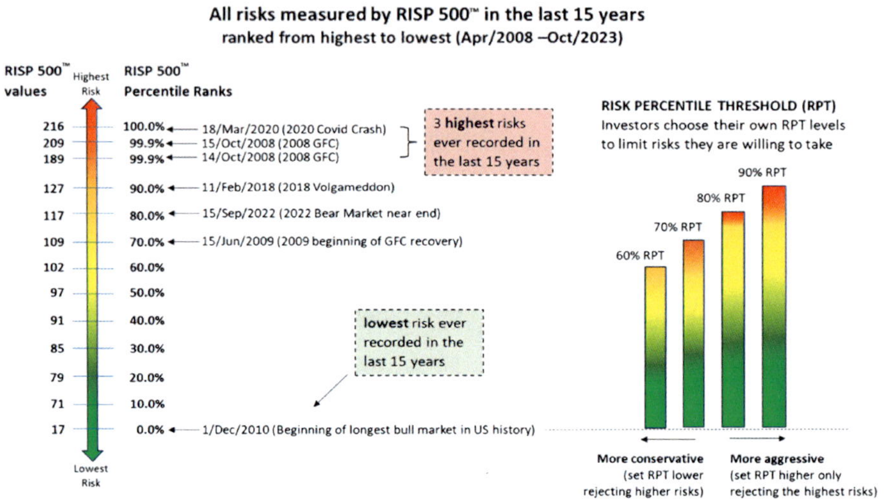

The **Percentile Rank** of a value of the RISP 500™ compares it to itself in the historical context. To do this, we ranked all risk values measured daily since April 29th, 2008 from the highest to the lowest. See diagram above. The highest ever measured (216) will correspond to the 100th percentile and the lowest (17) to the 0th percentile. For example, a RISP 500™ value of 117 has a Percentile Rank of 80.0% (or the 80th percentile). This means that 117 is greater than 80% of all values determined daily for the RISP 500™ since April 29th, 2008, when we started computing values. To put it another way, a value of 117 corresponds to a level of risk that is higher than those that occurred 80% of the time since we started measuring it.

Remember, risk is a relative concept. In absolute terms, risk doesn't have much useful meaning in this context. It only makes sense to say A is riskier than B or A is more volatile than B. Furthermore, we all see, perceive, and feel risks differently. Some people are conservative, preferring safety and not tolerating volatility well. Others want high returns and even seek riskier activities and behaviors.

Risk Percentile Threshold (RPT)

The RISP 500™ Personalized for Each Investor

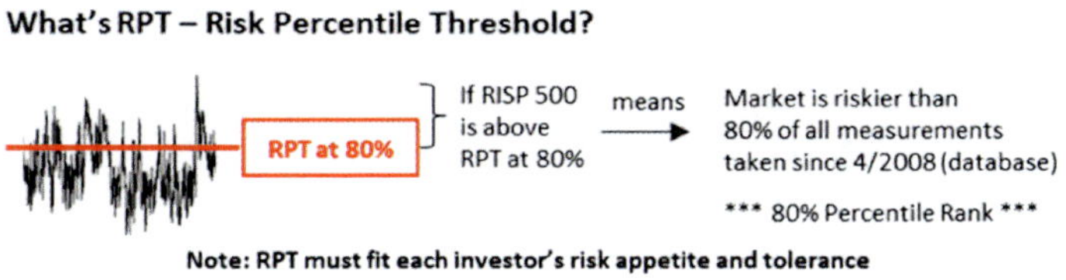

Here is where you determine your own personal **Risk Percentile Threshold (RPT)**. Let's start with the basic setup with two risk levels. In this case, you will have a Risk ON and a Risk OFF states. To distinguish them you will need to choose a Risk Percentile Threshold:

- If you are a **very conservative investor**, prefer a lower risk, and are fine with a lower return, you may want to choose a very low **Risk Percentile Threshold (RPT)** such as 66.7% (meaning you want to be out of the market in the $1/3^{rd}$ riskiest days), for example, or an even lower RPT.

- If you are a **very aggressive investor**, want a higher return, and are fine with a higher risk, you may want to choose a very high Risk Percentile Threshold (RPT) such as 90% (meaning you want to be out of the market only in the $1/10^{th}$ riskiest days), for example, or even higher.

***On a side note**: Buy & Hold investors are in the market 100% of the time but think it's the most conservative thing to do. How ironic! They couldn't be more wrong!*

- If you are a **moderate risk investor** and want a more balanced risk-return profile for your investments, you may want to choose a Risk Percentile Threshold (RPT) such as 70%, 75%, 80%, 85%, or any level in between that you feel most comfortable with.

To help you select the best RPT, we prepared a comprehensive study back-testing various RPT points and showed the statistics. Refer to the Simulation & Back-Testing Results section later in this book.

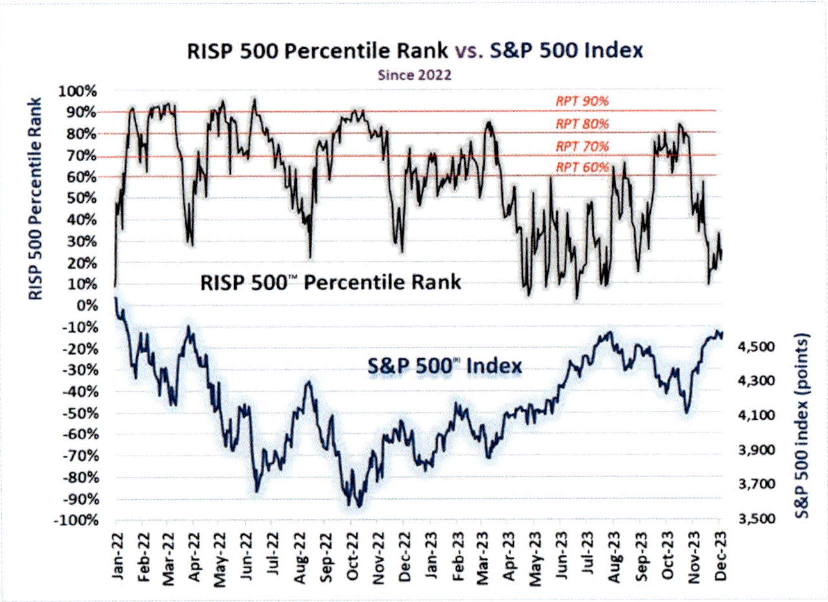

To see how the whole setup works in practice, refer to a case study showing how the system protected investors in a crash in the next section.

To wrap up this topic, here is a summary how to use RISP 500™ (two risk levels):

RISP 500™ Percentile Rank
- → RISP 500™ PR > RPT: Stay out or seek protection
- → RISP 500™ PR < RPT: Stay invested, safer market

Therefore, instead of telling you which Risk Percentile Threshold you should use, we only calculate the risk of the day for you and its percentile rank and we let you choose your own RPT that best fits your risk tolerance and goals. Don't worry if you don't know what RPT to select because we are going to guide you on making the best choice. We tested several scenarios and will show you the results to help you decide.

With the Percentile Rank of the RISP 500™, you can judge by yourself, based on your own risk tolerance, whether the measured risk in the market is worth taking or not

---

Fine-tuning: Once selected, we suggest you keep your RPT fixed, at least for some time, so you can judge your results. You can fine-tune it later by adjusting your RPT up or down as necessary. If you find that you can take a bit more risk to get a bit more return, just dial your RPT up a notch. With a higher RPT, you will accept taking up higher risks and be invested in risky assets in more days (more exposure). But if you feel you need to reduce your risk a little, given the results, just dial your RPT down a notch or two. In other words, now you have complete control right in your own hands! Remember, everyone gets the same RISP 500™ every day. What action we each will take and our results will depend on the RPT we each have selected.

Risk On, Risk Off: A Simple Two-Risk Level System

The simplest system that can be created is a two-risk level system. You will basically have a low and a high risk levels. You will have one RPT to choose, separating the two levels from each other. You can think of it like a two-weather system (good weather vs. bad weather) as illustrated below:

The most basic strategy you can adopt could be choosing an index ETF (e.g., S&P 500® or Nasdaq 100) to hold when risk is low and rotate it to cash when risk is high. See an example in the diagram below:

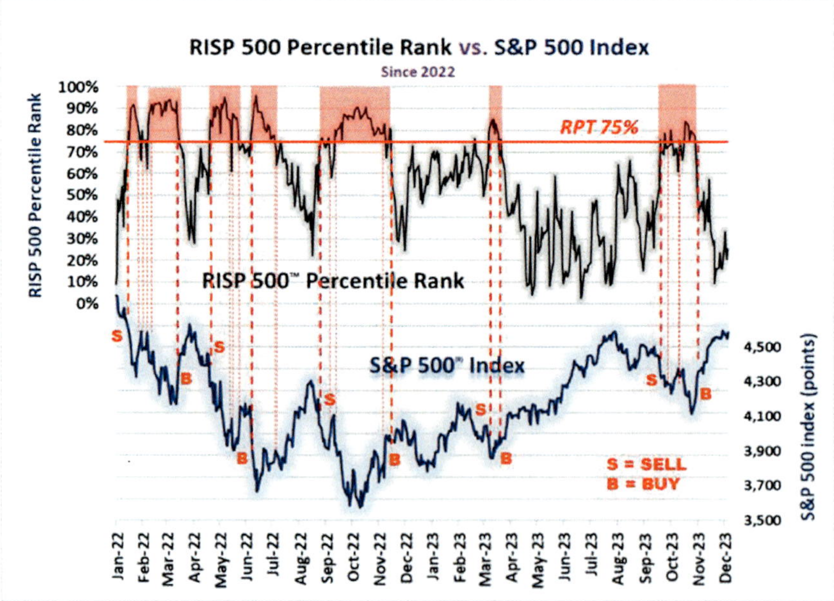

Note that every time the RISP 500™ line (black) crosses the RPT line (red), which marks the 75th percentile in this example, there is an action to take. If it crosses from below the RPT line, you would buy the risky asset. If it crossed from above, you would sell the risky asset and seek safety (rotate to the safe asset).

Three or more risk level systems

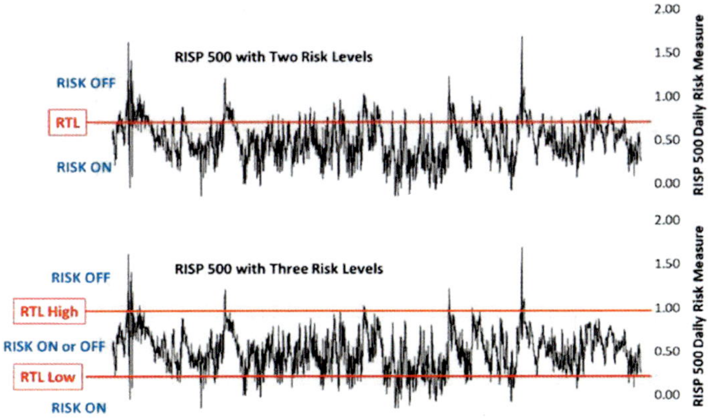

If you have decided for 3 risk levels instead, you would have to choose 2 RPTs.

In the intermediate risk level where risk is neither too high nor too low, you may choose to be either Risk ON or OFF, or better still, choose assets that perform better under such conditions.

But if you want 4 risk levels, choose 3 RPTs, and so on and so forth. That way, you will select the best assets for each risk level to explore the market conditions to the fullest for each level.

The best way to understand how all this works in practice is by seeing how the system performed in the real market. In the next section, we show how RISP 500™ combined with the RPT guided us to avoid the worst of the 2020 Coronavirus Crash and the 2008 GFC.

Notice how different levels of RPT signaled a market action (buy/sell) at different times. Notice also that a high RPT (90%) kept you exposed in the market longer than a low RPT (70%). Finally, notice how a low RPT guided you to safety sooner but a high RPT guided you back to the market to explore the recovery sooner.

SEE IT IN ACTION

How RISP 500™ Protects Investors from Market Crashes

Seeing is believing. Let's shed some light on details of the protection objective of the RISP 500™ by showing how a 2-risk level strategy with the most basic strategy (SPY or Cash) would have performed during two major crashes: the **2020 Coronavirus Crash** and the **2008 Global Financial Crisis**. We are going to illustrate three levels of RPT: 70%, 80%, and 90%. We are also reproducing the scenarios with real data.

Recall that the lower the RPT, the less risky the strategy is, and the move to safety action will be triggered more frequently. An RPT below 70% will meet the needs of conservative investors better. Conversely, the higher the RPT, the riskier the strategy is, and the move to safety action will be triggered less frequently. It's easier to see effect on the charts visually. The RPT line cuts through the RISP 500™ line higher or lower. It's like skimming off the top at a higher or lower cutoff level to be in a safety position.

In the series of charts below, the graph on top is the RISP 500™ Percentile Rank and the graph at the bottom is the S&P 500®. Green **B**s denote "Buy SPY" and red **S**s denote "Sell SPY". A trade is triggered every time the red RPT line is crossed. A cross from under the RPT line will result in a **S** and a cross from above the RPT line will result in a **B**. As a result, the moments when the strategy is holding the SPY (invested in the S&P 500®) are areas painted in red. The moments when the strategy is holding CASH are areas painted in green. Examine the charts carefully comparing the effects of each RPT on the results during serious market crashes. Which level of RPT you believe matches better your own investor profile? You can see exactly how you can easily customize RISP 500™ for your needs. Crystal ball? No! But the next best thing, we believe so!

* * * 2020 Coronavirus Crash * * *

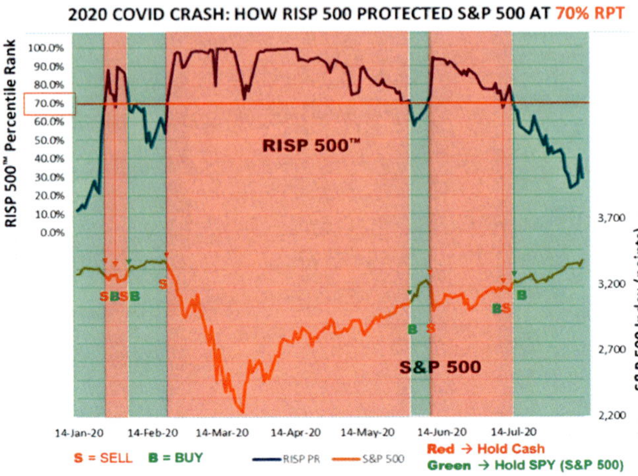

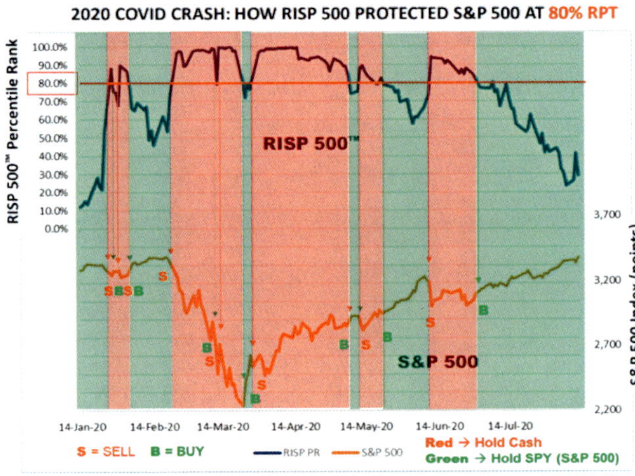

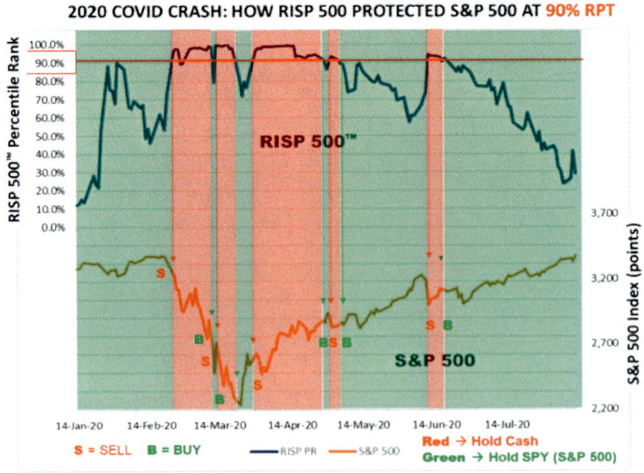

* * * 2008 Global Financial Crisis * * *

2008 GFC: HOW RISP 500 PROTECTED S&P 500 AT 70% RPT

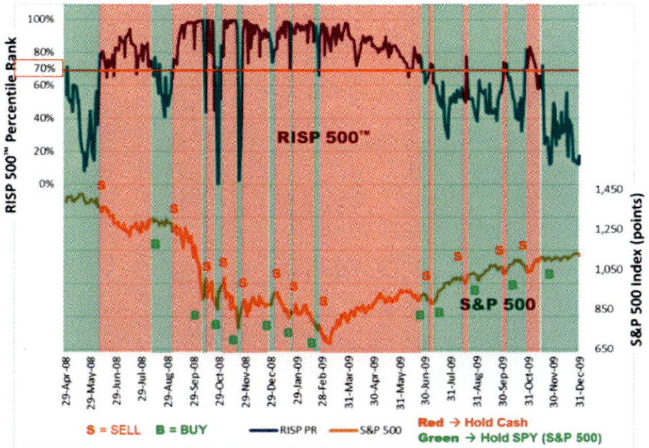

2008 GFC: HOW RISP 500 PROTECTED S&P 500 AT 80% RPT

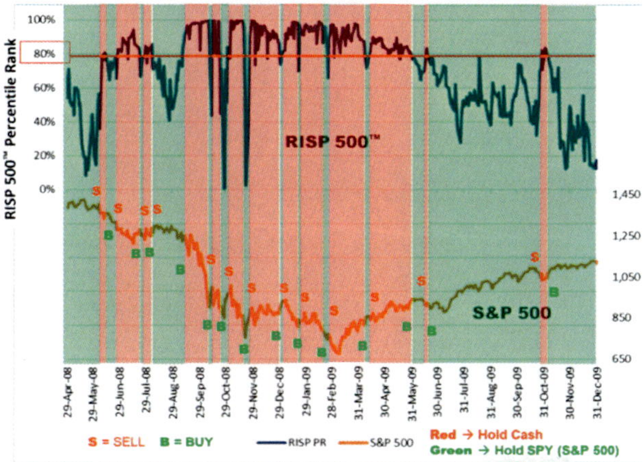

2008 GFC: HOW RISP 500 PROTECTED S&P 500 AT 90% RPT

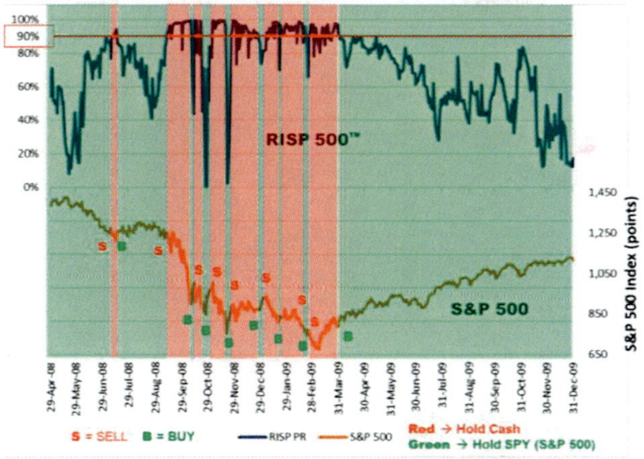

Understanding How RPT Affect Your Results

The RPT you choose will determine your results and it's very important that you understand this mechanism. It will also help you choose your own RPT. The good news is that it's quite easy to understand it visually. Let's envision two hypothetical two investors:

- Conservative Investor, who chose RPT = 70%
- Aggressive Investor, who chose RPT = 90%

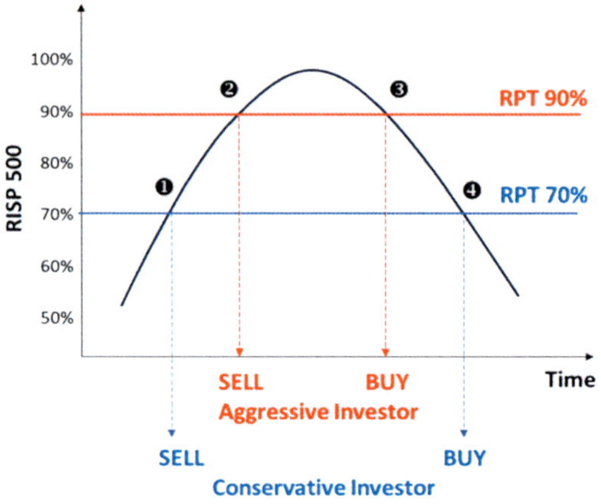

Let's see what happens if the RISP 500 Percentile Rank goes up to 95% and then goes down. On its way up, it must cross the 70% line before crossing the 90% line. But on its way down, it must cross the 90% line before crossing the 70% line. See image.

At point ❶, the Conservative Investor's RPT line (70%) gets crossed, so she will sell the risk asset to rotate to safety. At point ❷, the Aggressive Investor's RPT line (90%) gets crossed, so it's now his turn to sell the risk asset to seek safety. Note that conservative investors will typically seek safety selling the risk asset before aggressive investors when risks increase.

But the opposite happens when risks decrease. At point ❸, the Aggressive Investor's RPT line (90%) gets crossed, so he will buy the risk asset back to return to the market. At point ❹, the Conservative Investor's RPT line (70%) gets crossed, so it's now her turn to buy the risk asset back returning to the market too. Note that aggressive investors will typically return to the market buying back the risk asset before conservative investors when risks decrease.

Note also that the Aggressive Investor holds the risk asset longer than the Conservative Investor. In other words, the Aggressive Investor is exposed to market risks longer than the Conservative Investor.

This explains why in the charts of the two cases studies shown earlier, the red areas are wider than green areas for a lower RPT compared to that of a higher RPT.

Ironically, a Buy & Hold long-term passive investor is exposed 100% of the time and thinks that he is playing safe. Now you know that it is far from the truth. No wonder they suffer so much from the market's rollercoaster. They talk themselves into believing that in the long-term, it's ok to lose in a market crash, or multiple market crashes over a few decades, because *the market always goes up in the long run*. Well, I don't know about you but I would not bet my future or my retirement on it!

CHAPTER 5

5. The Science Behind the RISP 500™ Methodology

Mathematical relationships and memory of past events - In a nutshell, we analyze incoming new data and historical data to explore the relationships among a number of relevant variables directly observable or implied from various markets simultaneously. For example, the futures markets and volatility markets provide us with extremely valuable real-time information. Our algorithm then applies statistics and other analytical methods to crunch the data, treat it, filter out the noise, and capture key elements to determine the most accurate possible number representing the current risk in the stock market, represented by the RISP 500™ index.

As explained before, we rely heavily on hard data and data only, not opinions, forecasts, etc. We will explain some of the variables that help us compute the RISP 500™ index every day. We will dig a bit deeper into the technical aspects of the methodology here. If you aren't familiar with options, volatility, or related advanced concepts, and some things sound Greek to you, don't panic. Keep reading and take note of the parts you don't understand. Take our online courses (visit https://www.engineering-finance.com) to learn more and increase your financial IQ.

As soon as this book is published, we will start to produce on-demand online courses to help investors at all levels of proficiency (from beginner to advanced) gain this knowledge. Don't forget to sign up with your email to be notified when new courses, books, and workshops become available: https://www.engineering-finance.com. We will also offer a few mentorship opportunities for a more personalized experience, if interested.

Volatility Markets

We monitor the volatility world in the equity derivatives markets not just to trade awesome strategies there but also because they offer us a treasure of useful information about the underlying stock market. As explained earlier, volatility dealers are typically the most sophisticated in their class and those who provide hedge against market downturns to large institutional investors are often one step ahead of everyone else in the market. The reason is simple: for a price, volatility dealers sell protection to stock investors by taking up their downside risks. If the collective perception of risks increases by just a tiny bit, these dealers would be the first to detect. They are extremely sensitive. After all, they are in the business of buying and selling risk. That's great but can we capture this information from them?

We can actually "read their mind" by interpreting volatility information embedded in the pricing of their hedge products such as put options on the S&P 500® traded at CBOE. The volatility numbers extracted from option prices are called "implied volatilities". As the name suggests, "implied" means the volatility number that was actually used to price options offered and traded at the CBOE exchange. As we will discuss in a minute, "implied volatility" is not the same as actual volatility measured in the stock market and also not the same as historical volatility measured in the past. It's forward-looking and incorporates a certain margin for error as well as profit for taking up the risk. Naturally, options with high implied volatility have higher premiums.

Two important notes about implied volatilities: first, there is not one single implied volatility but many; i.e., one for each maturity (time period, e.g., 1 month, 3 months, 1 year, etc.) and "moneyness" (options are offered for multiple strike prices in-the-money, at-the-money, and out-of-the-money relative to the current price of the S&P 500®).

And second, there is a difference between implied volatilities and the actual volatility observed in the S&P 500®, or its historical volatility. Why? The best way to explain this concept is a little role play here, by placing yourself in the shoes of a protection seller or a put option seller (the dealer). The higher the volatility in the stock market, the more likely the option you sold will be exercised and you could lose money without limitation. Therefore, you would price the option premium higher assuming a higher volatility in your option pricing model. This higher volatility that you have just put in your pricing model is precisely the implied volatility. The difference between the implied volatility and the actual volatility of the S&P 500® is called Volatility Risk Premium (VRP). This is the first variable we use in our RISP 500™ model that we are going to explain in the next page.

Volatility Risk Premium (VRP)

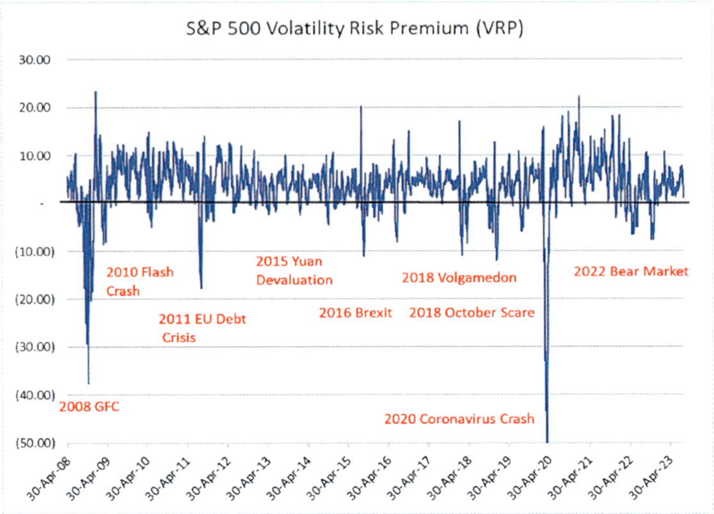

As we have just explained, VRP increases when the actual volatility of the stock market increases. This happens because option sellers need to protect themselves and still make a profit. Imagine you are a car insurance company insuring against a car collision. If traffic becomes chaotic and the number of accidents shoot up, you must increase the premiums you collect from car owners, or you will lose money. It's the same principle here. VRP exists and serves the purpose to protect hedge providers. Therefore, VRP must be a positive number, because implied volatility must always be greater than actual volatility, right? Not so fast! In normal times, yes, but in times of distress, no, because when risk in the stock market shoots up, actual volatility may outpace it and go above implied volatility. Thus, this is an important signal for us. Note in the chart that VRP is positive most of the time and turns negative during times of distress in the market. We can measure the VRP from options traded at the CBOE exchange. In summary:

Volatility Risk Premium (VRP)
- VRP > 0: Low risk in the stock market
- VRP < 0: High risk in the stock market

We actually don't use VRP directly and simplistically as shown above in our algorithm, but we treat the raw data converting it to a different format because of a few technicalities. First of all, taken alone, the VRP is not able to produce an early risk warning signal. We need an actionable signal that is produced very early. However, <u>taken together with other variables</u>, the VRP can offer us valuable clues. Another thing to note is that what we call actual volatility of the S&P 500® is not from the same day it is measured but over a recent period of a few days (7 days, 21 days, etc.) which is a look back number. However, implied volatility refers to a future period of time; i.e., a 30-day forward-looking number. By the way, such implied volatility is widely known as the **VIX**! The VIX is exactly the next variable we use in the RISP 500™ model, which we are going to discuss next. For the VRP analysis, we must make adjustments to make both numbers comparable. The VIX, extracted from options traded at CBOE, also needs to be treated or adjusted for a variable known as "**roll yield**", soon to be discussed as well.

Historical events offer compelling illustrations of VRP's significance in understanding market dynamics. During periods of economic uncertainty or market turmoil, such as the global financial crisis of 2008, VRP spiked sharply, reflecting heightened risk aversion among investors. Conversely, in bull markets or periods of low volatility, VRP remained subdued, signaling market confidence and low perceived risk. Again, taken alone, VRP is not without its limitations. Its effectiveness as a risk indicator is contingent upon market conditions. Moreover, VRP calculations rely on historical and forward-looking data, introducing potential lag and limiting real-time insights into market dynamics.

In summary, the VRP measures the compensation hedge sellers demand for bearing volatility risk. Research by academics and practitioners has shown that the VRP can be a useful predictor of future market returns in conjunction with other variables from the VIX world. When VRP is positive, it signifies relatively low perceived risk, as implied volatility exceeds realized volatility. Conversely, negative VRP indicates heightened risk and uncertainty, signaling potential market turbulence.

To delve deeper into the intricacies of VRP and its implications for financial markets, researchers and practitioners have produced a wealth of literature on volatility modeling, option pricing, and risk management. Notable studies have explored VRP's predictive power, its role in asset pricing models, and its implications for portfolio management strategies.

By incorporating these insights into your analysis of VRP, you gain a richer understanding of volatility dynamics and their implications for market participants. Whether navigating turbulent market conditions or capitalizing on periods of stability, VRP serves as a valuable tool for deciphering the language of market sentiment and risk perception.

References and Further Reading:

"The Volatility Risk Premium" by Tim Kroencke, Maik Schmeling, and Andreas Schrimpf (2015)

"The Volatility Risk Premium: A Practical Guide" by Simon Gervais, Ron Kaniel, and Dan Mingelgrin (2018)

"The Volatility Risk Premium Embedded in Stock Options" by Bryan Kelly, Hao Jiang, and Dacheng Xiu (2014)

"The Volatility Risk Premium" by Carol Alexander and Johannes M. Ordu

"The VIX, the Variance Premium and Stock Market Volatility" by Robert E. Whaley

VIX

The VIX was introduced by the Chicago Board Options Exchange (CBOE) in 1993. Initially, it tracked the Black-Scholes implied volatilities of options on the S&P 500® with near-the-money strikes. However, its rise to stardom came in 2003 when the CBOE redefined it as a model-free measure and released a time series of daily closing prices starting in January 1990. Its primary purpose is to serve as a fear gauge. When the VIX is high, it indicates heightened uncertainty and potential market turbulence. Conversely, a low VIX suggests calm and confidence. Nevertheless, we may use VIX as another piece of the puzzle in the construction of a risk measuring device to serve our purposes of an early signal of distress in the stock market.

Traders and investors monitor the VIX to gauge market sentiment. A rising VIX often accompanies stock market declines, as fear drives investors to seek protection. It helps identify potential market turning points. Extreme VIX spikes can signal market bottoms, while prolonged low VIX levels may precede market tops. In our formulation with the VIX, we go much beyond just that. Sophisticated traders employ VIX-based strategies, such as volatility arbitrage and volatility targeting. These strategies capitalize on discrepancies between implied and realized volatility. Institutions and individual investors use VIX-related products (such as VIX futures or options) to hedge their portfolios against market downturns. When the VIX rises, these products become more valuable, offsetting losses in other holdings.

Volatility is always equated to risk because a variable (e.g., a stock price) is volatile if it's uncertain. The uncertainty often leads to negative outcomes because investors dislike uncertainty and, more often than not, sell their stocks in droves (risk aversion). The VIX, or "the fear index," is a calculated index that measures the expected volatility of the S&P 500® index over the next 30 days but annualized. In other words, the VIX is the expected change within 1 standard deviation over the next 30 days expressed in annual terms. To convert the VIX into expected 1-day change in the S&P 500®, all you need to do is to multiply it by the square root of 252, which is the number of trading days in a year (remember the VIX number is annualized). For example, if the VIX is 10, the expected 1-day change implied by the VIX is 10% x √252 = ± 0.63% per day. A widely used rule of thumb is to consider a VIX of 30 to be the limit between a volatile market from a calm market. A VIX of 30 implies an expectation of 30% x √252 = ± 1.89% per day.

VIX	Daily S&P 500 +/- Change %
10	0.63%
20	1.26%
30	1.89%
40	2.52%
50	3.15%
60	3.78%
70	4.41%
80	5.04%
90	5.67%
100	6.30%

That said, remember that the VIX is actually greater than the expected volatility in the stock market in normal times because it includes the VRP.

As said earlier, the VIX is the implied volatility derived from call and put option prices traded on the CBOE. Note that the VIX index itself is not tradable, but a metric calculated through a given formula. There is a similar volatility index for the Nasdaq 100: the VXN.

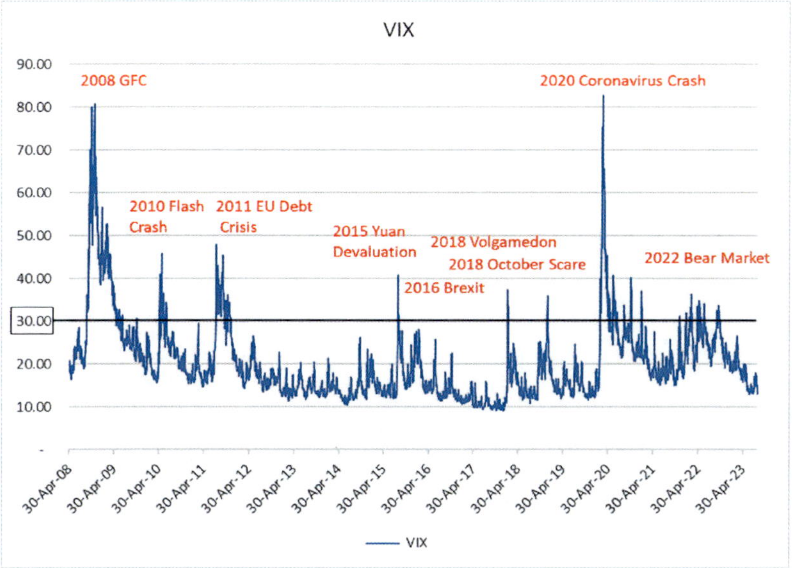

The VIX is called the fear index because it typically spikes during turbulent times and when uncertainty is high in the stock market. But not always though the correlation between the VIX and the underlying S&P 500® index is negative. The VIX index is directionless and measured as a standard deviation from a mean. Therefore, it's always plus or minus the amount of the standard deviation and not just minus as many people believe.

See in the historical chart above how the VIX peaked during periods of high uncertainty and distress in the markets. Real-life examples include the 2008 Financial Crisis when the VIX surged reaching unprecedented levels, which accurately reflected the panic and uncertainty prevailing in the markets at the time, and the 2020 COVID-19 pandemic when the VIX spiked sharply as the pandemic unfolded, signaling extreme fear and market turmoil.

Note that unlike stock prices, VIX and VXN do have mean-reversion attributes, making them useful to gauge risk. However, it's essential to note that while these indices provide valuable insights into market sentiment, they do not possess inherent predictive power when considered in isolation. As such, it may not always predict sudden shocks or black swan events and unfortunately don't work well as early warning signals. Many studies and back-testing have been done with the VIX in the hopes it offered early warning properties but not much predictive power was found, taken alone.

References and Further Reading:

"Understanding and Interpreting the VIX" by Christopher L. Culp and Anora Z. Mahmudova (2014)

"The Predictive Power of the VIX: Evidence from the S&P 500®" by Yingsha He and Tayfun Sönmez (2020)

"Trading VIX Derivatives: Trading and Hedging Strategies Using VIX Futures, Options, and Exchange-Traded Notes" by Russell Rhoads

"The VIX and its derivatives" by Enrique Sentana

CBOE's insights on the VIX and its indices

VIX Cash Term Structure Curve

A lot more key information can be extracted from the volatility world besides the VIX and the VRP. Adding the time dimension to VIX creates a whole new level for predictive power. Let's introduce the VIX cash term structure and the VIX futures term structure. Both provide a snapshot of market expectations regarding volatility over different time horizons but they are not the same. While the former estimates implied volatility into the future from the present day, the latter estimates VIX at future points in time. Let me clarify as it's a bit confusing. Remember the VIX is the estimation of implied volatility of options with maturity in the next 30 days (technically the CBOE will use out-of-the-money calls and puts on the S&P 500® expiring within 16 and 44 days). Additional data points using the same methodology can be created for the cash VIX term structure:

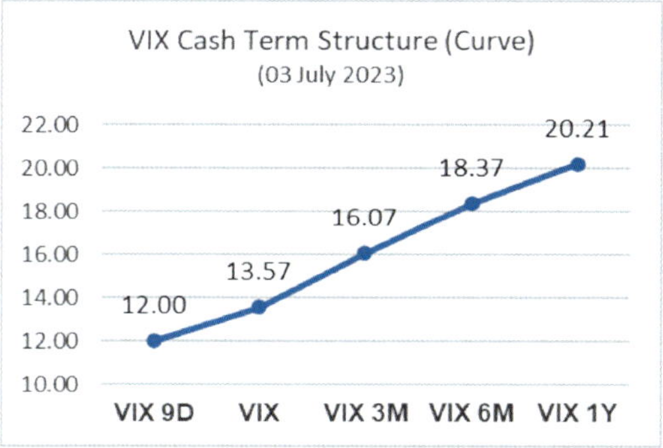

- VIX9D (9-day forward implied volatility)
- VIX (1-month forward implied volatility)
- VIX3M (3-month forward implied volatility)
- VIX6M (6-month forward implied volatility)
- VIX1Y (1-year forward implied volatility)

Plotted on a chart, the cash VIX term structure normally forms an upward sloping curve. But when risk increases, with higher uncertainty in the market, the curve may invert and become downward sloping because the near term will be priced at higher volatilities than the longer term. The VIX 9D moves the most and is also the fastest mover whereas VIX 1Y moves the least and is the slowest mover. Note that none of these variables are tradable. Just like the VIX, the others are calculated by the same methodology. On the other hand, VIX futures are tradable, which we will discuss next.

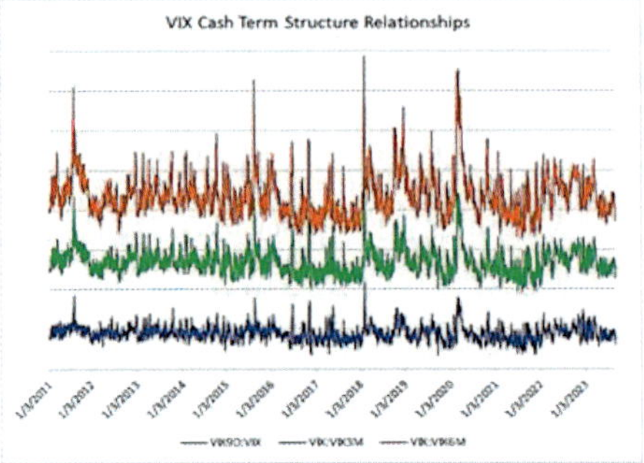

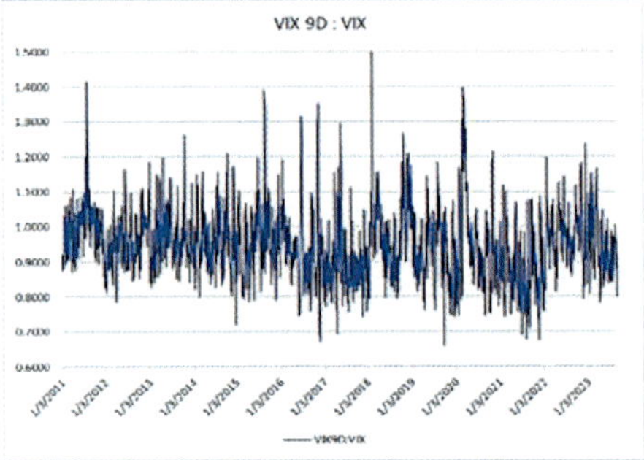

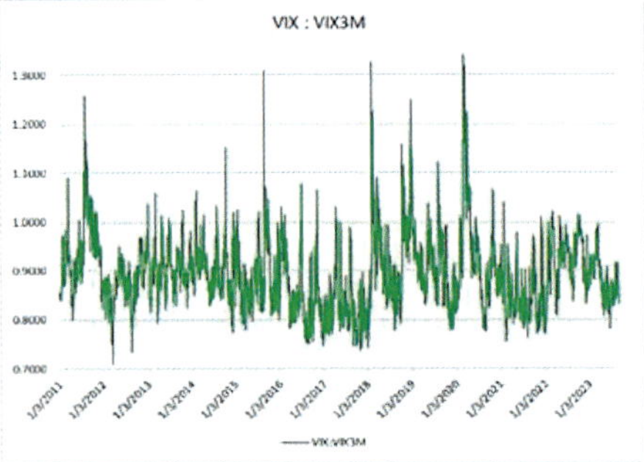

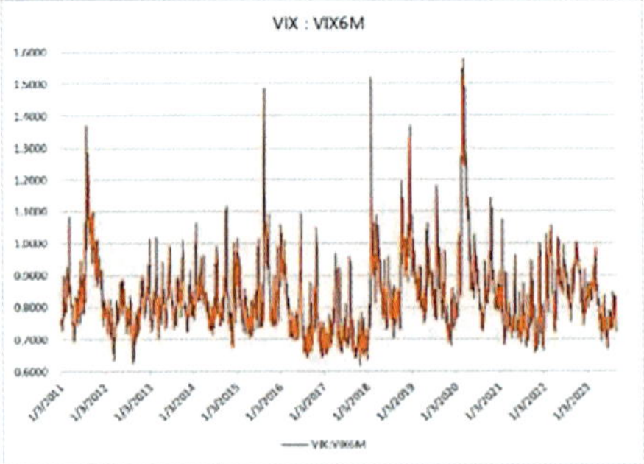

What we are interested in is not exactly the values along the VIX cash term structure curve but their relative positions along the curve (the shape of the curve). For this, we calculate the relative ratio of the value of each point along the curve to the VIX. For the example in the chart above taken on July 3rd, 2023, we have:

- VIX9D / VIX = 0.8843
- VIX / VIX3M = 0.8444
- VIX / VIX6M = 0.7387
- VIX / VIX1Y = 0.6714

Here is how historically these ratios have oscillated (see charts of ratios side by side).

For capturing the volatility for the shortest time frame (just 9 days), the VIX 9D / VIX is the fastest to react to changes in the market. If you want a fast-reacting signal, this is it. For the same reason, this indicator is the most volatile of them. In contrast, the VIX / VIX 1Y is the slowest to react. The other two sit in between. Which one you use or attribute more weight depends on your goals and time horizon. We use all of them, never in isolation, but always combined with many other indicators, as we had previously explained.

In a nutshell, several factors influence the VIX Cash Term Structure:

Market Sentiment: Bullish or bearish sentiment in the market can impact the shape of the term structure.

Economic Events: Significant economic releases, geopolitical events, central bank announcements, unexpected Fed´s interest rate policy and monetary policy, presidential elections, and unexpected events that cause a high degree of uncertainty can alter market expectations of future volatility.

Risk Appetite: Changes in risk appetite as well as anxiety facing uncertainty among investors can affect their demand for volatility protection, thereby influencing the shape of the term structure.

Market Liquidity: Liquidity conditions in VIX futures markets can impact the pricing of futures contracts and, consequently, the shape of the term structure.

VIX Futures Term Structure Curve

Both the VIX Cash Term Structure and the VIX Futures Term Structure, or volatility curve, refer to the relationship between the current spot VIX level and the expected future volatility levels as reflected in VIX futures prices over various expiration dates. They provide a snapshot of market expectations regarding volatility over different time horizons. The term structure can take different shapes, such as contango or backwardation. Contango occurs when longer-dated VIX futures trade at higher prices than near-term contracts, indicating expectations of increasing volatility in the future. Conversely, backwardation occurs when longer-dated futures trade at lower prices than near-term contracts, signaling expectations of decreasing volatility.

You can easily see the VIX Futures Term Structure at any time by visiting the site http://vixcentral.com/:

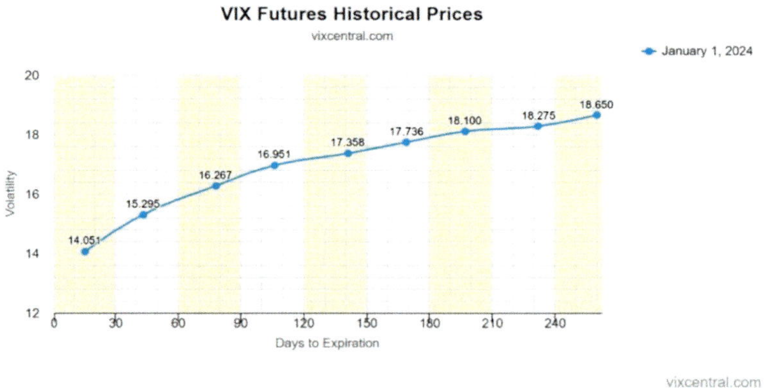

The same factors influence the VIX Futures Term Structure:

Market Sentiment: Bullish or bearish sentiment in the market can impact the shape of the term structure.

Economic Events: Significant economic releases, geopolitical events, central bank announcements, unexpected Fed´s interest rate policy and monetary policy, presidential elections, and unexpected events that cause a high degree of uncertainty can alter market expectations of future volatility.

Risk Appetite: Changes in risk appetite as well as anxiety facing uncertainty among investors can affect their demand for volatility protection, thereby influencing the shape of the term structure.

Market Liquidity: Liquidity conditions in VIX futures markets can impact the pricing of futures contracts and, consequently, the shape of the term structure.

But unlike the VIX cash term structure indicators, which are not tradable, VIX futures are actually traded at the CBOE exchange. Futures contracts expire on the 3rd Wednesday of each month. The first future (VX1) expires in up to one month, the second future (VX2) expires in up to two months, and so on and so forth. The VIX futures estimate the VIX on their respective expiration dates. For the same reasons as the VIX cash term structure, the VIX futures term structure is also normally upward sloping when plotted on a chart. We call this configuration a contango (VX1 < VX2 < VX3 < …). In turbulent and uncertain markets, when risk is high, the VIX futures curve becomes inverted and we call such a configuration a backwardation (VX1 > VX2 > VX3 >…). See charts below. The chart on top illustrates a **contango** situation on November 1st, 2019, before COVID-19 became a global concern. Contrast it with the chart on the bottom illustrating a **backwardation** on March 12th, 2020, well into the **Coronavirus market downturn**:

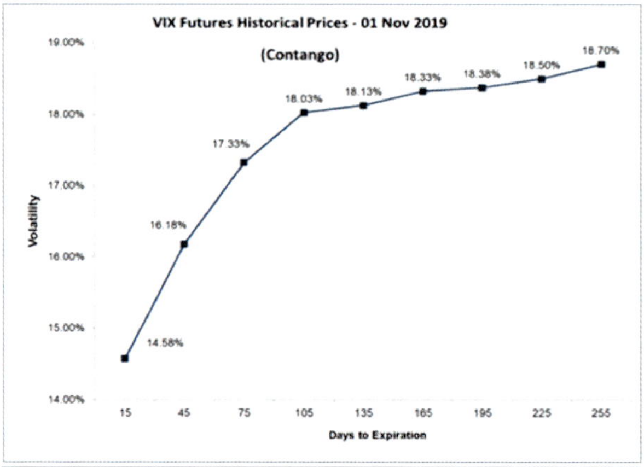

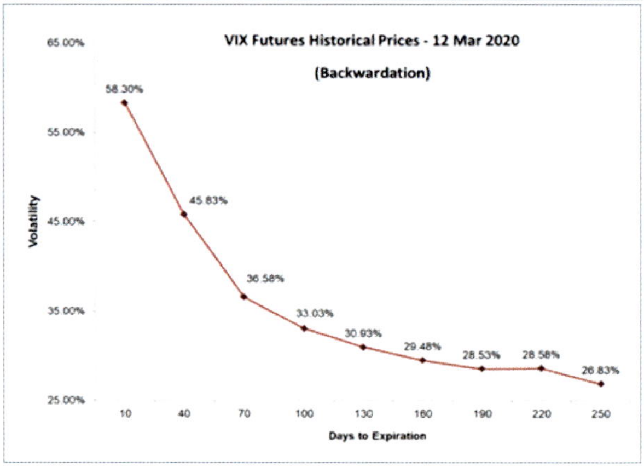

Note that not only the shape of the curve changed but also the absolute values of the volatility jumped to a whole new level with the coronavirus crisis. The shape itself may offer further clues. Often, during the transition between contango and backwardation, the shape of the curve may look very strange as VIX futures at different points in the time axis may fluctuate at different speeds and amplitudes.

The process of rolling futures contracts introduces **roll yield**, which can impact the performance of volatility-based strategies. This will be explained as our next variable from the volatility world.

How has the shape of the VIX Futures Curve helped anticipate the 2020 Coronavirus Crash

Let's examine how the shape looked along 14 points on the S&P 500 index price curve from November 1st, 2019 (before the Coronavirus Crash) to July 17th, 2020 on the chart below. We will also show a few additional points further forward in time (not depicted in the chart below).

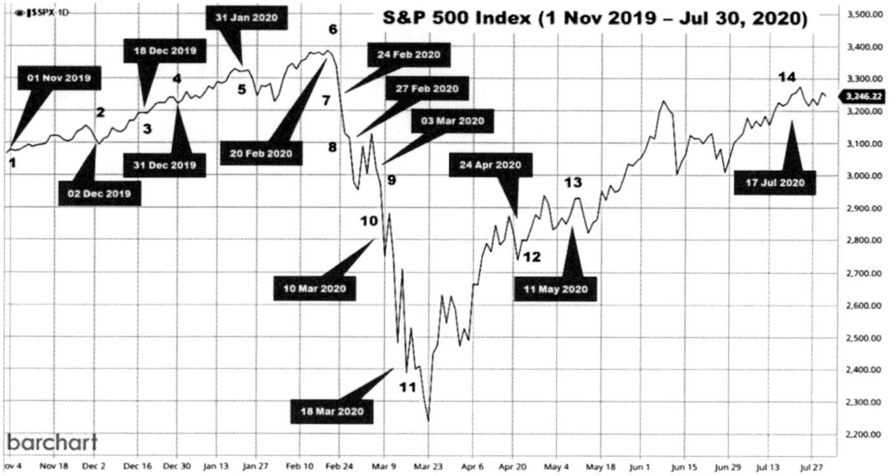

The Pre-Crash Phase

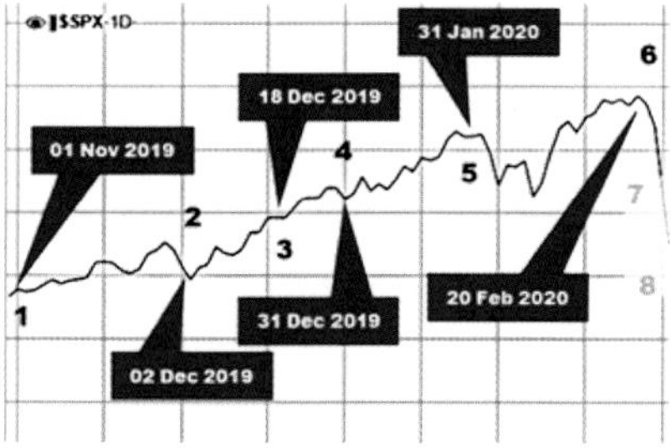

In the weeks leading up the 2020 Coronavirus, can you spot early and gradual indications of something very serious building up? Let's see snapshots of the VIX Futures Term Structure curve at 6 points in time before the crash.

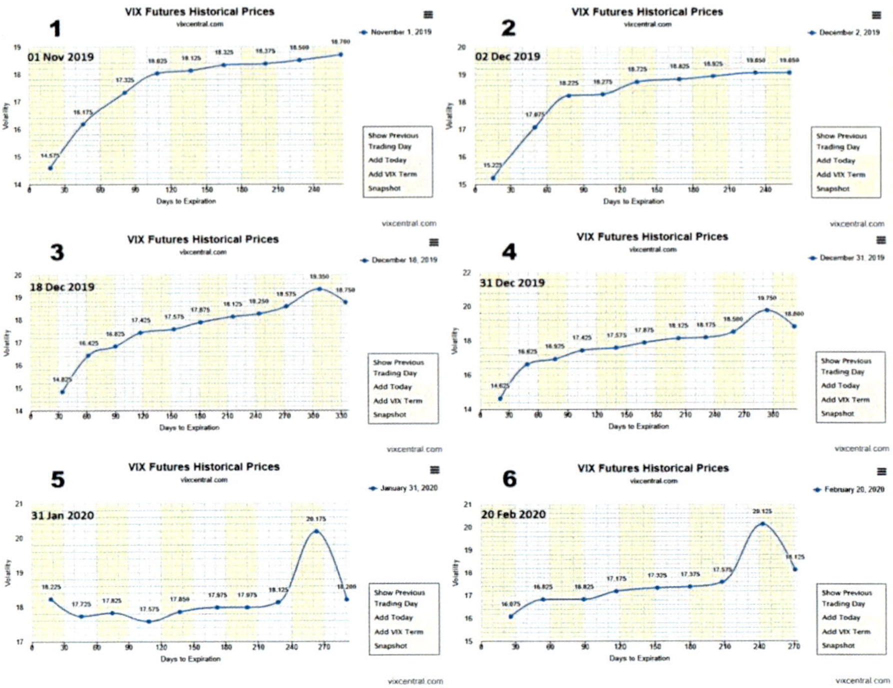

What do you notice in the 6 VIX Futures curves above? In November 2019 (Chart #1), the market was calm. The VIX Futures curve is a normal upward sloping one. In December 2019 (Chart #2), still more than 8 weeks ahead of the crash, the shape started to change. Pay attention not only at the shapes but also at the levels that have been gradually increasing lifting the entire curve higher, especially the near end. Besides, the curve hasn't really inverted in the wake of the crash but it has been markedly flattening.

The Crash

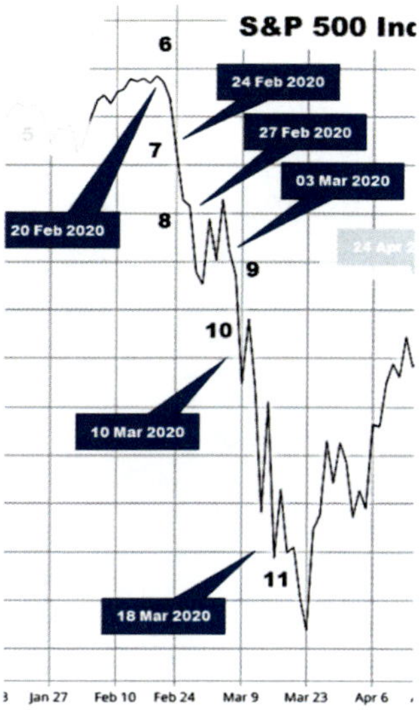

This is when the actual crash took place. In a matter of just 4 weeks, the S&P 500 lost about 35%. This is very fast even with the failed rebound attempts. Let's also examine 6 snapshots of the VIX Futures Term Structure curves along 6 points taken from the rapid descent of the index.

Note how the shape is going flat to downward sloping (inverted), starting from the nearest futures. In distress, near futures spike. The entire curve moves higher but more so in the near end of the curve. By the bottom of the market, the curve is totally inverted.

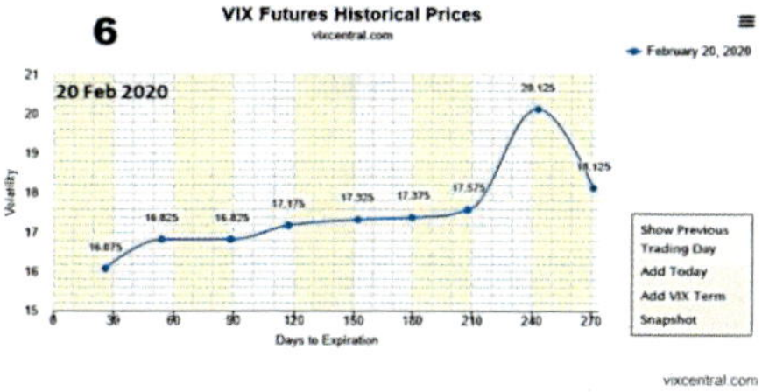

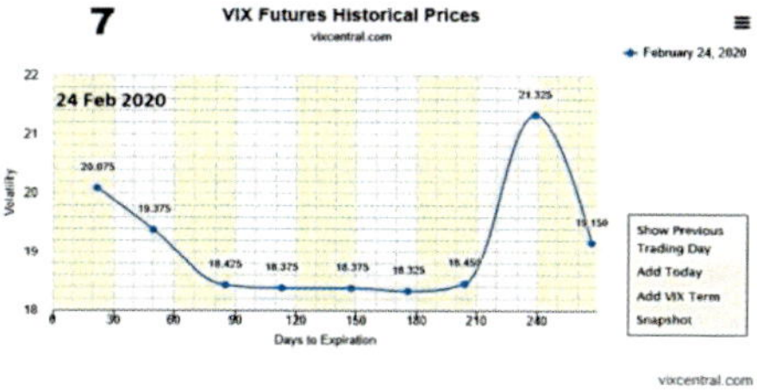

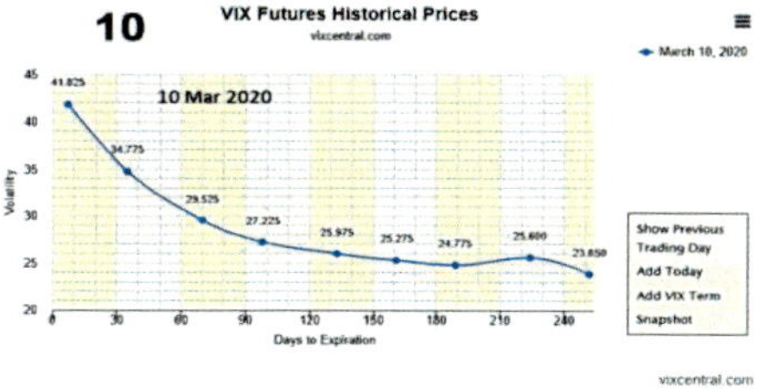

The Road to Recovery

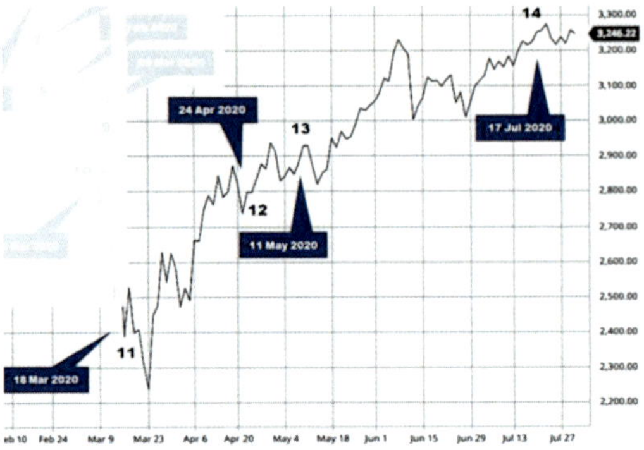

After reaching rock bottom, the market embarked on the recovery phase of the crash.

Observe how the curve's shape slowly and gradually returns to its normal shape. As market prices increase, demand for hedge decreases and volatilities decrease too.

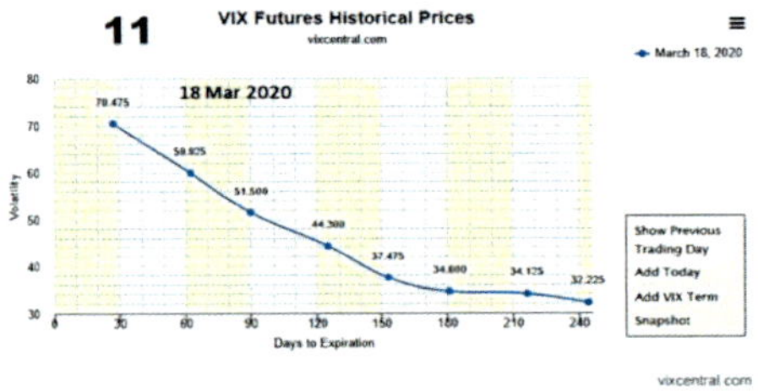

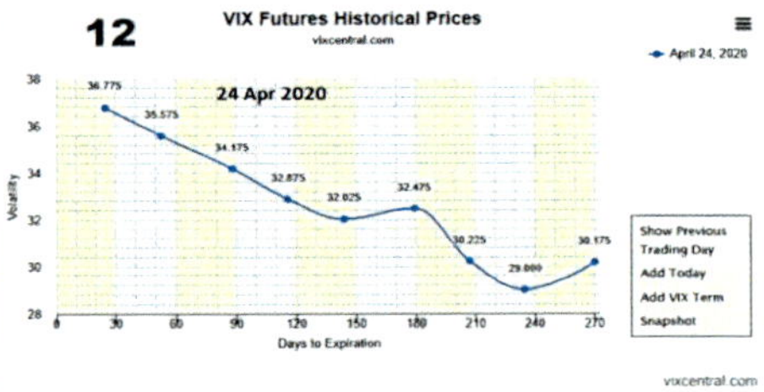

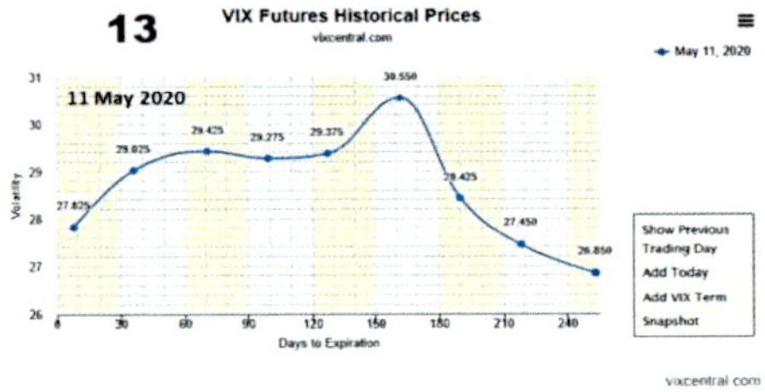

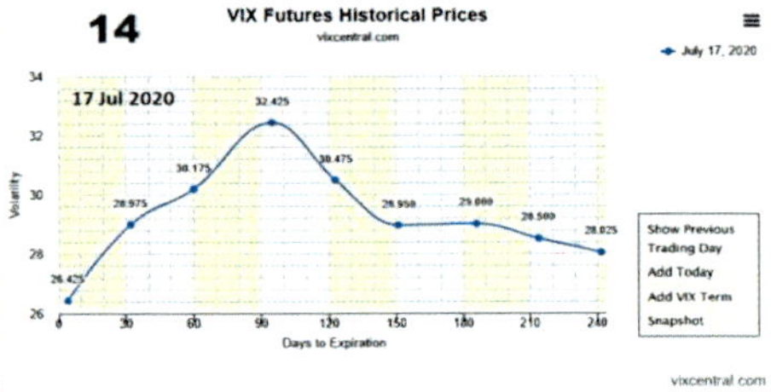

Note that by July 17th, although the worst of the Coronavirus Crash had long gone, there was still somewhat high volatilities embedded in option prices. Levels were still elevated and the shape was still an irregular one. The shape took several more months to be normalized. See charts below.

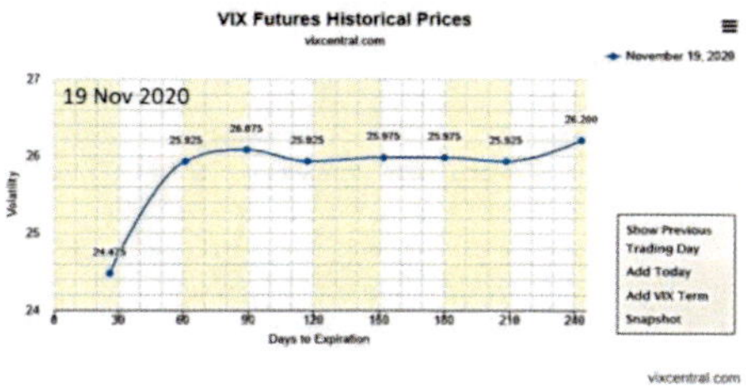

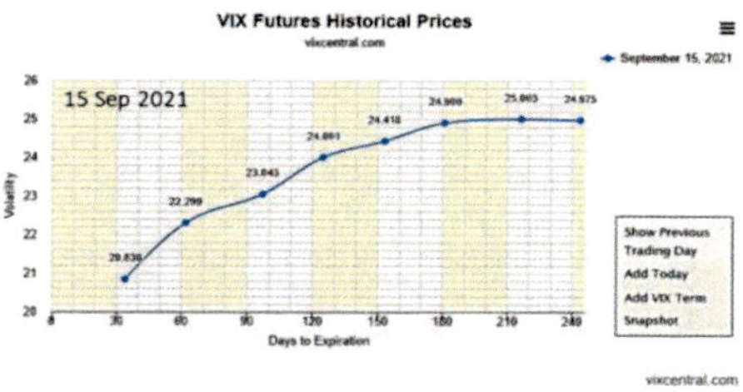

References and Further Reading:

"The Information Content of the VIX Term Structure" by Tim Bollerslev, Michael Gibson, and Hao Zhou (2009)

"Forecasting Volatility with the VIX: The Role of Investor Sentiment" by Carol Alexander and Dimitris Korovilas (2017)

"The Pricing of VIX Derivatives and the Term Structure of VIX Futures" by Geert Bekaert and Eric Engstrom (2010)

CBOE Term Structure Data: Provides real-time VIX term structure data and charts.

Roll Yield

Roll yield refers to the profit or loss generated from rolling futures contracts forward as they approach expiration. In the case of VIX futures, which are typically traded in monthly contracts, investors need to roll their positions from expiring contracts to contracts with later expiration dates to maintain exposure to volatility.

Futures traders are all too familiar with the concept of roll yield but it is a term often unknown to the public, so it's important to explain. With the passage of time, all futures contracts will expire, one by one, starting from the front month and so on and so forth. The first VIX future is VX1. For example, if we are in the month of January, the first VIX future, VX1, will expire on the 3rd Wednesday of February. The second VIX future, VX2, will expire on the 3rd Wednesday of March, and so on and so forth. Over time as expiration dates approach, VX1 converges to VIX, VX2 becomes VX1, VX3 becomes VX2, and so on so forth. The entire curve shifts every passing day and the differences between futures will converge over time. The gap will eventually close and **the rate at which the gap closes is known as roll yield**. In a contango situation, where VX1 > VIX, VX2 > VX1, we have a positive roll yield, and conversely, in a backwardation situation, where VX1 < VIX, VX2 < VX1, we have a negative roll yield. It can be shown that negative roll yields are typically associated with elevated risks in the underlying stock market. Contango/backwardation measures must also be adjusted by the roll with the passage of time. The ratio between the adjusted front futures has been shown to have solid predictive power. In summary:

VX1 < VIX → Positive Roll Yield → Contango → Safer market
VX1 > VIX → Negative Roll Yield → Backwardation → Riskier market

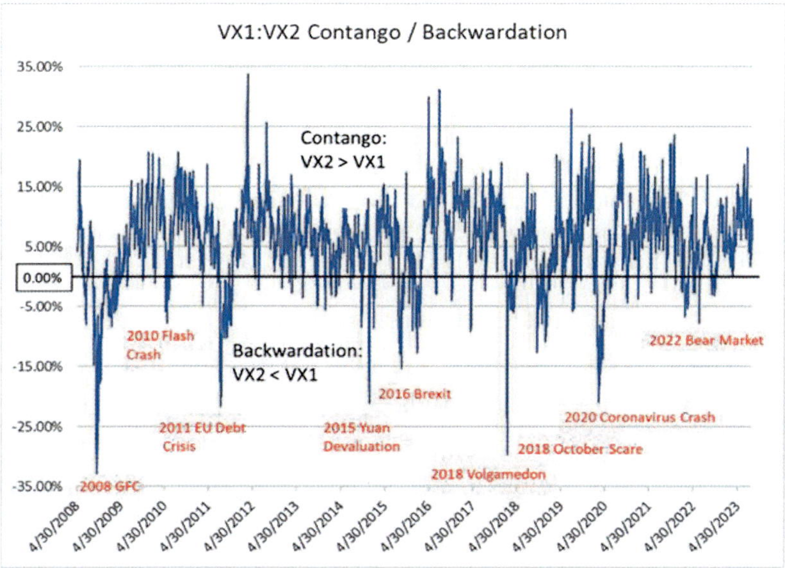

Roll yield can provide insights into future price movements in the underlying stock market through its relationship with the VIX futures term structure:

Contango and Market Expectations: Persistent contango in the VIX futures term structure may indicate market expectations of low volatility in the future. This could suggest complacency or optimism among investors, potentially signaling a period of calm or upward trend in the stock market.

Backwardation and Market Stress: Conversely, backwardation in the VIX futures term structure may signal market stress or uncertainty. This could indicate heightened expectations of future volatility, potentially signaling a period of turbulence or downward trend in the stock market.

As explained before, contango and backwardation ratios have to be adjusted by the time factor and roll yield to be used properly in our model because we always have to compare apples to apples. We are measuring the relationship between VX1 and VIX (or we can call it the spot VIX) and also the relationship between VX1 and VX2. Over time, VX1 will converge to VIX and upon expiration, the new VX1 will be replaced by VX2. In a contango situation, VX1 will **converge down** to VIX but in a backwardation situation, VX1 will **converge up** to VIX. Remember that the futures market runs simultaneously to the stock market.

Besides the spread (differential) between VX1 and VIX, we are also watching spreads along the rest of the VIX futures curve, as in VX3 and VX7, VX4 and VX8, etc. These measurements will further capture volatility expectations over different time frames to give us a better picture of the overall curve movements and risk expectations in the stock market at any given moment in time.

Roll yield is influenced by various factors, including interest rates and market dynamics, which can complicate its interpretation. Like the other variables previously presented, roll yield alone may not provide a reliable predictor of future stock market movements and should be considered alongside other indicators and market fundamentals.

References and Further Reading:

"The Roll Model Revisited: Evidence on Price Dynamics in S&P 500® Futures Contracts" by Gurdip Bakshi, Nikunj Kapadia, and Dilip Madan (2003)

"Roll Yield and Volatility Risk Premia" by Kewei Hou, Haitao Mo, and Chen Xue (2015)

"Understanding the Roll Yield of Futures Contracts" by Jan De Spiegeleer and Wim Schoutens (2017)

VVIX: Volatility of VIX

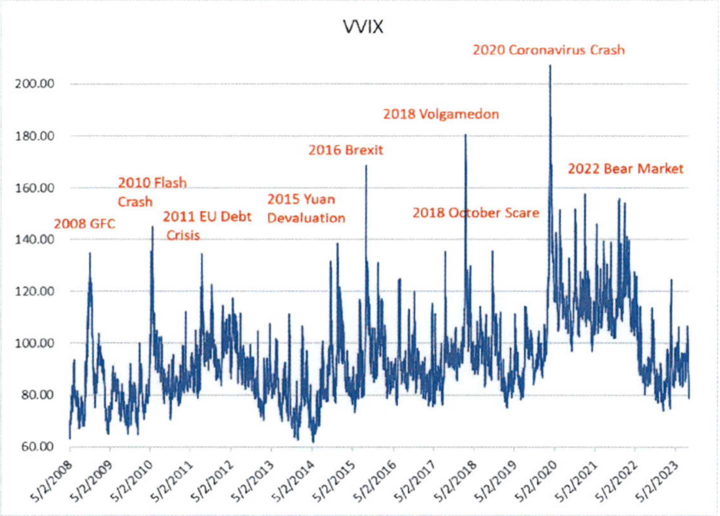

The VVIX, often referred to as the "volatility of volatility," is a metric that measures the expected volatility of the VIX itself. I know this may confuse people a bit, but in a nutshell, while the VIX gauges the expected volatility of the S&P 500®, the VVIX measures how volatile the VIX is anticipated to be. This can be thought of in physical terms as the difference between "speed" and "acceleration" — with the VVIX representing the "acceleration" of market volatility.

The VVIX is derived from the implied volatilities of VIX options, much like how the VIX is calculated from the implied volatilities of S&P 500® options. It provides a measure of the market's expectations for the variability in the VIX index over a specified period.

The VVIX is a crucial indicator of investor sentiment and market stress. High VVIX levels indicate that the market expects significant changes in volatility, often associated with periods of uncertainty and heightened risk aversion. Conversely, low VVIX levels suggest market stability and lower anticipated volatility fluctuations. For portfolio managers and traders, the VVIX serves as a valuable tool for risk management. By monitoring the VVIX, they can gain insights into the potential for sudden volatility spikes, allowing for more informed hedging and risk mitigation strategies. While the VVIX itself is not a direct predictor of market direction, its movements can provide clues about future volatility trends. Sharp increases in the VVIX often precede turbulent market conditions, making it a useful component in a comprehensive risk assessment framework.

Examining historical spikes in the VVIX can provide context for its behavior during significant market events. For instance, during the financial crisis of 2008 and the market turmoil triggered by the COVID-19 pandemic in early 2020, the VVIX saw substantial spikes, reflecting the heightened uncertainty and expected volatility in the VIX. While the VVIX offers unique insights, it is most powerful when used in conjunction with other indicators such as the VIX, VIX term structure, and volatility risk premium (VRP). Each of these metrics captures different aspects of market dynamics:

- **VIX**: Measures expected volatility of the S&P 500®.
- **VIX Term Structure**: Provides insights into market expectations over different time horizons.
- **VRP**: Highlights the premium for bearing volatility risk.
- **VVIX**: Gauges volatility of the volatility of the S&P 500®.

By integrating these indicators, a more holistic picture of market risk and sentiment emerges. Just like the previous indicators, VVIX adds more information to our model. As explained before, none of these indicators per se (taken alone) are good enough with sufficient predictive power to give us the complete picture of the risk in the stock market. But taken together with the addition of each one of them, a much clearer picture emerges. As you can see from the chart, the same crisis events are clearly distinguished by prominent spikes in the indicators. But the timing and scale for each indicator are different.

Some will shoot up earlier than others. Some may react more violently than others. That is why every piece of information contributes to the completeness of the puzzle. The job of the algorithm is to analyze every piece of information, filter out the noise, and calibrate the relative contribution of each variable for the overall risk measurement so that we can have a better understanding of the real risks in the market and produce the RISP 500™ index.

As you can see, the volatility world is a rich source of information for us stock investors. Unfortunately, most stock investors aren't even aware of its existence, let alone reading and understanding its power to help them excel at stock investing.

This is just a brief introduction to some of the variables we use from the VIX world. We can't cover all of them in this book or explain them in too much detail. We are presenting indicators from different markets, not only the volatility world. Most of them will give us a more medium-term insight into the risks of the stock market.

References and Further Reading:

"The Information in Option Volume for Future Stock Prices" by Pan, Poteshman (2006)

"Forecasting Volatility with VIX: The Role of Investor Sentiment" by Carol Alexander and Dimitris Korovilas (2017)

"Volatility Trading" by Euan Sinclair

"Option Volatility and Pricing: Advanced Trading Strategies and Techniques" by Sheldon Natenberg

Equity Risk Premium (ERP)

In a nutshell, the Equity Risk Premium (ERP) is the extra return that stocks are expected to pay above bonds to compensate investors for the higher risk associated with equity investments. In other words, this premium is essentially the reward for taking on the additional risk of investing in stocks rather than in safer assets like U.S. government treasury bonds. The basic formula for calculating the ERP involves subtracting the return on a risk-free asset, such as the 10-year U.S. Treasury note, from the return on a broad stock market index like the S&P 500®. ERP can be calculated in several ways giving rise to a number of combinations. Here are some ways to calculate ERP, leading to different interpretations:

- Historical ERP: This approach uses historical data to calculate the average return difference between stocks and bonds over a specific period.
- Forward-looking ERP: This method estimates future returns based on current stock prices, expected dividends, and expected growth rates.
- Adjusted for Inflation: ERP can also be calculated in real terms by adjusting for inflation, providing a more accurate reflection of purchasing power over time.
- Using P/E Ratios: The ERP can be derived from forward or trailing price-to-earnings (P/E) ratios to reflect market expectations about future earnings and risk.

However, the concept is the same. The ERP is a fundamental concept in finance and investing because it encapsulates the essence of why investors demand higher returns for taking on the added risk of equities. It underpins asset allocation decisions and is a critical input in models like the Capital Asset Pricing Model (CAPM), which helps determine the required rate of return for an investment. If you recall, this is the exact reason why measuring market risk is so indispensable for stock investors. You invest in riskier assets like stocks only because you want to make a better return than safer assets like U.S. government treasury bonds. You want to invest in stocks because you want to earn ERP.

Historically, the ERP has varied significantly depending on economic conditions, market sentiment, and geopolitical events. On average, the historical ERP for U.S. equities over the 20th century has been estimated to range between 4% and 6% per year. However, this average masks substantial variability over shorter time periods. Instances of below-average or negative ERP are usually associated with periods of instability in the markets:

Great Depression (1929-1939): The ERP turned negative during the Great Depression, as stock prices plummeted while government bonds provided relatively stable returns.

Dot-Com Bubble (2000-2002): During the burst of the dot-com bubble, the ERP fell significantly as the stock market experienced severe declines.

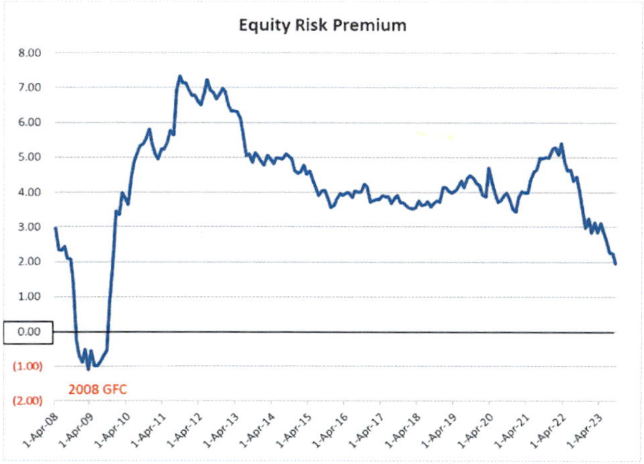

Great Financial Crisis (2008-2009): The ERP again turned negative during the financial crisis when the equity markets collapsed and investors flocked to the safety of government bonds.

You may ask, why not use ERP as the main risk indicator for investors? Look at the chart above. Although it's an important indicator, it does not provide us with an early warning by itself. During extreme crashes, ERP has not only narrowed significantly but even turned negative. While ERP is a crucial indicator of long-term market performance and investor expectations, taken alone it has serious limitations as a predictive tool by itself:

- **Lagging Indicator**: ERP often reacts to market conditions rather than predicting them. It can turn negative after a market crash, reflecting the realized losses rather than providing a forward-looking warning.
- **Variability**: ERP is influenced by numerous factors, including interest rates, inflation expectations, corporate earnings, and investor sentiment, making it volatile and sometimes difficult to interpret in the short term.

Nevertheless, taken in conjunction with other variables, it adds value to our algorithm by helping it confirm trends captured by variables with stronger predictive power.

References and Further Reading:

"The Equity Premium in 150 Textbooks" by Pablo Fernandez (2009): This paper reviews how ERP is presented across numerous textbooks, offering a comprehensive overview of its theoretical and practical applications.

"The Long-Run Equity Risk Premium" by John R. Graham and Campbell R. Harvey (2005): This study explores the historical ERP and its implications for future returns.

"Estimating the Equity Risk Premium" by Aswath Damodaran (2012): Methodologies for estimating the ERP using various approaches and datasets.

Yield Curve Inversions

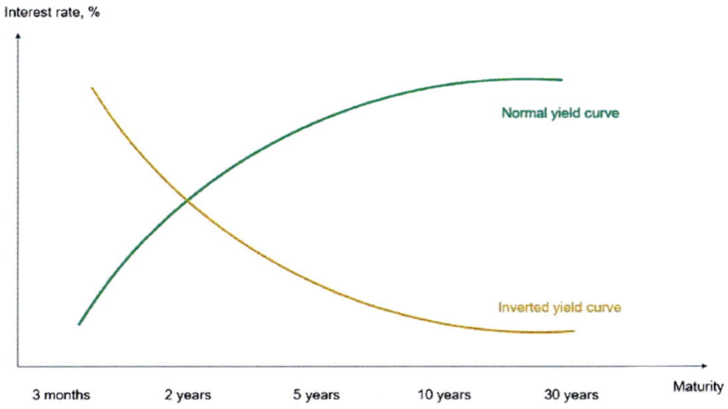

Credits: The Copenhagen Post

Interest rates affect all assets in the economy because interest rate changes reprice all assets. "Risk-free" interest rates, represented by U.S. Treasury bills, notes, and bonds, serve as the benchmark to measure returns of any investable assets. It is important to note that "risk-free" refers to the credit risk of the bond issuer, not its market risk or price risk.

The bond market offers many variables for us to read early signals. Historically, yield curve inversions have been associated with anticipating periods of recession.

Understanding the Yield Curve: The yield curve is a graphical representation of the interest rates on bonds of different maturities, typically from 3 months to 30 years. Under normal circumstances, the yield curve slopes upwards, indicating that longer-term bonds have higher yields compared to shorter-term bonds. This is because longer maturities involve greater risks, such as interest rate risk and reinvestment risk, which investors demand to be compensated for through higher yields.

Yield Curve Inversion Explained: A yield curve inversion occurs when short-term interest rates rise above long-term interest rates. This phenomenon is considered abnormal and signals that investors expect future economic growth to slow down, possibly leading to a recession. An inverted yield curve suggests that bond investors are more pessimistic about the near-term economy than the long-term, hence demanding higher returns for shorter maturities. See chart above. In normal circumstances, longer dated bonds will pay higher interest rates than shorter dated ones. This is natural because of time and reinvestment risk. However, the yield curve may get inverted at times. This usually happens when the Federal Reserve (Fed) is raising rates in the economy to combat inflation and cool down an overheated economy.

Rising interest rates means the cost of money is increasing, which in turn exerts a downward pressure on economic growth. See chart below.

Note that every time since the 1980s that the spread (interest rate differential) between the 10-year treasury note and the 2-year treasury note turned negative, a recession (marked in gray on the chart) followed after the spread stopped widening and started to return to more normal levels.

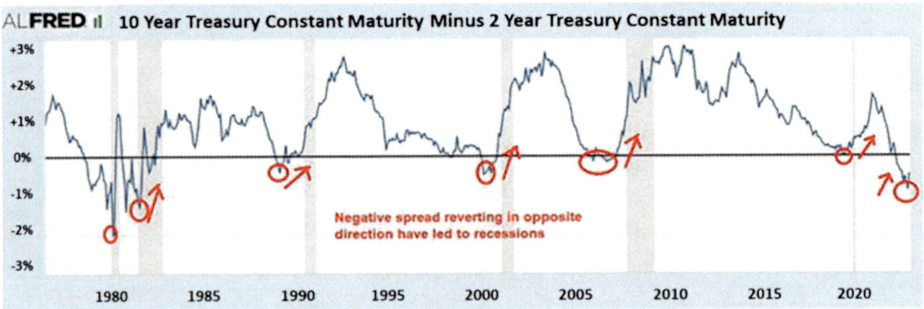

Key Historical Instances:

Early 1980s Recession: The yield curve inverted in late 1978, predicting the recession that began in 1980. This was a period marked by high inflation and aggressive rate hikes by the Federal Reserve.

2000 Dot-Com Bubble: The yield curve inverted in late 2000, preceding the economic slowdown and market crash in the early 2000s.

Global Financial Crisis (2007-2009): The yield curve inversion occurred in 2006-2007, preceding the severe economic downturn triggered by the housing market collapse and financial sector turmoil.

COVID-19 Pandemic: The yield curve briefly inverted in 2019, signaling concerns about economic stability. Although the recession was induced by the pandemic in 2020, the inversion highlighted underlying vulnerabilities.

Different Yield Spreads: While the 2-year/10-year spread is the most commonly cited, other spreads such as the 3-month/10-year or 5-year/30-year can also provide valuable insights. Each combination offers a different perspective on market expectations and economic conditions at diffeent points in time. Some traders use thresholds, such as 70% inversion across multiple spreads, to gauge the strength and reliability of the signal. The reaction time in the economy varies, though.

Predictive Power and Limitations: Although yield curve inversions are powerful indicators of economic recessions, they are not perfect predictors and have limitations:

- **Timing Variability**: The lag between an inversion and the onset of a recession can vary widely, ranging from a few months to a couple of years.
- **False Signals**: Occasionally, the yield curve may invert without leading to a recession, or it may briefly invert and then return to normal without significant economic impact.
- **Economic Interventions**: Central bank policies and other economic interventions can influence the yield curve, sometimes distorting its predictive power. But again, it's another piece of the puzzle in our tool arsenal.

Impact on the Stock Market: Yield curve inversions typically signal a risk-off sentiment in financial markets. As expectations of economic slowdown or recession rise, investors may shift from equities to safer assets like bonds, leading to stock market declines. Historical data shows that significant stock market corrections and bear markets often follow yield curve inversions, as investors anticipate reduced corporate earnings and economic activity.

References and Further Reading:

"The Yield Curve and Predicting Recessions" by Arturo Estrella and Frederic S. Mishkin (1996)

"Does the Yield Curve Signal Recessions?" by Estrella and Trubin (2006)

"The Evolving Predictive Power of the Yield Curve" by Michael Bauer and Thomas Mertens (2018)

"The Little Book of Market Indicators" by Kenneth L. Fisher and Lara Hoffmans

"Ahead of the Curve: A Commonsense Guide to Forecasting Business and Market Cycles" by Joseph H. Ellis

Bond Volatility (MOVE Index)

The equivalent of the VIX in the bond market is known as the MOVE Index, which stands for "Merrill Lynch Option Volatility Estimate." The MOVE Index measures the implied volatility of U.S. Treasury bonds and is derived from the prices of 1-month options on Treasury bonds with maturities ranging from 2 years to 30 years. This index provides a snapshot of the expected volatility in the bond market, similar to what the VIX does for the stock market.

MOVE Index

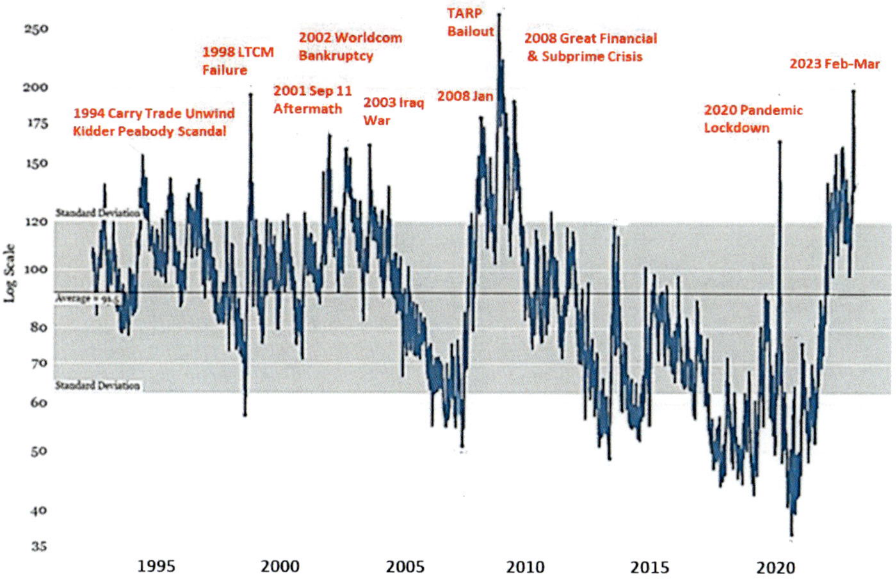

Credits: Bianco Research

The MOVE Index is calculated by aggregating the implied volatilities of various Treasury securities to create a single measure of bond market volatility. The index reflects the market's expectations for future volatility in interest rates, which are crucial for pricing bonds. The long-term mean of the MOVE Index is around 91.5, with deviations from this mean indicating varying levels of market stress or calm. The chart shows the MOVE with 1 standard deviation (gray area) around the long-term mean of 91.5. In times of distress in the bond markets, the MOVE typically shoots up, above 1 standard deviation during severe crises when the stock market also plummets. It's important to mention that the bond market and interest rates are more directly linked to the economy than stocks. This is because companies may adjust themselves to challenging economic conditions by adapting to them (e.g., cost control, downsizing, etc.) and still maintaining corporate profitability.

Historical Context and Economic Predictions:

Historically, the MOVE Index has been a valuable tool for gauging the bond market's sentiment and its implications for the broader economy. In times of economic uncertainty or distress, the MOVE Index typically spikes, signaling increased volatility and risk in the bond market. These spikes often coincide with significant economic events, such as financial crises or major shifts in monetary policy.

Key Historical Instances:

2008 Financial Crisis: During the 2008 financial crisis, the MOVE Index surged as investors flocked to safe-haven assets and the bond market experienced extreme volatility. This spike was an early warning of the turmoil that was to unfold in both bond and stock markets.

COVID-19 Pandemic: In early 2020, the MOVE Index saw significant spikes as the pandemic created unprecedented uncertainty and volatility across global markets. This rise in bond market volatility was a precursor to the dramatic movements seen in the stock market.

Monetary Policy Shifts: Major shifts in Federal Reserve policy, such as rate hikes or cuts, often result in increased volatility in the bond market, reflected in spikes in the MOVE Index. These movements can provide insights into the market's expectations for economic conditions and interest rate trajectories.

Predictive Power for the Stock Market: While the MOVE Index primarily reflects volatility in the bond market, its movements can offer valuable insights into broader financial market conditions. Elevated bond market volatility often indicates heightened uncertainty about economic conditions, which can spill over into the stock market. Historically, significant spikes in the MOVE Index have preceded stock market declines, as investors reassess risk and reallocate their portfolios.

Predictive Insights:

Risk Sentiment: A rising MOVE Index suggests increasing risk aversion among investors, which can lead to a flight to safety and reduced appetite for riskier assets like stocks, causing their prices to go down.

Interest Rate Expectations: The bond market's expectations for future interest rate movements, as indicated by the MOVE Index, can influence equity market valuations and investor behavior as a result.

Economic Stress: Spikes in the MOVE Index often coincide with periods of economic stress or uncertainty, providing an early warning signal for potential downturns in the stock market.

Practical Applications:

Risk Management: Investors and portfolio managers use the MOVE Index to gauge bond market volatility and assess the risk environment. Elevated MOVE readings may prompt adjustments to portfolio allocations, increasing exposure to safer assets.

Economic Forecasting: The MOVE Index is a useful tool for economists and analysts to predict economic cycles and potential shifts in monetary policy.

References and Further Reading:

"The MOVE Index and Bond Market Volatility" by John S. Hull and Alan White (1998)

"Interest Rate Volatility and the MOVE Index" by Andreas Schrimpf and Vladyslav Sushko (2019)

"Predicting Bond Market Volatility: The Role of the MOVE Index" by Yongjun Tang and Lu Liu (2015)

Leading Economic Indicators (LEI)

Conference Board's Leading Economic Indicators (LEI) has proven historically to be a pretty good predictor of recessions. Comprising 10 indicators that cover economic activity, employment, housing, and the stock market, LEI measures the state of the economy to **predict turning points in the business cycle**. On average, LEI level peaks about 1 year ahead of the peak in a business cycle. See chart. The gray areas are past recessions. An important threshold to notice is **LEI falling below -4% in 6 months**, indicating loss of momentum, which may likely lead to recession. There is also the diffusion index of LEI, which measures how widespread the weakness is (i.e., how many of LEI's 10 components are pointing down). The diffusion index ranges from 0 to 100. **If it's below 50, most of the components are weakening**. All this information taken together paints a more clear picture of what to expect from the economy in the months ahead. Note from the chart below that bottoming out of LEI has correlated well with bottoming out of the S&P 500®. Note also that in some instances, LEI moved ahead of the S&P 500® but not always.

Again, it's just one more piece of the puzzle for us. Remember, we watch many variables at the same time to produce the RISP 500™!

Leading Economic Indicators (LEI) Components

The LEI consists of ten key economic indicators that collectively provide a snapshot of future economic activity. Each component is chosen for its predictive power and sensitivity to changes in the business cycle. Here are the components, their ranges, and their

meanings:

Average Weekly Hours in Manufacturing

Range: Typically 38-42 hours.

Interpretation: Higher average hours indicate increased production in response to a strong demand. A decline suggests reduced production and potential economic slowdown.

Example: During the 2008 financial crisis, average weekly hours decreased, reflecting reduced demand and production cuts.

Average Weekly Initial Claims for Unemployment Insurance

Range: Typically 200,000-400,000 claims.

Interpretation: Lower claims indicate a healthy labor market, while increasing claims suggest rising unemployment and economic distress.

Example: Initial claims spiked during the early months of the COVID-19 pandemic, signaling a sharp economic downturn.

Manufacturers' New Orders for Consumer Goods and Materials

Range: Varies widely, typically measured in billions of dollars.

Interpretation: Higher new orders indicate strong consumer demand and economic growth. A decline suggests weakening demand and potential slowdown.

Example: New orders fell significantly before the 2001 and 2008 recessions, indicating reduced consumer spending.

ISM Index of New Orders

Range: 0-100

Interpretation: A reading above 50 indicates expansion in manufacturing activity, while below 50 signals contraction.

Example: The ISM New Orders Index fell below 50 in late 2000 and 2007, preceding the subsequent recessions.

Manufacturers' New Orders for Nondefense Capital Goods Excluding Aircraft

Range: Varies, typically measured in billions of dollars.

Interpretation: Higher orders suggest increased business investment, indicating economic confidence. A decline signals reduced investment and potential economic weakness.

Example: This component declined prior to the 2008 recession, reflecting reduced business investment.

Building Permits for New Private Housing Units

Range: Varies widely, typically measured in thousands of units.

Interpretation: Higher building permits indicate a robust housing market and economic growth. A decline suggests a weakening housing market and potential economic slowdown.

Example: Building permits fell sharply before the 2008 housing market crash, signaling impending economic trouble.

Stock Prices (S&P 500®)

Range: Varies with market conditions.

Interpretation: Rising stock prices indicate investor confidence and economic growth, while declining prices suggest economic concerns.

Example: The S&P 500® declined significantly before the 2001 and 2008 recessions, reflecting investor pessimism.

Leading Credit Index

Range: Typically between -10 and +10.

Interpretation: Positive values indicate favorable credit conditions, while negative values suggest tightening credit and potential economic stress.

Example: The Leading Credit Index turned negative before the 2008 financial crisis, indicating tightening credit conditions.

Interest Rate Spread (10-Year Treasury Bonds Less Federal Funds Rate)

Range: Typically between -2% and +4%.

Interpretation: A positive spread indicates a healthy economic outlook, while a negative spread (yield curve inversion) signals potential recession.

Example: The yield curve inverted before the 2001 and 2008 recessions, accurately predicting economic downturns.

Average Consumer Expectations for Business Conditions

Range: 0-100.

Interpretation: Higher values indicate consumer optimism, while lower values suggest pessimism.

Example: Consumer expectations declined significantly before the 2008 recession, reflecting widespread economic concern.

Diffusion Index of LEI

The diffusion index measures the proportion of the LEI components that are increasing versus decreasing. It ranges from 0-100, with values below 50 indicating more components are declining than rising.

Range: 0-100.

Interpretation: A diffusion index below 50 suggests widespread economic weakness, while a value above 50 indicates broad-based economic strength.

Example: Prior to the 2008 recession, the diffusion index fell below 50, signaling widespread economic deterioration.

Reading and Interpreting the LEI and Diffusion Index

Upward Trend: Indicates economic expansion and positive outlook. Investors may expect continued growth.

Downward Trend: Suggests economic slowdown or recession. Investors should be cautious and consider defensive strategies.

Critical Thresholds:

LEI Decline of More Than 4% in Six Months: Indicates significant loss of economic momentum and potential recession.

Diffusion Index Below 50: Signals widespread economic weakness, increasing the likelihood of a downturn.

These indicators are aggregated into a single composite index, which provides a snapshot of the economy's health and its likely trajectory over the coming months.

Historical Context and Predictive Power

2001 Recession: LEI declined in late 2000, providing an early warning of the impending recession. The diffusion index also fell below 50, signaling widespread economic weakness.

2008 Financial Crisis: The LEI began to drop in 2007, with a significant decline before the financial crisis. The diffusion index fell below 50, indicating broad-based economic distress.

COVID-19 Pandemic: The LEI saw a sharp decline in early 2020, ahead of the economic contraction caused by the pandemic. The diffusion index also fell below 50, reflecting widespread economic impact.

Predictive Power for the Stock Market:

The LEI's relationship with the stock market is complex but insightful. While not a perfect predictor, significant movements in the LEI often precede major stock market trends. This is because the stock market is forward-looking, and investors base their decisions on expected economic conditions.

Insights and Examples:

Correlation with Stock Market Bottoms: Historically, when the LEI bottoms out, the stock market often follows suit. For instance, the LEI bottomed out ahead of the S&P 500® during the 2008 financial crisis, indicating a subsequent recovery.

Early Warnings: Significant declines in the LEI, particularly drops of more than 4% over six months, have often preceded stock market downturns. This makes the LEI a valuable early warning signal for investors looking to mitigate risk.

Diffusion Index: The diffusion index of the LEI, which measures the breadth of weakness across its components, provides additional insights. A diffusion index below 50 indicates widespread weakness and can be a harbinger of broader economic and market challenges.

As said many times, we must take all the indicators together to extract the best information and predictive power. LEI is not different!

References and Further Reading:

"The Predictive Power of the Conference Board's Leading Economic Index" by Ataman Ozyildirim and Bart van Ark

"Leading Indicators for the 1990s" by Geoffrey H. Moore

"The Role of Leading Indicators in Economic Forecasting" by James H. Stock and Mark W. Watson

"Economic Indicators for Professionals: Understanding and Applying Economic Indicators to Maximize Investment Opportunities" by Charles Steindel

Fed Policy and Rate Hike/Cut/Hold Probabilities

The Federal Reserve's interest rate policy is a critical factor in the valuation of all assets in an economy. The stock market is highly sensitive to changes in interest rates, and at every Federal Open Market Committee (FOMC) meeting, professional investors scrutinize Fed officials' speeches for clues about their future intentions. Investors are keen to project the trajectory of future interest rates well beyond the next meeting.

The Fed Funds rate is the interest rate at which U.S. banks lend money to each other overnight to balance their daily cash positions. The Federal Reserve controls this rate by setting a target range during its policy meetings, which occur 8 times a year. This overnight rate has a ripple effect throughout the entire yield curve and the broader economy. Essentially, long-term interest rates are the market's projection of the compounded short-term rates over time. Therefore, by setting the Fed Funds rate, the Fed influences the entire yield curve.

MEETING PROBABILITIES — Source: CME

MEETING DATE	225-250	250-275	275-300	300-325	325-350	350-375	375-400	400-425	425-450
7/27/2022	19.1%	80.9%	0.0%						
9/21/2022	0.0%	0.0%	0.0%	19.1%	80.9%	0.0%	0.0%	0.0%	
11/2/2022	0.0%	0.0%	0.0%	0.0%	13.3%	62.2%	24.5%	0.0%	0.0%
12/14/2022	0.0%	0.0%	0.0%	0.0%	6.9%	38.9%	42.5%	11.7%	0.0%
2/1/2023	0.0%	0.0%	0.0%	0.0%	6.0%	34.6%	42.0%	15.8%	1.5%
3/15/2023	0.0%	0.0%	0.0%	2.0%	15.5%	37.1%	33.3%	11.0%	1.0%
5/3/2023	0.0%	0.0%	0.7%	6.6%	22.8%	35.8%	25.8%	7.7%	0.7%
6/14/2023	0.0%	0.3%	3.4%	14.1%	28.8%	31.2%	17.4%	[illegible]	0.4%
7/26/2023	0.1%	1.6%	7.8%	20.1%	29.8%	25.5%	12.1%	2.8%	0.2%

The Federal Reserve's interest rate policy affects the valuation of all assets in an economy. The stock market is very sensitive to interest rates and at every FOMC meeting, professional investors are paying attention to Fed officials' speeches for clues into their minds. The Fed often "telegraphs" its intention for the next meeting in advance to avoid unnecessary volatility around Fed meeting dates. However, investors want to project the trajectory of future interest rates. Long-term interest rates are no more than the projection of the compounding of the short rate and that is how the Fed ultimately influences the entire yield curve by setting the Fed Funds rate.

Check out the CME FedWatch Tool on their website to see the probabilities for future Fed action extracted from the Fed Funds Futures market at CME. For example, the probability matrix above was taken in June 2022. The market projected a 25 bp rate hike at the next meeting on July 27, 2022. It also expected the Fed to raise the rate to 3.75-4.00% by year-end and then it would pause for a month and start cutting in early 2023. We now know that it didn't happen as expected but the Fed Funds market is still the best place to gauge the market's collective expectations.

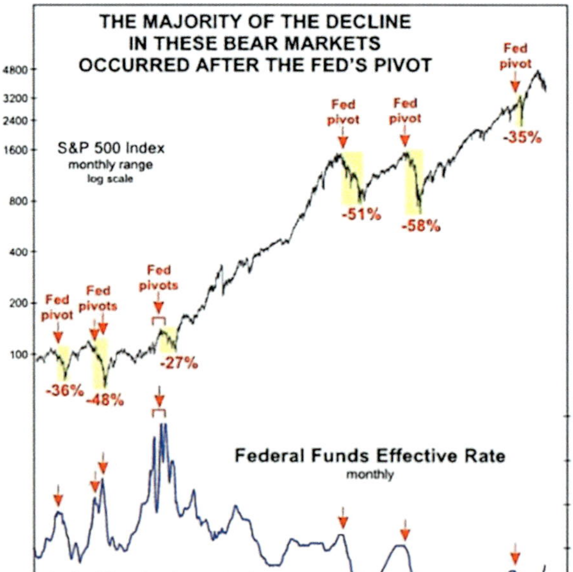

According to history, the stock market has reached the bottom of bear markets induced by Fed hiking campaigns only after the Fed's pivot moments (when the Fed reverses policy by starting to cut rates). See chart.

Understanding the Fed Funds Futures Market

The Fed Funds Futures Market, traded on the Chicago Mercantile Exchange (CME), is a valuable tool for investors to understand market expectations regarding future Federal Reserve actions. The CME FedWatch Tool aggregates data from these futures contracts to estimate the probabilities of different Fed rate actions at upcoming meetings.

How to read and interpret the CME FedWatch Tool

The CME FedWatch Tool provides a probability matrix that indicates the market's expectations for rate changes. Here's how to interpret this tool:

Probability of Rate Changes:

The tool shows the probabilities of various potential target ranges for the Fed Funds rate at upcoming FOMC meetings.

For instance, if the market expects a 25 basis points (bp) rate hike at the next meeting, the probability for that outcome will be prominently displayed.

Market Sentiment:

By analyzing these probabilities, investors can gauge the collective sentiment of the market regarding future monetary policy.

A high probability of rate hikes indicates that the market expects tighter monetary policy, which could signal concerns about inflation.

Conversely, a high probability of rate cuts suggests expectations of economic slowdown or recession.

Historical Context and Predictive Power

Historically, the Fed Funds Futures Market has been a reliable indicator of future Fed actions. However, it's important to note that while the market often accurately predicts the next immediate action, longer-term projections can be more uncertain due to the evolving economic landscape and unexpected events.

Often the market fails in predicting the Fed's next moves. For example, in June 2022, the market projected a 25 bp rate hike at the July 2022 meeting and expected the Fed to raise rates to 3.75-4.00% by year-end, followed by potential rate cuts in 2023. However, the actual path deviated as the economic conditions and inflation data influenced the Fed's decisions.

Fed's Pivot Moments

Historically, **the stock market often reaches the bottom of bear markets induced by Fed hiking campaigns only after the Fed pivots**; i.e., when it reverses policy by starting to cut rates. For example, during the 2008 financial crisis, the Fed began cutting rates aggressively after initially raising them, which helped stabilize the markets.

Calculating Probabilities from Fed Funds Futures Prices

Fed Funds Futures contracts are agreements to buy or sell the federal funds rate at a future date, typically one month in the future. The prices of these contracts reflect market participants' collective expectations for where the Fed Funds rate will be at that time. Here's a step-by-step explanation of how probabilities are derived:

Fed Funds Futures Contract Pricing: Each Fed Funds Futures contract is quoted as 100 minus the expected average federal funds rate for the delivery month. For example, if the market expects the average federal funds rate for a particular month to be 1.5%, the futures contract price will be 98.5 (i.e., 100 - 1.5).

Expected Average Rate Calculation: The price of the futures contract provides an estimate of the market's expectation for the average federal funds rate during the contract month. By looking at multiple contracts for different months, we can construct a timeline of expected rate changes.

Implied Probabilities: To calculate the probabilities of different rate outcomes, market analysts look at the current and expected rates embedded in the futures prices. Suppose the current Fed Funds rate is 1.5%, and the price of the futures contract for the next month implies an expected rate of 1.75%. This could suggest a high probability of a 25 basis points (bp) hike at the next FOMC meeting.

Interpreting the Probability Distribution: The CME FedWatch Tool simplifies this process by presenting the implied probabilities for various potential Fed rate changes. Here's how to interpret these probabilities:

Probability Distribution: The tool provides a probability distribution across possible rate changes in increments of 25 bp. For example, it might show probabilities for the rates staying the same, increasing by 25 bp, increasing by 50 bp, and so on. These probabilities add up to 100%, reflecting the market's collective assessment of all possible outcomes.

Reading the Probability Matrix: The matrix shows the probability of each potential target rate at the next FOMC meeting and for subsequent meetings. For example, a matrix might indicate a 70% probability of a 25 bp rate hike, a 20% probability of a 50 bp hike, and a 10% probability of no change.

Understanding Market Expectations: If a particular rate change (e.g., a 25 bp hike) has a very high probability, it suggests strong market consensus that this outcome is likely. Conversely, if the probabilities are more evenly distributed across several outcomes, it indicates greater market uncertainty about the Fed's next move.

Practical Application for Investors

Investors use these probabilities to make informed decisions about their portfolios:

Anticipating Rate Hikes: If the FedWatch Tool shows a high probability of a rate hike, investors might adjust their portfolios by reducing exposure to interest rate-sensitive assets such as bonds, utilities, and real estate investment trusts (REITs).

Assessing Economic Outlook: The probability distribution can also provide insights into the market's view of the economic outlook. A high probability of rate cuts might indicate concerns about an economic slowdown, prompting investors to seek safer investments.

Examples of Interpretation

Example 1: High Probability of Rate Hike
Current Rate: 1.5%
Next Meeting Probabilities:
No change: 10%
25 bp hike: 80%
50 bp hike: 10%

In this scenario, the market strongly expects a 25 bp hike at the next meeting. Investors might prepare for tighter monetary policy by adjusting their portfolios accordingly.

Example 2: Uncertain Market Conditions

Current Rate: 2.0%
Next Meeting Probabilities:
No change: 40%
25 bp hike: 30%
25 bp cut: 30%

Here, the probabilities are more evenly distributed, indicating market uncertainty. Investors might take a more cautious approach, awaiting further clarity from economic data or Fed communications.

Conclusion: Understanding how probabilities are calculated from Fed Funds Futures prices and interpreting these probabilities through tools like the CME FedWatch Tool allows investors to gauge market expectations for Federal Reserve actions effectively. This knowledge helps in making strategic investment decisions, managing risk, and anticipating economic conditions.

For more detailed information and live data on Fed rate hike/cut probabilities, visit the CME FedWatch Tool.

References and Further Reading:

Books:
"The Federal Reserve and the Financial Crisis" by Ben S. Bernanke
"Central Banking 101" by Joseph Wang

Research Papers:
"Market-Based Measures of Monetary Policy Expectations" by Refet Gürkaynak, Brian Sack, and Eric Swanson
"The Predictive Power of the Federal Funds Futures Market" by William R. Melick and Charles P. Thomas

Online Resources:
CME Group: Provides detailed information and tools for analyzing Fed Funds Futures.
Federal Reserve Economic Data (FRED): Offers comprehensive data on interest rates and economic indicators.

We conclude this chapter here after presenting several variables of interest that contribute to our best understanding of market risks. We watch many variables at the same time to produce the RISP 500™!

CHAPTER 6

6. Stock Market Investing Guided by RISP 500™ in Live Action

Back-Testing + Live Trading: Planning, Testing, and Performance Results

IMPORTANT DISCLAIMER: All testing results shown herein – Back-Tests and Live Trading – are intended to demonstrate the efficiency of the RISP 500™ in guiding investment decisions with risk management. Although the numbers are real and based on real market events and data, they are not intended to convince you that this is a fail-proof system in all situations, present and future, with guaranteed results. All systems, including those designed with artificial intelligence and neural networks, are not 100% fail-proof. The stock market is probabilistic in nature, not deterministic, thus outcomes can never be predicted nor guaranteed. Past performance also cannot guarantee future results. The RISP 500™ is not designed to eliminate 100% of risks or losses; otherwise, there would not be any meaningful return either. Instead, the goal of the RISP 500™ is to maximize return for the different levels of risk taken (optimize the return/risk ratio). The RISP 500™ is a risk management tool. As a tool that is highly customizable (e.g., choice of assets and risk tolerance levels or RPT), different users will invariably obtain different results from each other.

We are constantly putting the RISP 500™ to the test and analyzing test results. We are also testing and back-testing new strategies all the time. It's amazing how flexible the RISP 500™ tool is so that we could get a great deal of information: we were able to learn about how it behaved in a multitude of scenarios and different assets, figured out what is important and what is not, tested hypothesis, debunked myths, and in the process really learned about it like never before in my long career managing risks at the trading desks. In this book, however, we are going to present only two main studies. The first is the results and conclusion analysis of the initial back-test and the second is the results and conclusion analysis of live trading:

Back-Testing (BT): We back-tested 8 strategies carefully assembled for the period from **April 29th, 2008, to December 31st, 2021**. This is an almost **14 years** back-testing period. We could not go further back for lack of reliable data as some data sources the algorithm needs come from markets that did not exist or were not very reliable back then.

Live Trading (LT): We started trading the same 8 strategies live on **January 1st, 2022**. We are still trading them today and counting.

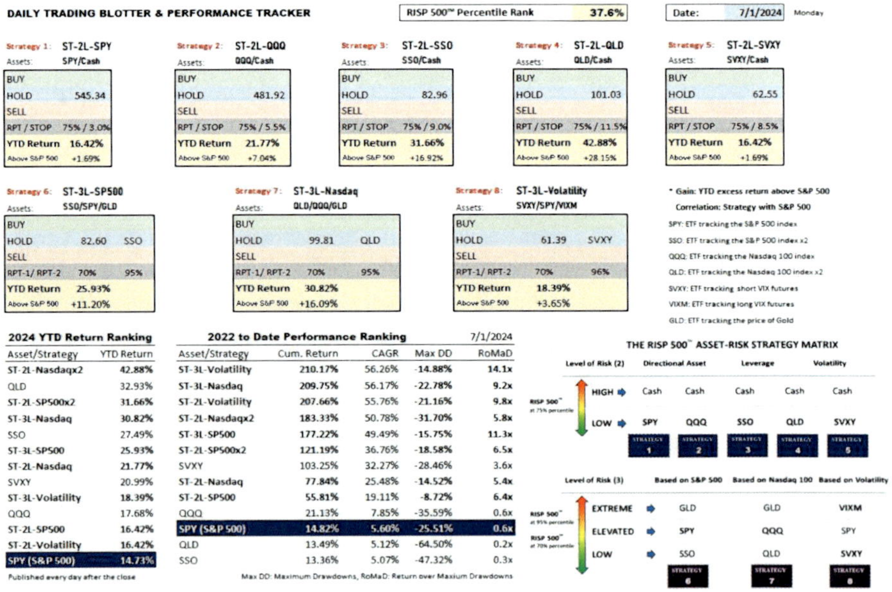

DAILY TRADING BLOTTER & PERFORMANCE TRACKER | RISP 500™ Percentile Rank 37.6% | Date: 7/1/2024 Monday

	Strategy 1: ST-2L-SPY	Strategy 2: ST-2L-QQQ	Strategy 3: ST-2L-SSO	Strategy 4: ST-2L-QLD	Strategy 5: ST-2L-SVXY
Assets:	SPY/Cash	QQQ/Cash	SSO/Cash	QLD/Cash	SVXY/Cash
BUY					
HOLD	545.34	481.92	82.96	101.03	62.55
SELL					
RPT / STOP	75% / 3.0%	75% / 5.5%	75% / 9.0%	75% / 11.5%	75% / 8.5%
YTD Return	16.42%	21.77%	31.66%	42.88%	16.42%
Above S&P 500	+1.69%	+7.04%	+16.92%	+28.15%	+1.69%

	Strategy 6: ST-3L-SP500	Strategy 7: ST-3L-Nasdaq	Strategy 8: ST-3L-Volatility
Assets:	SSO/SPY/GLD	QLD/QQQ/GLD	SVXY/SPY/VIXM
BUY			
HOLD	82.60 SSO	99.81 QLD	61.39 SVXY
SELL			
RPT-1/ RPT-2	70% 95%	70% 95%	70% 96%
YTD Return	25.93%	30.82%	18.39%
Above S&P 500	+11.20%	+16.09%	+3.65%

* Gain: YTD excess return above S&P 500
Correlation: Strategy with S&P 500
SPY: ETF tracking the S&P 500 index
SSO: ETF tracking the S&P 500 index x2
QQQ: ETF tracking the Nasdaq 100 index
QLD: ETF tracking the Nasdaq 100 index x2
SVXY: ETF tracking short VIX futures
VIXM: ETF tracking long VIX futures
GLD: ETF tracking the price of Gold

2024 YTD Return Ranking

Asset/Strategy	YTD Return
ST-2L-Nasdaqx2	42.88%
QLD	32.93%
ST-2L-SP500x2	31.66%
ST-3L-Nasdaq	30.82%
SSO	27.49%
ST-3L-SP500	25.93%
ST-2L-Nasdaq	21.77%
SVXY	20.99%
ST-3L-Volatility	18.39%
QQQ	17.68%
ST-2L-SP500	16.42%
ST-2L-Volatility	16.42%
SPY (S&P 500)	14.73%

Published every day after the close

2022 to Date Performance Ranking 7/1/2024

Asset/Strategy	Cum. Return	CAGR	Max DD	RoMaD
ST-3L-Volatility	210.17%	56.26%	-14.88%	14.1x
ST-3L-Nasdaq	209.75%	56.17%	-22.78%	9.2x
ST-2L-Volatility	207.66%	55.76%	-21.16%	9.8x
ST-2L-Nasdaqx2	183.33%	50.78%	-31.70%	5.8x
ST-3L-SP500	177.22%	49.49%	-15.75%	11.3x
ST-2L-SP500x2	121.19%	36.76%	-18.58%	6.5x
SVXY	103.25%	32.27%	-28.46%	3.6x
ST-2L-Nasdaq	77.84%	25.48%	-14.52%	5.4x
ST-2L-SP500	55.81%	19.11%	-8.72%	6.4x
QQQ	21.13%	7.85%	-35.59%	0.6x
SPY (S&P 500)	14.82%	5.60%	-25.51%	0.6x
QLD	13.49%	5.12%	-64.50%	0.2x
SSO	13.36%	5.07%	-47.32%	0.3x

Max DD: Maximum Drawdowns, RoMaD: Return over Maxium Drawdowns

THE RISP 500™ ASSET-RISK STRATEGY MATRIX

Level of Risk (2)	Directional Asset		Leverage		Volatility
HIGH	Cash	Cash	Cash	Cash	Cash
LOW	SPY	QQQ	SSO	QLD	SVXY
	STRATEGY 1	STRATEGY 2	STRATEGY 3	STRATEGY 4	STRATEGY 5

RISP 500™ at 75% percentile

Level of Risk (3)	Based on S&P 500	Based on Nasdaq 100	Based on Volatility
EXTREME	GLD	GLD	VIXM
ELEVATED	SPY	QQQ	SPY
LOW	SSO	QLD	SVXY
	STRATEGY 6	STRATEGY 7	STRATEGY 8

RISP 500™ at 95% percentile
RISP 500™ at 70% percentile

At the time of this writing, we are reporting the last data point as of **July 1st, 2024**. We already have **2.5 years**-worth of data and results.

We are also making YTD and ITD performance results available on Facebook: www.facebook.com/risp500 and our site: www.risp500.com. As you know, every post on a social media platform has a date stamp, so you can trust the exact date and time we posted our daily results.

In this project, we trade no more than only **once a day**, usually between 10:00 a.m. and 2:00 pm (New York time/ET) when we take the official measurement of the day's RISP 500™. We actually measure the RISP 500™ all day long, even before and after the NYSE is closed, but for this project we take a measurement only once a day. The reason is that we want to prove that non-professional investors, who don't have the time to be watching markets and trading all day, can also be very successful – much more than they are right now – by reading the RISP 500™ (and taking action if necessary) only once a day. On most days, there will be no trades, which is perfect for most people.

Both testing methods are valuable tools to put the entire RISP 500™ project to the test of time to prove whether SMIGRM really works or not, to see it working in live action, and to see how it guides stock market investing to long-term success. Both tests together are giving us **16.5 years** of performance data for the same 8 strategies until the time of this writing. These strategies cover a wide spectrum of risk-return profiles from the most conservative to the moderate and the most aggressive. They were designed that way to show you the real capabilities of the RISP 500™. You will see that it not only helps conservative investors reduce risks but also boosts returns for the most aggressive investors just as well. The success of RISP 500™ is the success of the entire Stock Market Investing Guided by Risk Management (SMIGRM) method.

8 Strategies, 7 Assets Tested

We tested 5 two-risk level and 3 three-risk level SMIGRM strategies, totaling 8 strategies with 7 assets. For our tests, we selected the following assets:

SPY: ETF tracking the S&P 500® index

SSO: ETF tracking the S&P 500® index x2 (leveraged 2x)

QQQ: ETF tracking the Nasdaq 100 index

QLD: ETF tracking the Nasdaq 100 index x2 (leveraged 2x)

SVXY: ETF tracking short VIX futures

VIXM: ETF tracking long VIX futures

GLD: ETF tracking the price of gold

And we designed the following strategies:

Strategy 1 (ST-2L-SP500):
2-risk level strategy based on the S&P 500® (SPY/Cash)

Strategy 2 (ST-2L-Nasdaq):
2-risk level strategy based on the Nasdaq 100 (QQQ/Cash)

Strategy 3 (ST-2L-SP500x2):
2-risk level strategy based on the S&P 500® x2 (SSO/Cash)

Strategy 4 (ST-2L-Nasdaqx2):
2-risk level strategy based on the Nasdaq 100 x2 (QLD/Cash)

Strategy 5 (ST-2L-Volatility):
2-risk level strategy based on VIX Futures (QLD/Cash)

Strategy 6 (ST-3L-SP500):
3-risk level strategy based on the S&P 500® (SSO/SPY/GLD)

Strategy 7 (ST-3L-Nasdaq):
3-risk level strategy based on the Nasdaq 100 (QLD/QQQ/GLD)

Strategy 8 (ST-3L-Volatility):
3-risk level strategy based on the VIX Futures (SVXY/SPY/VIXM)

THE RISP 500™ ASSET-RISK STRATEGY MATRIX

	Level of Risk (2)	Directional Asset		Leverage		Volatility
	HIGH	Cash	Cash	Cash	Cash	Cash
RISP 500™ at 75% percentile						
	LOW	SPY	QQQ	SSO	QLD	SVXY
		STRATEGY 1	STRATEGY 2	STRATEGY 3	STRATEGY 4	STRATEGY 5

	Level of Risk (3)	Based on S&P 500	Based on Nasdaq 100	Based on Volatility
	EXTREME	GLD	GLD	VIXM
RISP 500™ at 95% percentile				
	ELEVATED	SPY	QQQ	SPY
RISP 500™ at 70% percentile				
	LOW	SSO	QLD	SVXY
		STRATEGY 6	STRATEGY 7	STRATEGY 8

Rationale: Why were these assets selected and why were these strategies created for our test?

THE MOST BASIC STRATEGY

"Safer Day"

RISP 500™ PR < RPT
Buy or hold SPY
(Risk ON → low risk to invest)

"Riskier Day"

RISP 500™ PR > RPT
Sell SPY and hold CASH
(Risk OFF → high risk, seek safety)

First, we want to keep things as simple as possible. Everybody understands what the S&P 500® is. The most basic strategy is a 2-risk level strategy with just the SPY and Cash. That's it. SPY is the most popular S&P 500® index tracker ETF. In layman's terms, it's holding the S&P 500® when risks are low and rotating to Cash whenever risks increase above the chosen tolerance level (RISP 500™ moving above your chosen RPT). That is exactly **Strategy 1**, designed for conservative investors looking for a lower risk long-term successful investing and simplicity. We did not want strategies based on any individual stock or anything complicated for the most basic strategies. The idea is to keep it simple, easy to understand, and still capable of delivering powerful results in the long run by avoiding deep corrections and market crashes. It is ideal for passive index investors holding a S&P 500® index fund for the long run.

For investors who are slightly less conservative and want exposure to Nasdaq, we designed **Strategy 2**, which is exactly like Strategy 1, but we use QQQ instead of SPY to track the Nasdaq 100 index. In the sequence, we added the 2x-leveraged versions of both the S&P 500® and Nasdaq 100, respectively the SSO and QLD ETFs, to create **Strategy 3** and **Strategy 4**. Since both strategies involve leveraged ETFs, they involve more risk. Therefore, they are not suitable for very conservative investors.

Side Note: If we didn't have the RISP 500™ guiding us and the SMIGRM method, we would never ever have invested in leveraged ETFs because of the risk. Remember, if the S&P 500® increased by 1%, the SSO would increase by 2%, but the reverse is also true: if the S&P 500® decreased by 1%, the SSO would decrease by 2%. We feel it's just too risky for us. But since we do have the RISP 500™ guiding us and protecting us from high risk situations, we feel confident enough to invest in leveraged strategies. We just wanted to take this opportunity to highlight the importance of SMIGRM in our lives, allowing us **the unique opportunity to explore assets that we would have otherwise snubbed, potentially letting us achieve much higher returns with lower risks and drawdowns**.

Strategy 5 is intended to explore the volatility world. As volatility traders, we know that because the stock market is going up *most of the time*, the VIX is low *most of the time*. Because of this fact, volatility traders extract a kind of income from the market, sort of speaking, by constantly shorting options or VIX futures. The SVXY ETF tracks a short position on VIX futures. Buying SVXY is essentially taking a short position on the VIX. Holding SVXY during normal times and bull markets typically makes money for investors. But be careful! When the volatility of the S&P 500® spikes and during bear markets, investors may lose a lot of money and fast! It wouldn't make sense to give away all the money earned back to the market (and some more) when the market trend suddenly reverses. Again, this is another high risk investment that we accepted only because we practice SMIGRM with the RISP 500™ protecting us and leading the way.

Strategies 1 through 5 are two-risk level strategies. As you can see, they have only two assets – a risky asset and cash. When the RISP 500™ increases above the chosen RPT level, we rotate to Cash and hold it there until the RISP 500™ decreases below the chosen RPT for us to rotate back to the risky asset. In our two-risk level strategies, the safe asset is always Cash. Plain and simple. Yes, we could have chosen bonds, gold, a money market fund, T-bills, etc. but we selected Cash purely for simplicity. For risky assets we selected SPY, QQQ, SSO, QLD, and SVXY for strategies 1 through 5 respectively. Only one RPT level is required to separate the two levels of risk (High and Low).

Strategies 6 through 8 are three-risk level strategies. They will have not one RPT, but two! They require two RPTs to separate the three levels of risk (Extreme, High, and Low) - see diagram above. **Strategy 6** is based on the S&P 500®. In Low risk situations, we hold the SSO. In High risk situations, we hold the SPY, and in Extreme risk situations, we hold GLD (Gold ETF). We chose GLD for the safe asset, but again, we could have chosen other safe assets, e.g. cash, etc. **Strategy 7** is identical in principle to Strategy 6, except that it is based on the Nasdaq 100 instead of the S&P 500®. In Low risk situations, we hold the QLD. In High risk situations, we hold the QQQ, and in Extreme risk situations, we hold GLD (Gold ETF).

Strategy 8 is a three-risk level strategy based on volatility aimed at exploring the VIX futures markets. In Low risk situations, we hold the SVXY (short volatility). In High risk situations, we hold the SPY (S&P 500®), and in Extreme risk situations, we hold VIXM (long volatility). It is important to note why we chose VIXM to be long volatility only in extremely high risk situations. In normal times in the stock market and during low volatility, you should never hold VIXM; it's dangerous and it will make you lose money for sure. We reserve VIXM to be used only in extreme situations, like when the markets are crashing, to profit from such risky environments. With 3 risk levels, we can design bolder strategies suitable for more aggressive investors.

Again, without SMIGRM and the RISP 500™ guiding us, we would never navigate in such troubled waters! But with SMIGRM and the RISP 500™ guiding us, we can be confidently bolder to explore higher yielding and riskier strategies we would have never even considered before. Having the right tools is crucial to take you further and enable you to achieve higher, much higher goals than ever before.

The above 8 strategies are ordered by increasing risk and return

Strategy 1 is the simplest, based on the S&P 500® index alone. In terms of risk and return, Strategy 1 has the lowest expected (and realized) return among the 8 strategies but also has the lowest risk among them. On the other hand, Strategy 8 is the most advanced involving volatility, and together with the leveraged-ETF Strategies 6 and 7, have the highest expected (and realized) returns and also the highest risks.

Strategies 1 and 2, involving no leverage and no volatility, are more appropriate for conservative stock investors. Strategies 3 through 6 are appropriate for moderate risk investors as they involve leverage and volatility to boost expected returns with somewhat higher risks. Strategies 7 and 8 are most appropriate to aggressive and advanced investors only. As we said before, the 8 strategies cover a wide spectrum of risk-return profiles.

New strategies are constantly being tested and developed by us. We will gradually introduce them to our followers and SMIGRM practitioners as our research and testing activities advance and results pass our minimum quality standards.

Note that the two-risk level strategies will have only one RPT while the three-risk level strategies have two RPTs. Every time the RISP 500™ percentile rank crosses a RPT line, it triggers an action to change the asset previously held (rotation). It signals a change in risk environment. This rotation of the most appropriate assets matching risk environments is exactly the Context-Dependent Dynamic Asset Allocation in live action!

Back-Testing Results and Conclusion Analysis

During the year 2021, the RISP 500™ project started to take shape as a spinoff from earlier projects. Back-testing produced very encouraging signs. We back-tested with data stretching as far back as **April 29, 2008**, which is about **14 years' worth of data** at that time. Here is how we did it. First, we reproduced the daily RISP 500™ data running the algorithm and ranked them from the riskiest reading to the least risky.

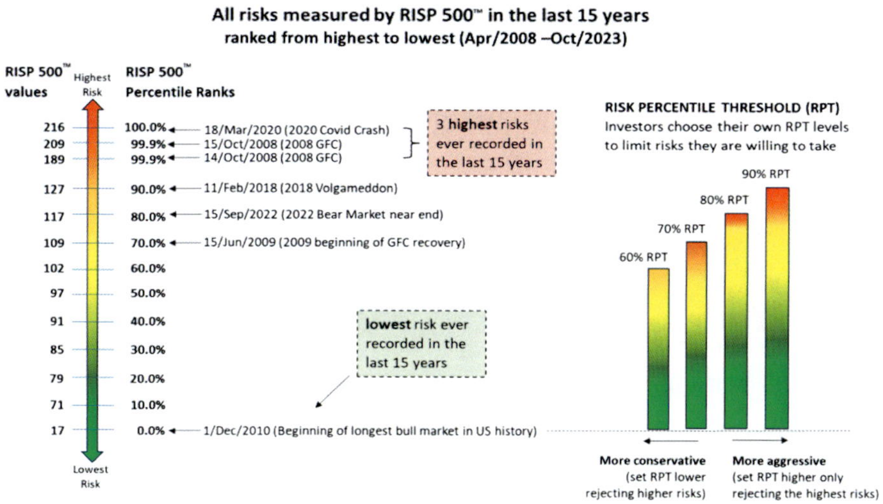

Thus, we could determine the percentile rank of each data point. The 0th percentile corresponds to the lowest risk ever measured in our 14-year database and the 100th percentile corresponds to the highest. We could map out exactly what happened with the S&P 500® at every risk level (decile) that has occurred. That is why we needed a very long period of time for the data, covering periods of bull markets, bear markets, corrections, crashes, and everything in between. Everyone can speculate what assets perform best in what risk environment but back-testing studies can help us confirm or reject the hypotheses. Some of the conclusions of the study will remain proprietary to allow for continuous improvement and calibration of the model algorithm, but the most relevant conclusions will be shown and discussed here.

Back-testing for a long period of almost **14 years** (from **April 29, 2008** to **December 31, 2021**) gave us some invaluable insights and we would like to share with you so you get a better idea of RISP 500™ and how we can better use it to significantly improve the outcomes of our investments over the long run.

How back-testing was conducted and its limitations

The goal was to recreate the same conditions to the extent possible as if this were live trading. But it is not — we can't go back in time — so there will be approximations, errors, and limitations on what we can do with back-testing. But every professional trader knows that back-testing is a very powerful and essential tool. We first reconstructed the RISP 500™ percentile rank every day and once a day for the back-testing period based on actual market closing prices (from multiple markets). This is obviously not perfect due to intraday volatility, but this simplification of the model can be acceptable for back-testing purposes. Every day, an action to buy, hold, or sell was taken by comparing the RISP 500™ percentile rank with the chosen RPT resulting in the corresponding action. We tested a few levels of RPT that a prior sensitivity analysis revealed to be relevant for our study: we tested RPTs from 70% to 95% in 5% increments. In some cases, we also simulated other RPT levels as appropriate. We have also set up an automatic trailing stop loss level for Strategies 1 through 5. Trailing stops move up with the market but remains fixed when market prices aren't going up. Trailing stops have the advantage to lock in profits already earned, not giving them back when executing the stop. For the back-test, trade prices (both sides) are assumed to be the midpoint of the day's high and low. The day's P/L is calculated assuming no idle or excess cash sitting around unused. This is to be consistent when comparing to the benchmark (e.g., S&P 500®, Nasdaq 100, etc.). Remember, the study is to be taken in relative terms. We are testing all 8 strategies against their respective benchmarks as a basis for comparison. Absolute numbers may not be accurate or mean much in the study, but relative comparisons with the benchmarks should be very close to reality. That was the purpose of the Back-Test. We wanted to see how much better SMIGRM fared against simply holding the index ETFs (or benchmarks) in the long run. Because all 8 strategies and their respective benchmarks were tested under the exact same conditions, we should only make conclusions on a relative basis.

Also, notice that in the Back-Test, we are adopting days to be the basic temporal units. RISP 500™ can measure risks continually all day long, even when the market is technically closed. But for simplicity, we aren't considering intraday variations of the RISP 500™ in the back-test and adopting days to be the basic units of time. As you can see from the results, this simplification has not caused any tangible loss to the power of the method, and again, remember to consider things on a relative basis.

How we are judging performance

We are looking at not only the annual returns, or the value the investment has reached in about 14 years (starting from $1,000 on January 1st, 2022), or how much each strategy outperformed its respective benchmark, but we are also paying special attention to the drawdowns (average and maximum during the period) and the RoMaD ratio. Remember, we need to look at both sides of the coin: return and risk. RoMaD helps us judge whether the risk taken was worth it to earn the realized return over the period.

Why are we using drawdowns and not Sharpe ratio, volatility, etc. as our preferred metric for our risk minimization goal? - you might be asking. Yes, we aren't even showing Sharpe ratio and volatility in our Back-Testing studies for an important reason: both the Sharpe ratio and volatility take into account not only the negative dispersion of returns around the mean but also the positive. For risk management purposes, we are really interested in the negative side or potential losses. Secondly, in our practical experience over the years, we know that what really causes problems for investors are the drawdowns. Investors suffer because of drawdowns. They are the direct causers of losses. Good investment plans and strategies (especially long-term ones) are destroyed because of drawdowns. Sharpe ratio and volatility are both great metrics to have, especially before making investments, but in the end, what ultimately cause investors to lose sleep, stop out of investments, and damage their bottom line are the drawdowns. For these reasons, we decided to use only drawdowns to help us judge the merits of an investment.

Note that drawdowns depend on the period of consideration. Whether a big drawdown (e.g. 2008 financial crisis, 2000 internet bubble, etc.) was or was not included in the period of consideration makes a huge difference. That is why you may hear people out there presenting different drawdown numbers for the same asset, especially the S&P 500®. In our Back-Test, we are considering the period since April 29, 2008.

To judge whether a strategy is good or bad in comparison with other strategies or common investments out there, we prefer to use RoMaD (Return over Maximum Drawdown). There are other variations that can be easily derived from this basic formula such as using average instead of maximum or averaging the top 3 drawdowns above a certain percentage, etc. Either way, you got the idea. We want to be properly compensated as investors for the risks we take. The higher the RoMaD or another form of ratio between return and risk, the better. For a RoMaD of 1, which means you are risking a potential maximum drawdown of the same size of the potential return you are expecting to earn, is usually fine with many investors. Anything below 1 starts to quickly look very unfavorable from the return-risk standpoint. We believe RoMaD can be a very good metric to help make investment decisions involving both risk and return in a simple, easy to calculate formula.

We tested RPTs from 70% to 95% in 5% increments. Sensitivity analyses have shown this range is where RISP 500™ could most meaningfully impact investment outcomes in the direction we are looking for. And what direction is it? We want to maximize returns while minimizing drawdowns (DD), which is the main goal. We would also like to keep trading frequency low, not only to reduce costs but also to make it easier for non-professional traders. We present the results from the Back-Testing below:

	S&P 500	STRATEGY 1 - SPY or Cash					
	SPY	RPT at 70%	RPT at 75%	RPT at 80%	RPT at 85%	RPT at 90%	RPT at 95%
Year	Annual Return	Annual Return	Annual Return	Annual Return	Annual Return	Annual Return	Annual Return
2008*	(35.12%)	8.18%	7.20%	15.13%	29.80%	54.30%	51.50%
2009	23.49%	15.54%	18.01%	26.44%	51.68%	51.65%	78.87%
2010	12.84%	15.19%	11.88%	12.32%	20.35%	18.47%	14.44%
2011	(0.20%)	(4.87%)	(1.19%)	3.49%	(0.82%)	8.09%	15.09%
2012	13.47%	4.57%	8.57%	10.67%	12.39%	13.47%	13.47%
2013	29.69%	12.13%	19.00%	22.27%	20.03%	24.68%	29.69%
2014	11.29%	(5.03%)	(0.39%)	0.40%	1.93%	2.92%	3.92%
2015	(0.81%)	(4.49%)	(7.82%)	(7.27%)	(6.61%)	(4.69%)	(1.51%)
2016	9.64%	10.75%	9.27%	12.56%	8.55%	8.87%	10.05%
2017	19.38%	19.28%	18.80%	18.83%	19.40%	18.35%	19.38%
2018	(6.35%)	4.34%	(0.55%)	3.29%	4.25%	0.90%	(3.09%)
2019	28.79%	18.91%	18.38%	19.72%	26.23%	26.37%	27.86%
2020	16.16%	26.98%	22.12%	33.22%	50.29%	52.48%	57.95%
2021	27.04%	19.23%	23.25%	20.47%	25.28%	26.32%	27.04%
Max DD	(52.39%)	(14.67%)	(19.54%)	(18.47%)	(15.85%)	(15.36%)	(16.36%)
Avg DD	(7.85%)	(3.80%)	(3.64%)	(3.39%)	(3.09%)	(2.88%)	(2.72%)
Avg Return	10.67%	10.05%	10.47%	13.68%	18.77%	21.58%	24.62%
RoMaD	0.2x	0.7x	0.5x	0.7x	1.2x	1.4x	1.5x
Value	3,415	3,616	3,816	5,658	9,690	13,160	17,562
Profit		201	401	2,243	6,275	9,745	14,147
Gain above S&P 500		+6%	+12%	+66%	+184%	+285%	+414%

(Legend: DD = Drawdowns / 2008*: since April 29, 2008 / First column = Benchmark. Value = value reached on December 31, 2021 from investing $1,000 on April 29, 2008. Profit/Gain from S&P 500 = how much Value of the strategy is greater than Value of S&P 500)

Year	Nasdaq	STRATEGY 2 - QQQ or Cash					
	QQQ	RPT at 70%	RPT at 75%	RPT at 80%	RPT at 85%	RPT at 90%	RPT at 95%
	Annual Return	Annual Return	Annual Return	Annual Return	Annual Return	Annual Return	Annual Return
2008*	(37.52%)	2.38%	4.45%	10.11%	20.70%	44.25%	36.55%
2009	53.83%	19.64%	21.85%	35.07%	59.70%	71.47%	99.00%
2010	19.04%	21.41%	16.95%	13.79%	26.69%	24.85%	20.54%
2011	2.52%	(2.30%)	(0.33%)	6.22%	0.52%	9.69%	18.58%
2012	16.66%	7.04%	10.37%	12.65%	15.38%	16.66%	16.66%
2013	35.05%	18.33%	25.04%	28.02%	24.48%	30.45%	35.05%
2014	17.38%	(2.45%)	4.10%	5.67%	8.14%	11.92%	11.76%
2015	8.34%	2.89%	(0.65%)	0.22%	(0.22%)	9.52%	12.71%
2016	5.92%	9.59%	8.03%	12.57%	5.55%	2.67%	5.00%
2017	31.47%	28.70%	28.39%	28.58%	30.49%	29.46%	31.47%
2018	(0.96%)	6.81%	(0.20%)	4.54%	6.74%	4.12%	1.86%
2019	37.83%	28.33%	27.28%	27.55%	34.91%	34.29%	36.52%
2020	47.57%	34.01%	31.15%	37.76%	56.45%	69.08%	75.33%
2021	26.81%	19.47%	24.82%	19.68%	27.42%	27.53%	26.81%
Max DD	(49.44%)	(18.32%)	(21.79%)	(21.25%)	(19.61%)	(16.08%)	(19.68%)
Avg DD	(6.15%)	(4.05%)	(4.12%)	(3.56%)	(3.34%)	(3.04%)	(3.06%)
Avg Return	18.85%	13.85%	14.37%	17.32%	22.64%	27.57%	30.56%
RoMaD	0.4x	0.8x	0.7x	0.8x	1.2x	1.7x	1.6x
Value	8,358	5,718	6,107	8,736	15,039	25,319	32,895
Profit		(2,641)	(2,251)	378	6,681	16,961	24,537
Gain above Nasdaq 100		-32%	-27%	+5%	+80%	+203%	+294%

Year	S&P 500 x2	STRATEGY 3 - SSO or Cash					
	SSO	RPT at 70%	RPT at 75%	RPT at 80%	RPT at 85%	RPT at 90%	RPT at 95%
	Annual Return	Annual Return	Annual Return	Annual Return	Annual Return	Annual Return	Annual Return
2008*	(63.98%)	10.08%	6.48%	26.14%	122.83%	197.30%	183.03%
2009	45.57%	33.22%	39.38%	57.99%	82.97%	80.40%	140.56%
2010	25.65%	31.87%	25.91%	23.84%	18.09%	13.07%	3.62%
2011	(3.45%)	(6.69%)	(1.28%)	7.62%	1.94%	20.90%	36.07%
2012	30.09%	9.45%	17.75%	22.33%	(2.65%)	0.00%	0.00%
2013	69.94%	28.32%	43.31%	51.14%	(23.70%)	(12.63%)	0.00%
2014	25.11%	(9.05%)	(0.29%)	1.17%	(20.86%)	(14.46%)	(11.76%)
2015	(1.80%)	(10.52%)	(15.30%)	(14.26%)	(12.29%)	(7.08%)	0.11%
2016	20.86%	23.06%	19.42%	26.36%	(4.14%)	(4.52%)	(0.37%)
2017	43.72%	41.70%	40.52%	40.53%	(0.72%)	(2.43%)	0.00%
2018	(15.18%)	7.49%	(2.57%)	5.20%	21.67%	15.10%	7.25%
2019	62.51%	40.33%	38.61%	40.46%	(6.74%)	(6.82%)	(1.81%)
2020	21.12%	58.69%	43.09%	67.55%	90.53%	94.38%	112.74%
2021	60.23%	35.77%	48.40%	41.51%	(4.23%)	(1.76%)	(0.00%)
Max DD	(81.12%)	(29.47%)	(37.65%)	(34.69%)	(30.05%)	(25.81%)	(32.26%)
Avg DD	(18.62%)	(7.42%)	(7.28%)	(6.79%)	(6.41%)	(5.23%)	(5.05%)
Avg Return	22.88%	20.98%	21.67%	28.40%	18.76%	26.53%	33.53%
RoMaD	0.3x	0.7x	0.6x	0.8x	0.6x	1.0x	1.0x
Value	8,028	11,690	12,652	26,500	78,422	154,786	254,141
Profit		3,662	4,624	18,472	70,394	146,758	246,113
Gain above S&P 500 x2		+46%	+58%	+230%	+877%	+1828%	+3066%

Year	Nasdaq x2 QLD Annual Return	STRATEGY 4 - QLD or Cash RPT at 70% Annual Return	RPT at 75% Annual Return	RPT at 80% Annual Return	RPT at 85% Annual Return	RPT at 90% Annual Return	RPT at 95% Annual Return
2008*	(67.24%)	0.71%	3.41%	13.23%	34.25%	89.25%	69.53%
2009	121.20%	41.36%	46.40%	78.78%	147.19%	179.32%	275.73%
2010	36.90%	42.86%	33.13%	29.03%	58.58%	50.80%	40.43%
2011	0.04%	(5.97%)	(1.81%)	9.97%	(2.96%)	16.13%	34.06%
2012	34.57%	13.34%	20.72%	25.78%	31.93%	34.57%	34.57%
2013	81.72%	40.12%	56.33%	63.71%	54.57%	69.75%	81.72%
2014	37.29%	(4.93%)	8.05%	11.37%	16.42%	25.61%	24.77%
2015	14.61%	4.59%	(1.96%)	(0.34%)	(1.40%)	8.49%	14.61%
2016	9.90%	19.89%	16.14%	25.81%	10.38%	4.10%	8.32%
2017	70.30%	63.64%	62.73%	63.18%	67.99%	65.18%	70.30%
2018	(8.37%)	11.48%	(3.10%)	5.88%	10.20%	4.35%	(0.55%)
2019	81.41%	60.72%	57.49%	57.18%	75.33%	73.12%	78.61%
2020	88.88%	73.62%	64.75%	80.18%	130.71%	169.18%	187.71%
2021	54.67%	37.08%	49.56%	38.47%	56.47%	56.42%	54.67%
Max DD	(78.75%)	(34.08%)	(40.07%)	(39.70%)	(37.56%)	(30.92%)	(36.76%)
Avg DD	(13.83%)	(8.30%)	(8.23%)	(7.08%)	(6.80%)	(6.22%)	(6.34%)
Avg Return	39.70%	28.46%	29.42%	35.87%	49.26%	60.45%	69.60%
RoMaD	0.5x	0.8x	0.7x	0.9x	1.3x	2.0x	1.9x
Value	34,706	25,262	28,118	55,967	154,605	376,886	611,345
Profit		(9,444)	(6,588)	21,262	119,899	342,181	576,640
Gain above Nasdaq x2		-27%	-19%	+61%	+345%	+986%	+1662%

Year	Volatility SVXY Annual Return	STRATEGY 5 - SVXY or Cash RPT at 70% Annual Return	RPT at 75% Annual Return	RPT at 80% Annual Return	RPT at 85% Annual Return	RPT at 90% Annual Return	RPT at 96% Annual Return
2011*	24.18%	23.96%	21.43%	7.79%	(5.01%)	3.78%	12.84%
2012	150.38%	51.34%	102.31%	117.02%	137.85%	150.38%	150.38%
2013	106.17%	12.66%	28.22%	43.03%	30.83%	63.74%	106.17%
2014	(1.25%)	(40.95%)	(23.62%)	(30.38%)	(30.58%)	(26.14%)	(10.16%)
2015	(17.51%)	14.39%	(16.15%)	(13.76%)	(3.51%)	(13.85%)	(5.48%)
2016	80.34%	105.20%	91.66%	114.58%	83.99%	92.24%	103.68%
2017	181.84%	182.37%	169.67%	167.36%	193.38%	154.05%	181.84%
2018	(91.75%)	(30.87%)	(37.72%)	(31.28%)	(24.16%)	(24.38%)	(37.93%)
2019	54.21%	40.05%	35.26%	41.45%	53.76%	49.50%	51.60%
2020	(36.47%)	24.47%	(2.98%)	3.24%	22.35%	13.43%	12.96%
2021	48.53%	22.88%	41.39%	29.65%	50.50%	46.26%	48.53%
Max DD	(95.25%)	(67.72%)	(55.29%)	(61.85%)	(60.11%)	(61.08%)	(58.51%)
Avg DD	(44.94%)	(22.96%)	(21.34%)	(19.65%)	(16.45%)	(16.10%)	(15.92%)
Avg Return	45.33%	36.86%	37.22%	40.79%	46.31%	46.27%	55.86%
RoMaD	0.5x	0.5x	0.7x	0.7x	0.8x	0.8x	1.0x
Value	2,924	11,243	11,059	13,762	21,064	22,763	41,146
Profit		8,319	8,135	10,838	18,140	19,839	38,222
Gain above SVXY		+285%	+278%	+371%	+620%	+679%	+1307%

Year	S&P 500 SPY Annual Return	STRATEGY 6 - SSO or SPY or GLD RPT-2 at 85% RPT-1 at 70% Annual Return	RPT-2 at 90% RPT-1 at 75% Annual Return	RPT-2 at 90% RPT-1 at 70% Annual Return	RPT-2 at 95% RPT-1 at 65% Annual Return	RPT-2 at 95% RPT-1 at 75% Annual Return	RPT-2 at 95% RPT-1 at 70% Annual Return
2008*	(35.12%)	33.27%	34.75%	60.32%	46.79%	7.00%	28.42%
2009	23.49%	95.65%	75.56%	92.97%	121.64%	109.30%	130.07%
2010	12.84%	48.48%	38.57%	43.87%	26.62%	35.37%	40.55%
2011	(0.20%)	0.78%	15.59%	8.61%	26.84%	22.12%	14.75%
2012	13.47%	11.73%	23.73%	13.15%	5.03%	23.73%	13.15%
2013	29.69%	38.21%	34.61%	37.03%	36.87%	43.12%	45.68%
2014	11.29%	(7.20%)	(4.17%)	(6.14%)	(8.50%)	(0.64%)	(2.69%)
2015	(0.81%)	(3.83%)	(2.03%)	(1.65%)	(2.35%)	(3.45%)	(3.38%)
2016	9.64%	31.20%	29.88%	28.82%	24.05%	30.08%	29.01%
2017	19.38%	48.41%	47.90%	47.22%	48.60%	49.85%	49.16%
2018	(6.35%)	40.13%	31.39%	31.08%	21.50%	23.55%	23.01%
2019	28.79%	83.88%	71.89%	82.24%	67.76%	74.15%	84.51%
2020	16.16%	109.73%	92.50%	119.84%	103.61%	97.01%	119.74%
2021	27.04%	71.63%	88.53%	74.94%	71.90%	89.34%	75.69%
Max DD	(52.39%)	(26.12%)	(31.43%)	(23.73%)	(24.87%)	(36.22%)	(26.21%)
Avg DD	(7.85%)	(5.13%)	(4.32%)	(4.76%)	(4.83%)	(4.45%)	(4.71%)
Avg Return	10.67%	43.00%	41.34%	45.16%	42.17%	42.90%	46.26%
RoMaD	0.2x	1.6x	1.3x	1.9x	1.7x	1.2x	1.8x
Value	3,415	97,089	93,286	120,538	88,271	98,391	124,534
Profit		93,674	89,870	117,123	84,856	94,976	121,119
Gain above S&P 500		+2743%	+2632%	+3430%	+2485%	+2781%	+3547%

Year	Nasdaq QQQ Annual Return	STRATEGY 7 - QLD or QQQ or GLD RPT-2 at 90% RPT-1 at 65% Annual Return	RPT-2 at 90% RPT-1 at 70% Annual Return	RPT-2 at 90% RPT-1 at 75% Annual Return	RPT-2 at 95% RPT-1 at 65% Annual Return	RPT-2 at 95% RPT-1 at 70% Annual Return	RPT-2 at 95% RPT-1 at 75% Annual Return
2008*	(37.52%)	70.15%	47.28%	28.88%	33.43%	15.50%	(0.14%)
2009	53.83%	113.09%	116.28%	95.83%	154.61%	158.42%	133.98%
2010	19.04%	43.15%	62.14%	52.01%	38.59%	56.98%	47.17%
2011	2.52%	25.66%	10.17%	12.77%	36.21%	19.41%	22.24%
2012	16.66%	10.28%	20.89%	28.73%	10.28%	20.89%	28.73%
2013	35.05%	44.14%	51.10%	47.89%	54.24%	60.65%	57.23%
2014	17.38%	(2.80%)	2.09%	4.44%	0.22%	5.26%	7.68%
2015	8.34%	17.13%	15.36%	16.87%	14.74%	13.01%	15.22%
2016	5.92%	16.46%	20.23%	22.67%	17.49%	21.29%	23.76%
2017	31.47%	75.99%	76.32%	76.83%	79.84%	80.17%	80.70%
2018	(0.96%)	39.05%	41.01%	46.63%	31.46%	33.32%	39.07%
2019	37.83%	89.79%	109.98%	92.80%	90.93%	114.40%	96.52%
2020	47.57%	136.43%	157.49%	120.56%	138.57%	159.82%	126.96%
2021	26.81%	69.19%	75.13%	85.20%	67.92%	73.82%	83.82%
Max DD	(49.44%)	(27.83%)	(27.27%)	(33.68%)	(27.83%)	(28.93%)	(40.32%)
Avg DD	(6.15%)	(5.39%)	(5.22%)	(5.16%)	(5.42%)	(5.32%)	(5.51%)
Avg Return	18.85%	53.41%	57.53%	52.29%	54.90%	59.49%	54.50%
RoMaD	0.4x	1.9x	2.1x	1.6x	2.0x	2.1x	1.4x
Value	8,358	255,376	346,432	251,839	266,517	364,588	269,158
Profit		247,018	338,074	243,481	258,159	356,230	260,799
Gain above Nasdaq 100		+2955%	+4045%	+2913%	+3089%	+4262%	+3120%

	S&P 500	STRATEGY 8 - SVXY or SPY or VIXM					
		RPT-2 at 96%	**RPT-2 at 96%**	**RPT-2 at 96%**	**RPT-2 at 97%**	**RPT-2 at 97%**	**RPT-2 at 98%**
	SPY	**RPT-1 at 75%**	**RPT-1 at 80%**	**RPT-1 at 85%**	**RPT-1 at 80%**	**RPT-1 at 85%**	**RPT-1 at 80%**
Year	Annual Return	Annual Return	Annual Return	Annual Return	Annual Return	Annual Return	Annual Return
2011*	11.71%	20.90%	36.88%	40.54%	36.88%	40.54%	36.88%
2012	13.47%	104.55%	114.74%	138.58%	114.74%	138.58%	114.74%
2013	29.69%	33.78%	37.40%	26.45%	37.40%	26.45%	37.40%
2014	11.29%	(25.25%)	(32.92%)	(39.25%)	(28.51%)	(35.26%)	(28.07%)
2015	(0.81%)	15.17%	13.13%	23.46%	17.59%	28.33%	33.98%
2016	9.64%	148.43%	168.86%	152.29%	157.10%	141.26%	157.10%
2017	19.38%	208.36%	199.60%	217.29%	199.60%	217.29%	199.60%
2018	(6.35%)	(13.42%)	(12.26%)	(7.76%)	(14.58%)	(8.14%)	(8.84%)
2019	28.79%	75.24%	81.06%	78.99%	90.56%	88.38%	89.67%
2020	16.16%	202.30%	213.90%	196.47%	191.60%	175.78%	114.91%
2021	27.04%	106.23%	87.45%	73.40%	87.45%	73.40%	87.45%
Max DD	(34.10%)	(46.35%)	(57.49%)	(59.28%)	(56.19%)	(58.04%)	(55.92%)
Avg DD	(2.77%)	(10.24%)	(11.05%)	(11.42%)	(10.42%)	(10.61%)	(9.86%)
Avg Return	14.55%	79.66%	82.53%	81.86%	80.90%	80.60%	75.89%
RoMaD	0.4x	1.7x	1.4x	1.4x	1.4x	1.4x	1.4x
Value	4,228	206,399	230,793	216,055	232,715	223,127	208,814
Profit		202,171	226,565	211,827	228,487	218,899	204,586
Gain above S&P 500		+4782%	+5359%	+5010%	+5404%	+5178%	+4839%

Here are some important conclusions and takeaways from the Back-Test:

SMIGRM significantly reduces drawdowns and increases returns: In all 8 strategies, we can clearly see both maximum drawdown and average drawdown getting significantly reduced with the introduction of SMIGRM led by RISP 500™. By strategically rotating to cash when risks increase (as measured by RISP 500™) above chosen RPT levels, we see drawdowns getting reduced to around half or less. As you can see from the results, this happened to all 8 strategies. At the same time, returns got a decent boost too! This is the first indication from the back-test that we were on the right track.

For two-risk level strategies, since cash is in the asset rotation, we are basically comparing a simple buy & hold (*permahold*) of the asset vs. investing in the same asset with SMIGRM. For three-risk level strategies, we added a bit more sophistication and cash is no longer in the rotation. But still we can compare with the assets each of them is based on (SPY, QQQ, SVXY). As you can see from the Back-Test results, their drawdowns were also significantly reduced from their corresponding base assets' drawdowns. And just like two-risk level strategies, three risk-level strategies also experienced a significant boost in terms of returns compared to their corresponding base assets' returns.

The logic is simple: by reducing drawdowns or losses, net returns must naturally improve as a direct result. We can use a sports analogy. It is similar to winning games with a strong defense. This is because a strong defense enables the offense to shine with confidence knowing their backs are well protected. When your team has a reliable defense, the offense can even play bolder taking more risks. That is why leveraged ETF strategies and volatility strategies can earn proportionately higher returns while keeping drawdowns at acceptable levels.

SMIGRM improves Return Over Max Drawdown ratio: You can also see that the RoMaD for all 8 strategies have significantly improved. Note that we are measuring RoMaD for the entire 14-year period considering the maximum drawdown that occurred during this period and the corresponding cumulative return during the same period for its calculation. It turned out that in the back-testing, the RoMaD for all 8 strategies were significantly above 1 while the RoMaD for all the base assets (SPY, QQQ, SSO, QLD, with the exception of SVXY) had RoMaD below 1. This is another strong indication we are on the right track.

Why are max drawdowns such a big deal?

Remember the asymmetry between percentage gains and losses? If you're caught in a big drawdown (like most people were during the 2008 GFC), it's really hard to recover (it may take years just to undo the damage). A -20% drawdown requires a subsequent gain of +25% to break even, but a -50% will require a +100% subsequent gain to recover, which is exponentially harder. Shrinking your drawdown is indeed a VERY big deal!

Can SMIGRM erase risk completely? Nope, and we don't want that! Risk cannot be 100% eliminated while maintaining a high return or even the same return. That is because we live in a probabilistic world! As a result, you cannot eliminate drawdowns and losses 100% unless you give up on returns too! Unless you are content with miniscule returns, the best that anyone can and should do is to optimize the return-risk ratio. As you can see from the results of both back-testing and live trading, we proved how the SMIGRM led by the RISP 500™ was able to do just that: optimize the risk-return ratio.

Higher RPT leads to higher returns but also higher risks: We can also clearly see that a higher RPT leads to higher returns and higher drawdowns as well. This is consistent with our expectations. This happens because by rotating to safe assets only at higher levels of risk, you would be holding risky assets longer. Naturally a longer exposure to risks will get you more drawdowns. But on the other hand, you would also get more return in return (pun not intended). By choosing an RPT level, you are essentially setting up a risk stop level, beyond which you are not willing to be exposed to greater risks. If you set this bar high, you are essentially accepting more risks on the expectation of higher returns as well. We can see that in the 14-year period of the Back=Test, higher RPTs (e.g. 90% or 95%) would have resulted in exceptionally high returns. This can actually be explained by the impressive decades-long bull market experienced by the American stock market since the end of World War II. The capitalistic economy centered on value creation for shareholders also contributed to the decades-long bull market in U.S. equities. Market crashes or strong corrections did occur with some frequency but it has been essentially a bull market, a fact no one can deny. That is why a very high RPT would have led to oversized returns as SMIGRM would have protected investors only from the really serious drawdowns while keeping them exposed to risk most of the time. Nevertheless, in choosing an appropriate RPT, we should think beyond only the results from the Back-Test alone. If we did, we would have simply embraced 95% as our official RPT for our live trading. We didn't.

Again, RPT should be selected based on each investor's own risk-return appetite. Investors should not only look at returns when selecting their RPTs. They must balance it with the size of potential drawdowns they are actually comfortable with facing. For example, say you like a strategy with a maximum drawdown of 20%. Ask yourself if you would be comfortable if such a drawdown happens again while you are holding the asset. Would you be suffering too much emotionally or you would face it alright without pulling the plug? If the answer is the former, you should choose an RPT that produces lower drawdowns or even another asset or strategy. Remember, just like playing a game or sports, you want to invest seriously but also having fun and in a relaxed way so that your rational brain can work best for you. You don't want to be doing this under pressure all the time (this is what happens to most folks all the time, pros and non-pros alike). When I'm trading or making investments, I want to have fun in the activity and be on top of it enjoying the activity. Your sanity is important. Avoid putting yourself in cornered situations, such as being forced to stop out of positions because losses became too unbearable for you. All of us have experienced being in such situations at least once in our lives (if you haven't, you haven't been in the market long enough). But if we can avoid such situations by planning ahead with a tool like the RISP 500™, it will get you disciplined naturally, without all that unnecessary suffering.

Does the SMIGRM have an Achilles' heel? In what type of situations might it not deliver results as intended? It's absolutely important to map out the weaknesses of any system or method, no matter how strong and robust they are, so you can find solutions around it to minimize the effects. Despite all the great results delivered by SMIGRM in almost all situations (bull market, bear market, etc.), we found that there is one particular situation, which is when the market is very undecided on direction and moves in such an extreme whipsaw fashion that it may create an Achilles' heel for the system. When stock prices and the risk measured fluctuate too frequently, especially around your chosen RPT levels, it triggers a frequent rotation between risky and safe assets in a rapid succession of buy and sell transactions. Changing positions back and forth too frequently may be costly and affect your performance numbers. If you think about it, it is not the fault of the model or system per se because it is still doing its job as designed, trying to protect you from harm. But if you are in a market that is volatile, directionless, and oscillates too much around RPT levels for a persistently long period of time, the cost of the protection may eat up your profits. Fortunately, these situations are not very common. But they do happen once in a while. From the system's construction, we may anticipate that those using high RPTs should have fewer problems with a whipsaw market than those using low RPTs, but again, it depends at what risk level the whipsaw is actually centered around.

If you think about it, this is a situation that happens in daily life to everyone. Think of a time you have been very undecided about a difficult choice you had to make. Sometimes we may struggle and take hours, or days, or even longer to make up our minds. The same can happen with markets, which, in the end, are moved by a collective of human minds. Any system reading the markets would be confused by a constant change of mind.

Some suggested solutions if it happens: A workaround investors may employ in this situation is to "desensitize" the system a bit in response to the high volatility experienced with frequent triggering for asset rotation. Dial up RPT a notch or two. This way you will essentially be accepting higher risks or higher volatility for a limited period of time while the situation persists. As a result of a higher RPT, you will be less frequently triggered to rotate assets. This is similar to what pilots do when the aircraft encounters annoying turbulence: fly at a higher altitude.

A word of caution, though: only do this if the market is directionless, essentially moving sideways. If the market has a strong possibility of going south, or if you are unsure, just simply hold the safe asset or cash while the situation persists. Avoid this market altogether and wait it out on the sidelines until the storm is gone. A whipsaw won't make you rich anyway; but it can make you poor! – so no problem simply avoiding it. That is exactly the right thing intelligent investors would do in a highly uncertain situation anyway, right? Common sense still applies, folks, always! A smart warrior can always fight another day. In general, avoid RPT below 70% if you experience too frequent rotations (switching position back and forth in a succession of many days) and/or a significant drop in performance.

Even if we decided not to take any of the above precautions to make adjustments, SMIGRM should still be able to deliver us a strong performance over the long run. This is because we will most likely have some good years, some spectacular years, some 'ok' years, but most importantly no horribly bad years, which are so common investing without SMIGRM, unless you consciously choose to run great risks such as a very high RPT (95% or greater). For investors who can't afford losing much especially, being wiped out by a crash may mean game over for them. Although future performance can never be guaranteed, SMIGRM was designed to avoid that scenario.

Lower RPT leads to more frequent trades: Lower RPTs would invariably cause investors to trade more frequently. That happens because the lower RPT is equivalent to a more sensitive risk detector, in a way. Visually on a chart, you can see that a lower RPT line crosses the daily RISP 500™ percentile rank line more often than a high RPT line. If investors are too busy and/or not willing to trade often, and provided they are willing to accept slightly higher risks, they may decide for a slightly higher RPT and stay in the market longer. A word of caution: avoid choosing a RPT that is too low (below 50% or 60%) as it may lead you to lose the benefits of SMIGRM. A sensitivity analysis suggested the optimal range: 70% to 95%.

Back-testing is not live trading: Although we try to recreate the same conditions as if we could go back in time and trade, it is just not the same. That is why we make our analysis and draw conclusions on a relative, not absolute basis. Gladly, we have at least two years of live trading experience to share with you (next section!) and results have been very impressive too.

Live Trading Results and Conclusion Analysis

On **January 1st, 2022**, real-time live trading debuted for the RISP 500™ project. This is completely different and more accurate to reality than back-testing. For privacy reasons about our personal investments, we are presenting a hypothetical initial amount of $1,000 invested in the 8 strategies after preliminary back-testing results were considered highly satisfactory to justify live trading with real money. In live trading, decisions are made in real time. RISP 500™ is calculated usually between the hours the market is most active (we prefer between 10 a.m. and 2 p.m. New York time or EST) and trading is executed right after, if there is a trade.

In this book, we are presenting results obtained until the writing has concluded and getting ready to be published. Today is Monday, July 1st, 2024. Thus, the results of our live trading presented here covers the **period between January 1st, 2022 and July 1st, 2024**. But we will continue trading, of course! It won't end here. If you're interested in learning how we are doing, we are making our daily blotter and performance results available on Facebook and on our websites:

- www.Facebook.com/risp500
- www.risp500.com

By the time of this writing, all 8 strategies have performed above expectations in live trading. We have chosen a RPT of 75% for all 5 two-risk level strategies. For the three-risk level strategies, we have chosen RPT-1 at 70% and RPT-2 at 95%.

Note 1: The choice of RPTs, as discussed earlier, is highly personal - they must match each investor's own risk-return profile. Conservative investors should select lower RPTs and aggressive investors can use higher RPTs.

Note 2: RPTs don't have to be fixed; they can be made variable by users according to market regime, etc. but the choice must be minimally validated by back-testing first. For simplicity, we can work with fixed RPTs, unless strategies aren't working as intended or we are in a whipsaw market with too frequent rotations as we discussed earlier.

Note 3: For performance results, we are calculating daily P/L and adding it up over time. Daily P/L is calculated by investing the full amount of the price of the asset without any excesses or cash to be sitting idle unused. This means investing the full amount. This is not how mutual funds or hedge funds calculate their daily returns because they will always have excess cash sitting idle. We are calculating daily returns as if we were deploying the exact amount needed to buy or sell the assets. Well, first of all, we are not funds investing clients' money. The reason we chose to do it this way is threefold:

1. It makes it fairer to compare with the S&P 500® index or any other index as a benchmark because the indexes don't consider any unutilized cash in their return calculation as well. This way, we have a direct apples-to-apples comparison.

2. We chose not to disclose the exact amounts we are investing personally, so there is no reason to have any idle cash in the studies. After all, we are not doing this to boast about anything but only to prove a technical concept: that SMIGRM works!

3. Everyone will have a different amount of unused cash when they invest anyway as everyone has different investable amounts.

Therefore, we believe the approach is more than reasonable, the difference is probably negligible, but we want to make this disclaimer. Let's now present the results of the live trading that continues up to this day and will continue further:

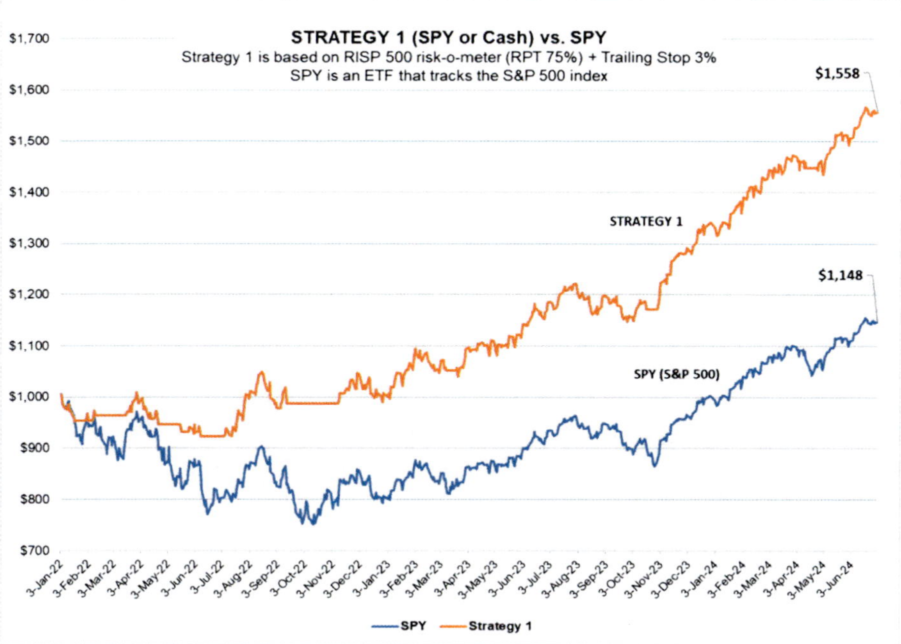
STRATEGY 1 (SPY or Cash) vs. SPY
Strategy 1 is based on RISP 500 risk-o-meter (RPT 75%) + Trailing Stop 3%
SPY is an ETF that tracks the S&P 500 index
$1,558
$1,148
STRATEGY 1
SPY (S&P 500)
$1,700
$1,600
$1,500
$1,400
$1,300
$1,200
$1,100
$1,000
$900
$800
$700
3-Jan-22 3-Feb-22 3-Mar-22 3-Apr-22 3-May-22 3-Jun-22 3-Jul-22 3-Aug-22 3-Sep-22 3-Oct-22 3-Nov-22 3-Dec-22 3-Jan-23 3-Feb-23 3-Mar-23 3-Apr-23 3-May-23 3-Jun-23 3-Jul-23 3-Aug-23 3-Sep-23 3-Oct-23 3-Nov-23 3-Dec-23 3-Jan-24 3-Feb-24 3-Mar-24 3-Apr-24 3-May-24 3-Jun-24
SPY
Strategy 1

STRATEGY 2 (QQQ or Cash) vs. QQQ
Strategy 2 is based on RISP 500 risk-o-meter (RPT 75%) + Trailing Stop 5.5%
QQQ is an ETF that tracks the Nasdaq index
$1,778
$1,211
STRATEGY 2
QQQ (NASDAQ 100)
$2,000
$1,800
$1,600
$1,400
$1,200
$1,000
$800
$600
3-Jan-22 3-Feb-22 3-Mar-22 3-Apr-22 3-May-22 3-Jun-22 3-Jul-22 3-Aug-22 3-Sep-22 3-Oct-22 3-Nov-22 3-Dec-22 3-Jan-23 3-Feb-23 3-Mar-23 3-Apr-23 3-May-23 3-Jun-23 3-Jul-23 3-Aug-23 3-Sep-23 3-Oct-23 3-Nov-23 3-Dec-23 3-Jan-24 3-Feb-24 3-Mar-24 3-Apr-24 3-May-24 3-Jun-24
QQQ
Strategy 2

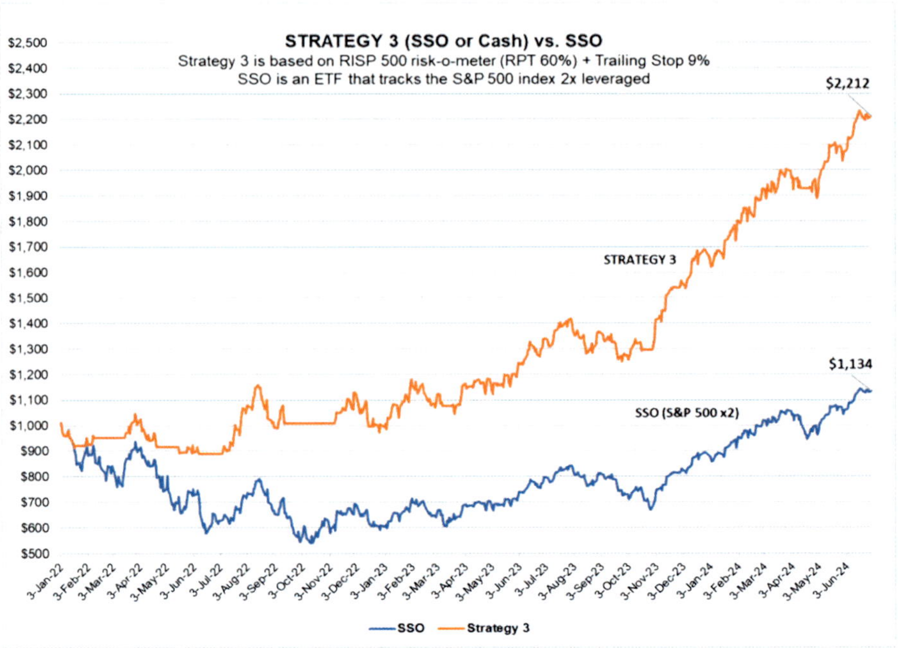
STRATEGY 3 (SSO or Cash) vs. SSO
Strategy 3 is based on RISP 500 risk-o-meter (RPT 60%) + Trailing Stop 9%
SSO is an ETF that tracks the S&P 500 index 2x leveraged
$2,212
STRATEGY 3
$1,134
SSO (S&P 500 x2)
SSO
Strategy 3

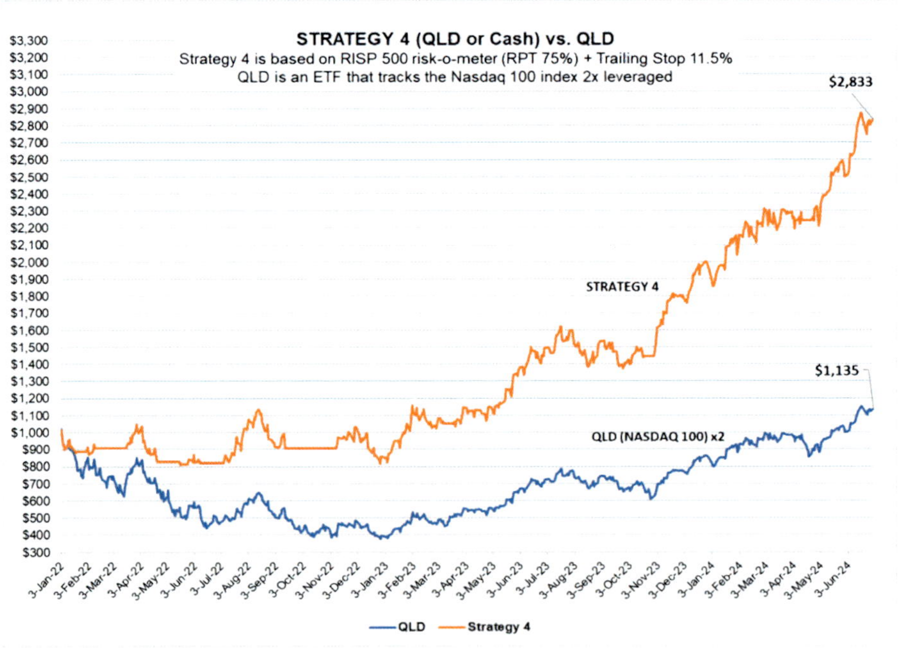
STRATEGY 4 (QLD or Cash) vs. QLD
Strategy 4 is based on RISP 500 risk-o-meter (RPT 75%) + Trailing Stop 11.5%
QLD is an ETF that tracks the Nasdaq 100 index 2x leveraged
$2,833
STRATEGY 4
$1,135
QLD (NASDAQ 100) x2
QLD
Strategy 4

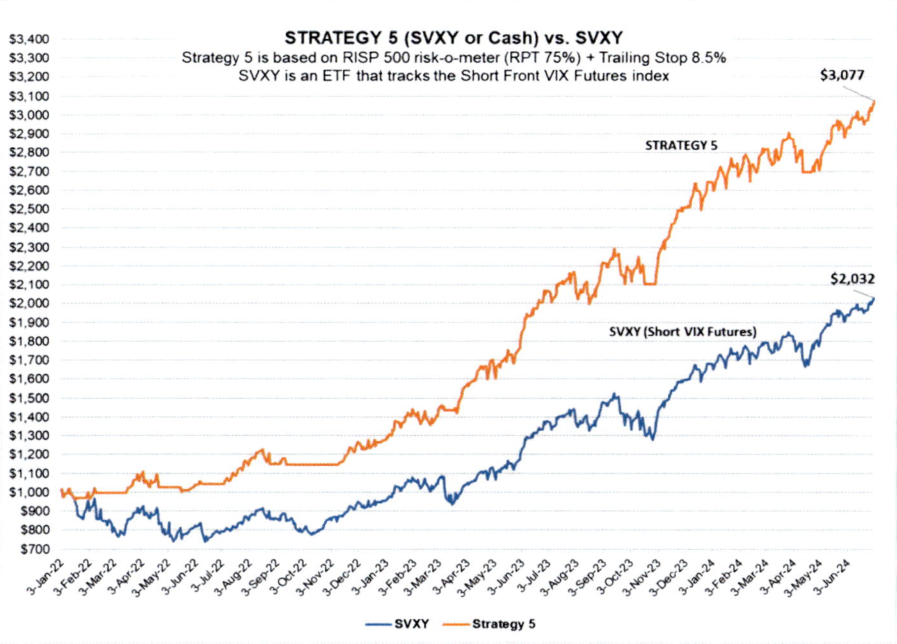
STRATEGY 5 (SVXY or Cash) vs. SVXY
Strategy 5 is based on RISP 500 risk-o-meter (RPT 75%) + Trailing Stop 8.5%
SVXY is an ETF that tracks the Short Front VIX Futures index
$3,077
STRATEGY 5
$2,032
SVXY (Short VIX Futures)
SVXY
Strategy 5

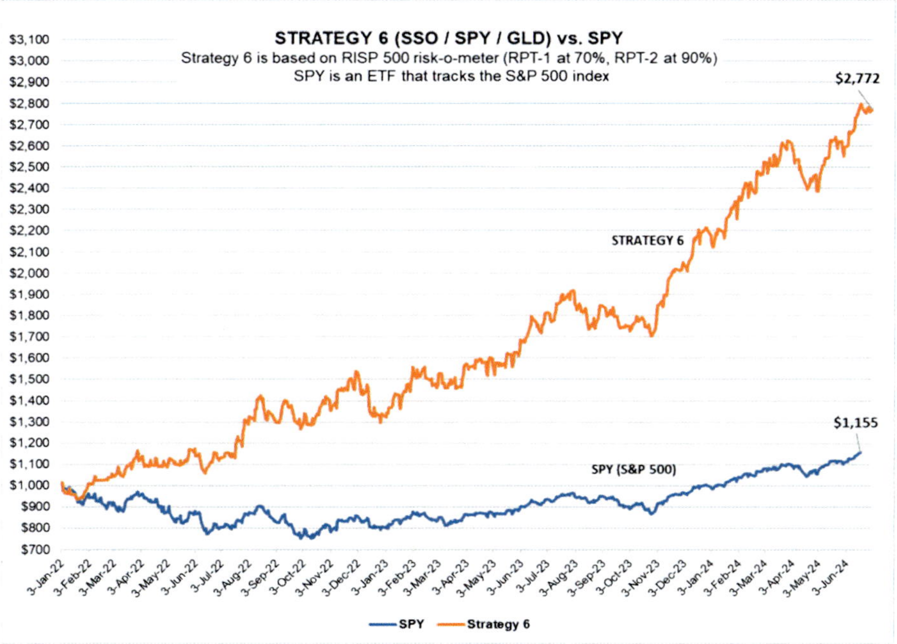
STRATEGY 6 (SSO / SPY / GLD) vs. SPY
Strategy 6 is based on RISP 500 risk-o-meter (RPT-1 at 70%, RPT-2 at 90%)
SPY is an ETF that tracks the S&P 500 index
$2,772
STRATEGY 6
$1,155
SPY (S&P 500)
SPY
Strategy 6

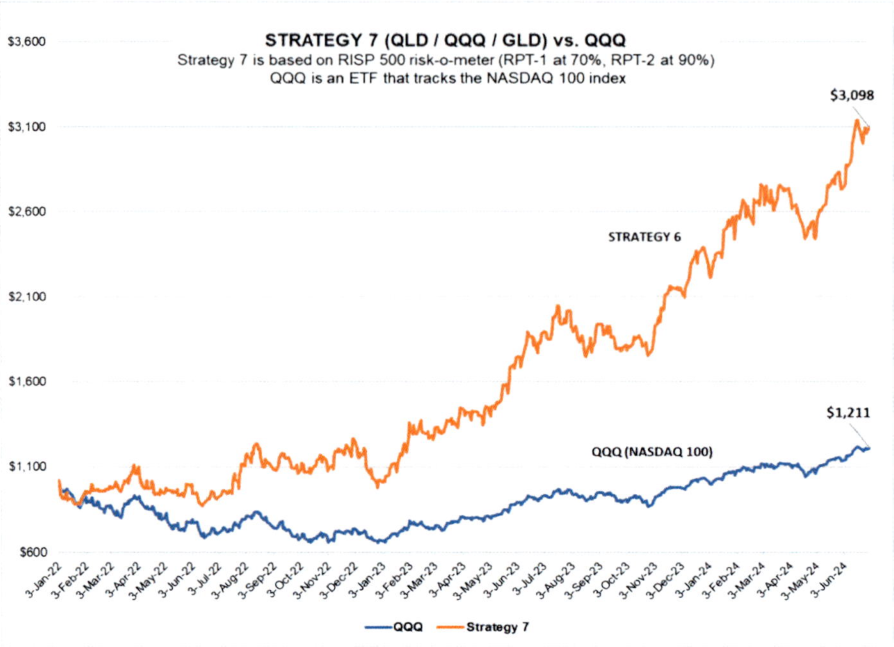
STRATEGY 7 (QLD / QQQ / GLD) vs. QQQ
Strategy 7 is based on RISP 500 risk-o-meter (RPT-1 at 70%, RPT-2 at 90%)
QQQ is an ETF that tracks the NASDAQ 100 index
$3,098
STRATEGY 6
$1,211
QQQ (NASDAQ 100)
QQQ
Strategy 7

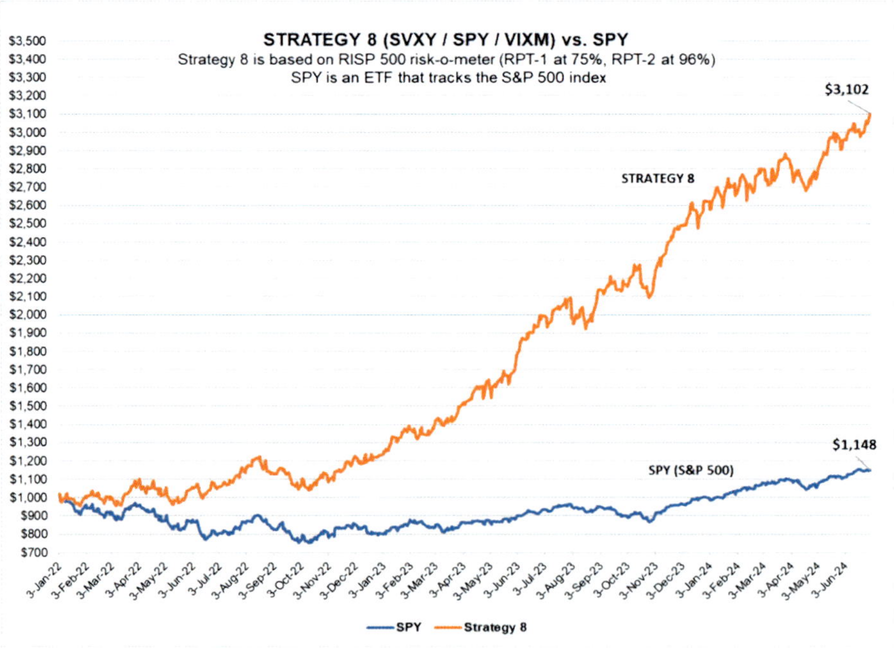
STRATEGY 8 (SVXY / SPY / VIXM) vs. SPY
Strategy 8 is based on RISP 500 risk-o-meter (RPT-1 at 75%, RPT-2 at 96%)
SPY is an ETF that tracks the S&P 500 index
$3,102
STRATEGY 8
$1,148
SPY (S&P 500)
SPY
Strategy 8

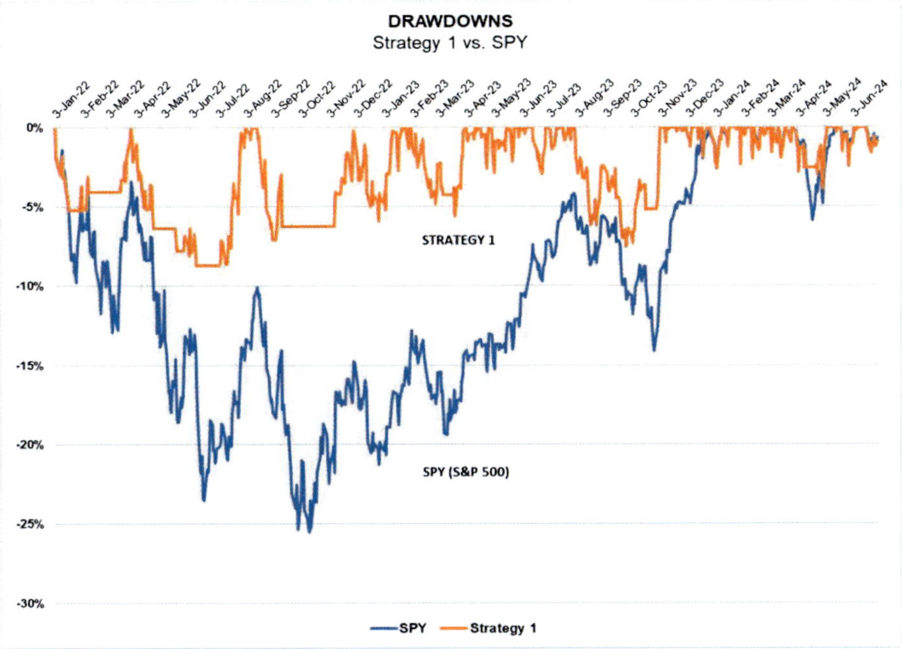
DRAWDOWNS
Strategy 1 vs. SPY
STRATEGY 1
SPY (S&P 500)
0%
-5%
-10%
-15%
-20%
-25%
-30%
SPY
Strategy 1

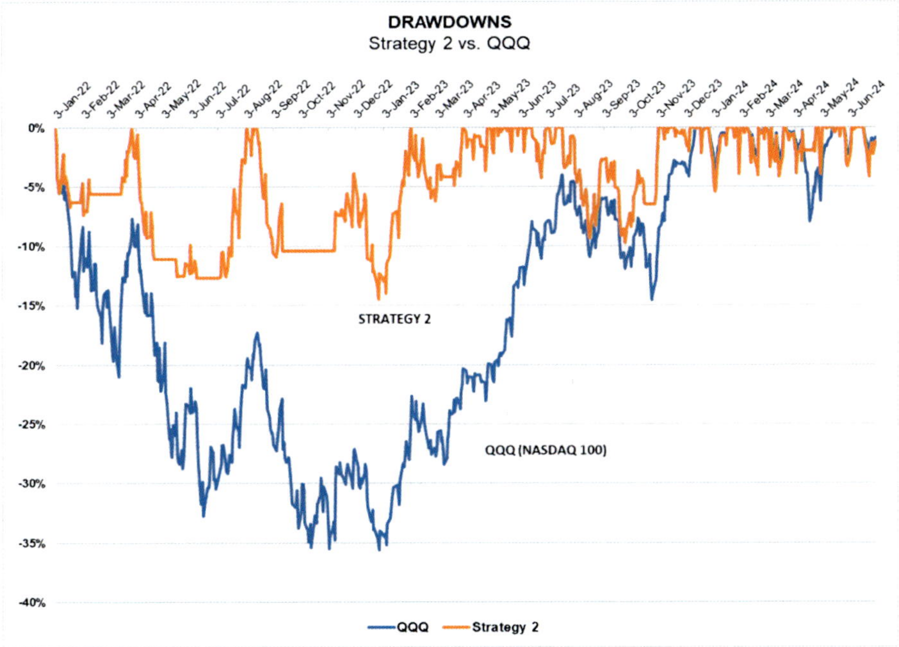
DRAWDOWNS
Strategy 2 vs. QQQ
STRATEGY 2
QQQ (NASDAQ 100)
0%
-5%
-10%
-15%
-20%
-25%
-30%
-35%
-40%
QQQ
Strategy 2

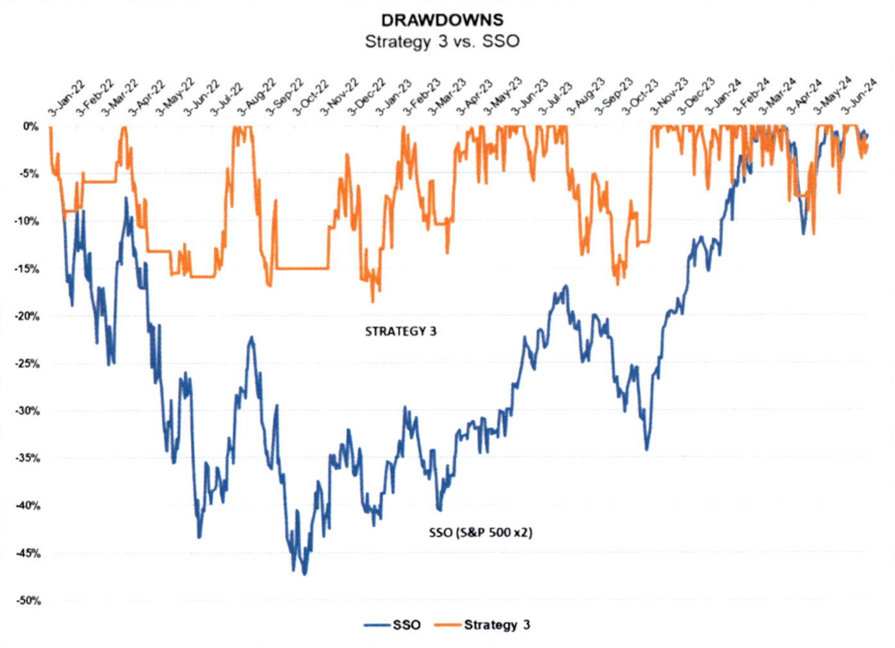
DRAWDOWNS
Strategy 3 vs. SSO
STRATEGY 3
SSO (S&P 500 x2)
SSO
Strategy 3

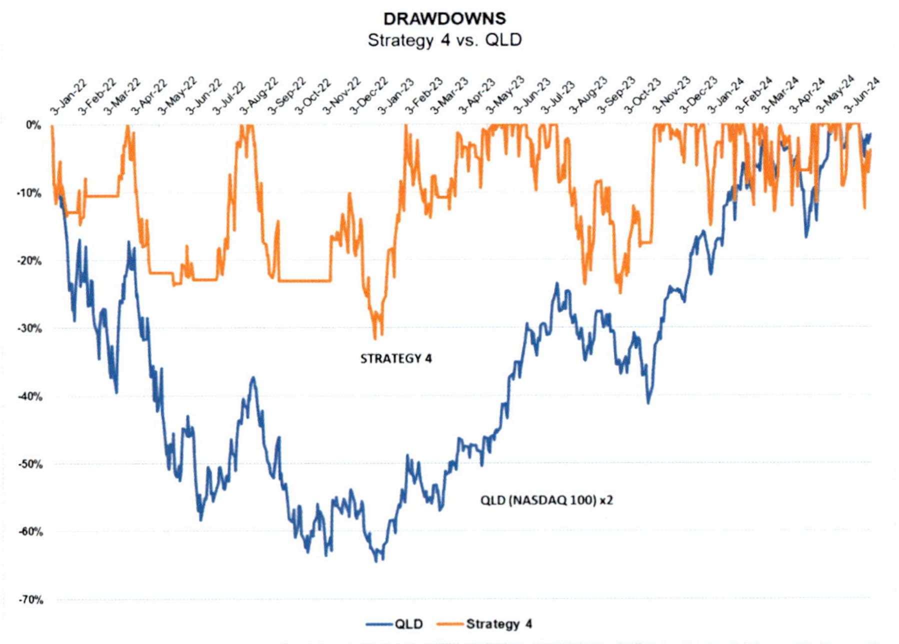
DRAWDOWNS
Strategy 4 vs. QLD
STRATEGY 4
QLD (NASDAQ 100) x2
QLD
Strategy 4

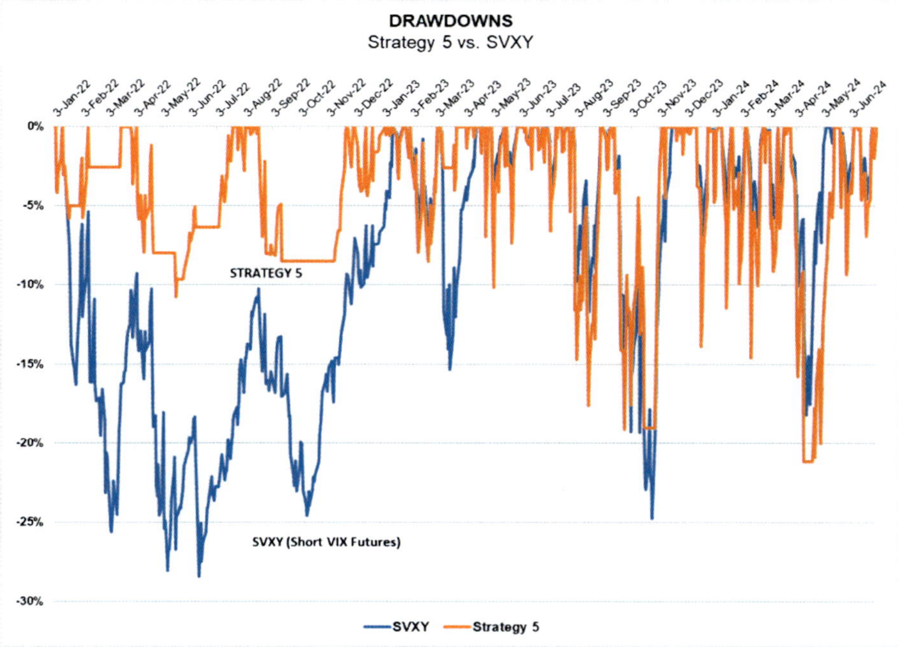
DRAWDOWNS
Strategy 5 vs. SVXY
STRATEGY 5
SVXY (Short VIX Futures)
0%
-5%
-10%
-15%
-20%
-25%
-30%
SVXY
Strategy 5

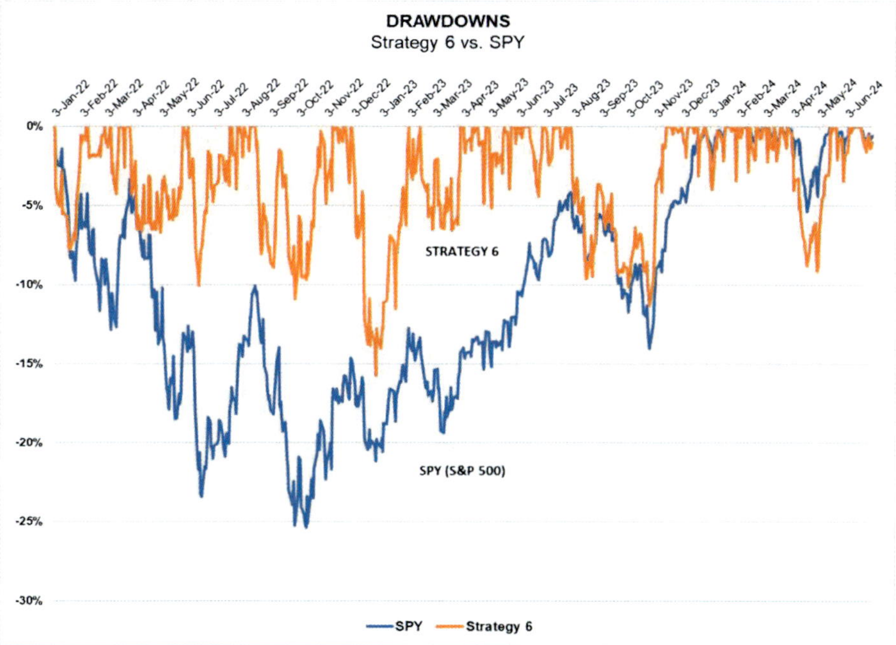
DRAWDOWNS
Strategy 6 vs. SPY
STRATEGY 6
SPY (S&P 500)
0%
-5%
-10%
-15%
-20%
-25%
-30%
SPY
Strategy 6

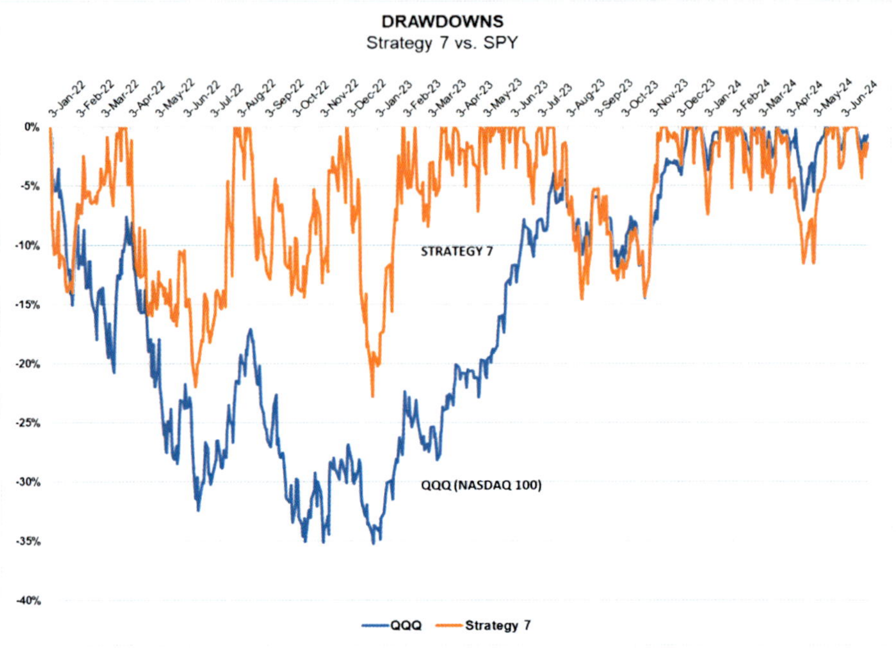
DRAWDOWNS
Strategy 7 vs. SPY
3-Jan-22
3-Feb-22
3-Mar-22
3-Apr-22
3-May-22
3-Jun-22
3-Jul-22
3-Aug-22
3-Sep-22
3-Oct-22
3-Nov-22
3-Dec-22
3-Jan-23
3-Feb-23
3-Mar-23
3-Apr-23
3-May-23
3-Jun-23
3-Jul-23
3-Aug-23
3-Sep-23
3-Oct-23
3-Nov-23
3-Dec-23
3-Jan-24
3-Feb-24
3-Mar-24
3-Apr-24
3-May-24
3-Jun-24
0%
-5%
-10%
-15%
-20%
-25%
-30%
-35%
-40%
STRATEGY 7
QQQ (NASDAQ 100)
QQQ
Strategy 7

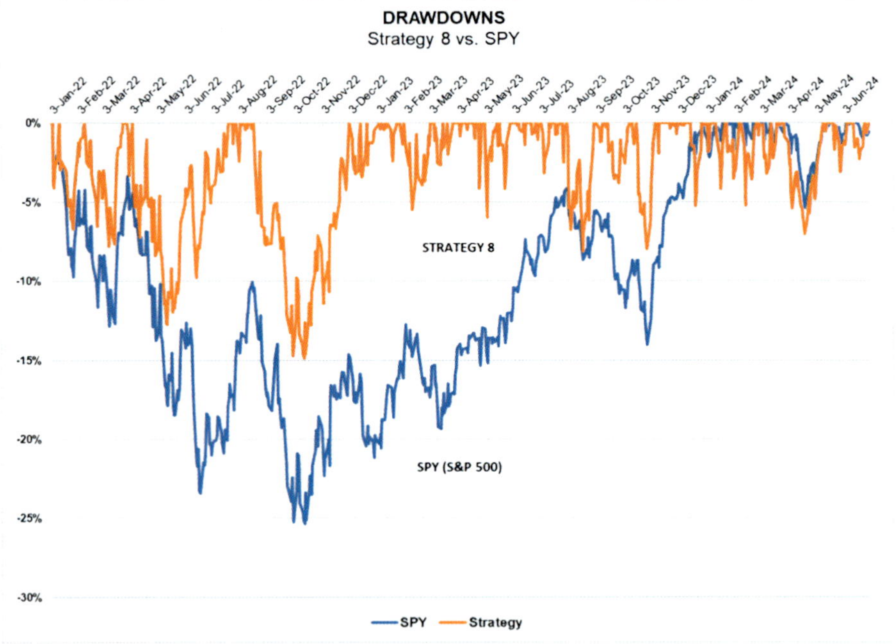
DRAWDOWNS
Strategy 8 vs. SPY
3-Jan-22
3-Feb-22
3-Mar-22
3-Apr-22
3-May-22
3-Jun-22
3-Jul-22
3-Aug-22
3-Sep-22
3-Oct-22
3-Nov-22
3-Dec-22
3-Jan-23
3-Feb-23
3-Mar-23
3-Apr-23
3-May-23
3-Jun-23
3-Jul-23
3-Aug-23
3-Sep-23
3-Oct-23
3-Nov-23
3-Dec-23
3-Jan-24
3-Feb-24
3-Mar-24
3-Apr-24
3-May-24
3-Jun-24
0%
-5%
-10%
-15%
-20%
-25%
-30%
STRATEGY 8
SPY (S&P 500)
SPY
Strategy

2024 YTD Return Ranking	
Asset/Strategy	YTD Return
ST-2L-Nasdaqx2	**42.88%**
QLD	32.93%
ST-2L-SP500x2	**31.66%**
ST-3L-Nasdaq	**30.82%**
SSO	27.49%
ST-3L-SP500	**25.93%**
ST-2L-Nasdaq	**21.77%**
SVXY	20.99%
ST-3L-Volatility	**18.39%**
QQQ	17.68%
ST-2L-SP500	**16.42%**
ST-2L-Volatility	**16.42%**
SPY (S&P 500)	**14.73%**

Published every day after the close

2022 to Date Performance Ranking				1-Jul-2024
Asset/Strategy	Cum. Return	CAGR	Max DD	RoMaD
ST-3L-Volatility	**210.17%**	56.26%	**-14.88%**	**14.1x**
ST-3L-Nasdaq	**209.75%**	56.17%	**-22.78%**	**9.2x**
ST-2L-Volatility	**207.66%**	55.76%	**-21.16%**	**9.8x**
ST-2L-Nasdaqx2	**183.33%**	50.78%	**-31.70%**	**5.8x**
ST-3L-SP500	**177.22%**	49.49%	**-15.75%**	**11.3x**
ST-2L-SP500x2	**121.19%**	36.76%	**-18.58%**	**6.5x**
SVXY	103.25%	32.27%	-28.46%	3.6x
ST-2L-Nasdaq	**77.84%**	25.48%	**-14.52%**	**5.4x**
ST-2L-SP500	**55.81%**	19.11%	**-8.72%**	**6.4x**
QQQ	21.13%	7.85%	-35.59%	0.6x
SPY (S&P 500)	**14.82%**	**5.60%**	**-25.51%**	**0.6x**
QLD	13.49%	5.12%	-64.50%	0.2x
SSO	13.36%	5.07%	-47.32%	0.3x

Max DD: Maximum Drawdowns, RoMaD: Return over Maxium Drawdowns

Here are some important conclusions and take-aways from the Live Trading results:

1. SMIGRM significantly reduces drawdowns and increases returns: Live trading has confirmed what we have seen in back-testing. The 2022-2023 period was actually great to prove the whole concept. 2022 started with a bear market since the very first few days of the year. Some call it the burst of the Everything Bubble that took place post-pandemic. Not only did the stock market go down but also the bond market, destroying in its path balanced stock-bond portfolios. The S&P 500® returned -19.64% in 2022 (the SPY ETF tracking the S&P 500® returned -19.48%). It gave us a bear market year to test SMIGRM right at the start. Then we had 2023 and 2024, which, up to the moment of this writing in late-June 2024, were essentially bull market years. Therefore, we were able to test SMIGRM in a bear and bull market to make important observations. First, all 8 strategies delivered great returns and they all outperformed the S&P 500®, some by substantial margins. Just the volatility-based strategies (Strategies V and VIII) aren't beating the S&P 500® in 2024 YTD by a tiny margin; however, both strategies significantly outperformed the S&P 500® in both 2022 and 2023.

In terms of drawdowns, all 8 strategies experienced significant reductions, especially in the bear market year of 2022.

Check the **2022 to Date Performance Ranking table** above. Six SMIGRM strategies occupy the top of the ranking with triple-digit returns. Since the market went up during the period despite the 2022 bear market, leveraged strategies and volatility-based strategies guided by the RISP 500™ avoiding high risk situations delivered the best performance. In 2024, volatility-based strategies haven't performed so well after two spectacular years. The market has essentially gone up with low volatility and a few hiccups along the way. But leveraged strategies are still at the top of this year's ranking, delivering more return than twice the S&P 500®. Overall, the

2022 - 2024 YTD ANNUAL PERFORMANCE CONTROL **1-Jul-2024**

Year	S&P 500 Annual Return	STRATEGY 1 Annual Return	Gain over S&P 500	STRATEGY 2 Annual Return	Gain over S&P 500
2022	-19.48%	0.53%	20.01%	-7.61%	11.87%
2023	24.29%	33.13%	8.84%	58.07%	33.78%
YTD 2024	14.73%	16.42%	+1.69%	21.77%	+7.04%
Year	S&P 500 Annual Return	STRATEGY 3 Annual Return	Gain over S&P 500	STRATEGY 4 Annual Return	Gain over S&P 500
2022	-19.48%	0.18%	19.66%	-14.32%	5.16%
2023	24.29%	67.71%	43.42%	131.44%	107.15%
YTD 2024	14.73%	31.66%	+16.92%	42.88%	+28.15%
Year	S&P 500 Annual Return	STRATEGY 5 Annual Return	Gain over S&P 500	STRATEGY 6 Annual Return	Gain over S&P 500
2022	-19.48%	27.33%	46.81%	33.42%	52.91%
2023	24.29%	107.55%	83.26%	64.99%	40.71%
YTD 2024	14.73%	16.42%	+1.69%	25.93%	+11.20%
Year	S&P 500 Annual Return	STRATEGY 7 Annual Return	Gain over S&P 500	STRATEGY 8 Annual Return	Gain over S&P 500
2022	-19.48%	2.37%	21.85%	22.99%	42.47%
2023	24.29%	131.29%	107.00%	113.02%	88.73%
YTD 2024	14.73%	30.82%	+16.09%	18.39%	+3.65%

performance over the entire two and half years since live trading has started has been well above the S&P 500®.

2. SMIGRM significantly improves Return Over Max Drawdown ratio (RoMaD): Therefore, as expected given higher returns and lower drawdowns experienced by live trading, the ratio between them (expressed by RoMaD – Return over Maximum Drawdown) for all 8 strategies during the recent 2.5 year period exceeded S&P 500®'s RoMaD by a very large margin! In other words, much higher returns for the same risk taken with the same asset. This proves the real value and power of the SMIGRM method.

Remember, we want RoMaD greater than 1 and the higher, the better. See the 2022 to Date RoMaD Ranking below, ordered from the highest to the lowest:

2022 to Date Performance Ranking 1-Jul-2024

Asset/Strategy	Cum. Return	CAGR	Max DD	RoMaD
ST-3L-Volatility	**210.17%**	56.26%	**-14.88%**	**14.1x**
ST-3L-SP500	**177.22%**	49.49%	**-15.75%**	**11.3x**
ST-2L-Volatility	**207.66%**	55.76%	**-21.16%**	**9.8x**
ST-3L-Nasdaq	**209.75%**	56.17%	**-22.78%**	**9.2x**
ST-2L-SP500x2	**121.19%**	36.76%	**-18.58%**	**6.5x**
ST-2L-SP500	**55.81%**	19.11%	**-8.72%**	**6.4x**
ST-2L-Nasdaqx2	**183.33%**	50.78%	**-31.70%**	**5.8x**
ST-2L-Nasdaq	**77.84%**	25.48%	**-14.52%**	**5.4x**
SVXY	103.25%	32.27%	-28.46%	3.6x
QQQ	21.13%	7.85%	-35.59%	0.6x
SPY (S&P 500)	**14.82%**	**5.60%**	**-25.51%**	**0.6x**
SSO	13.36%	5.07%	-47.32%	0.3x
QLD	13.49%	5.12%	-64.50%	0.2x

As you can see from the above results, the S&P 500® had a maximum drawdown of -25.51% experienced during the lowest point of the 2022 bear market. You can also see that except for the twice-leveraged Nasdaq 100 strategy, all other 7 strategies guided by the

RISP 500™ had experienced lower drawdowns than the S&P 500®. Remember that most of these strategies, including the twice-leveraged Nasdaq 100 strategy, achieved much greater returns than the S&P 500®. As a result, no wonder all their RoMaDs turned up so much better than that of the S&P 500®.

3. SMIGRM means more money in your pocket: SMIGRM guided by the RISP 500™ turned every $1,000 invested in each strategy on January 1st, 2022 into the following amounts by July 1st, 2024:

How Much Has $1,000 On 01/Jan/2022 Turned Into:	
Asset/Strategy	**Amount on 01/Jul/2024**
ST-3L-Volatility	$3,101.70
ST-3L-Nasdaq	$3,097.52
ST-2L-Volatility	$3,076.62
ST-2L-Nasdaqx2	$2,833.30
ST-3L-SP500	$2,772.24
ST-2L-SP500x2	$2,211.92
SVXY (VIX Futures)	$2,032.49
ST-2L-Nasdaq	$1,778.39
ST-2L-SP500	$1,558.15
QQQ (Nasdaq 100)	$1,211.31
SPY (S&P 500)	$1,148.18
QLD (Nasdaq 100 x2)	$1,134.91
SSO (S&P 500 x2)	$1,133.57

Given stronger RoMaDs, stronger everything, all 8 strategies under the guidance of the RISP 500™ returned us more money than the S&P 500® and the other ETFs investing without the guidance of the RISP 500™.

Remember that the S&P 500® lost almost 20% in 2022 and it took the entire year of 2023 to recover completely! See when the blue line crossed $1,000 in the chart below. Also see in the chart how Strategy I avoided that dip so it could spend the same year of 2023 building up gains.

4. How the RISP 500™ helped boost the results of the strategies? Let's visualize this on the Strategy I vs. S&P 500® chart below. The same logic applies for all other strategies. Let's first discuss the chart below:

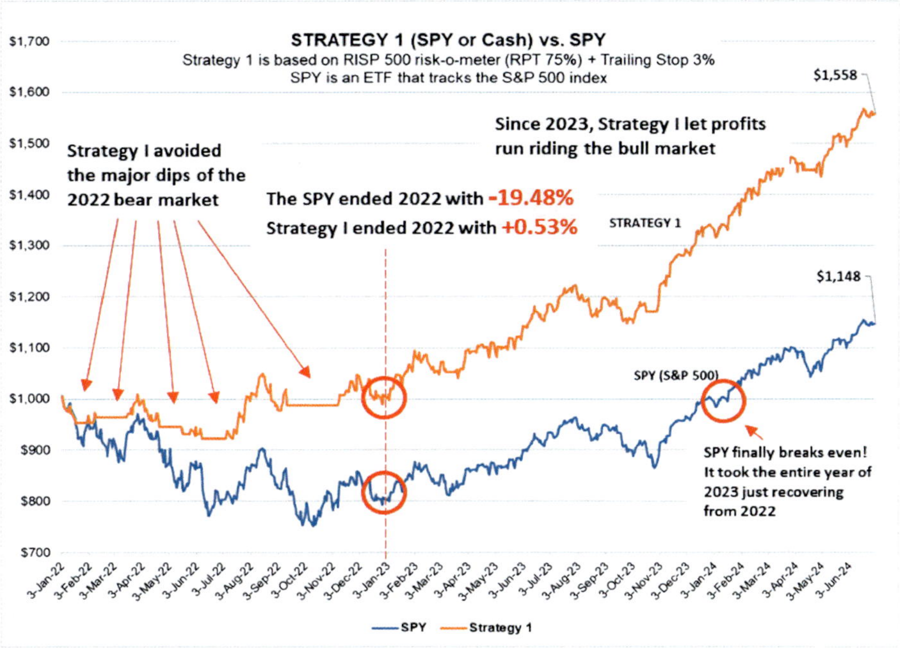

First note that both lines depart from $1,000 on January 1st, 2022. Then right at the start, the S&P 500® (blue line) encountered headwinds and started a descent, slowly and gradually at first but rapidly later on. Strategy I (orange line) also went down a little with it when the descent was still small and slow, but before the most significant dips, it plateaus. Note that the several plateaus, indicated with the arrows, correspond exactly to the most significant dips of the S&P 500® (blue line). This is exactly SMIGRM in real action!

By avoiding the worst of the 2022 bear market, all 8 strategies ended the year outperforming the S&P 500®, most of which by as much as two and three-digit percentage point returns!

In 2023, you don't see many plateaus and none that lasted too long. This is because the RISP 500™ hasn't detected as much danger as the previous year and the market went up and up well into 2024. This is the logic of the RISP 500™: take you out of the market when risk is high (and probability of losses is high) and let you hold your position to explore the upside of the market when the risk measured is low (and probability of gains is high). It's a simple logic that works if you have a tool like the RISP 500™ guiding the way, as you can see.

And you see that the same has reflected on the Drawdowns chart below. Note how Strategy I's drawdowns (orange line) have plateaus (as indicated by the arrows) exactly when the RISP 500™ indicated risks above our RPT, enabling us to avoid the worst drawdowns of the S&P 500® (blue line) during the year of 2022. The RISP 500™ helped us avert the largest dips, keeping drawdowns low relatively to the S&P 500®. Long-term passive index investors will experience the blue line drawdowns. If that sounds like you, this may be your lucky day. You are learning a powerful lesson that can change your life.

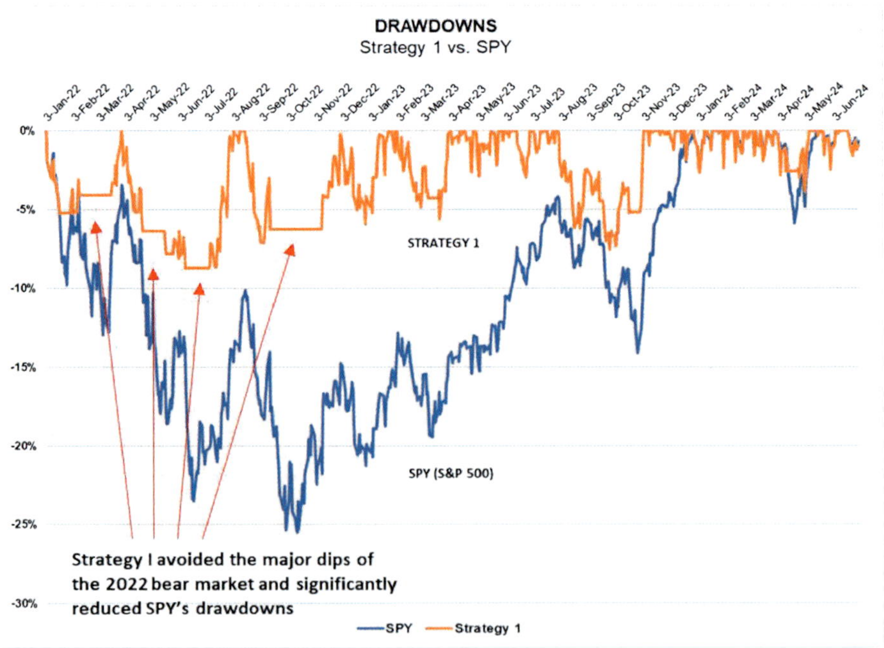

Looking through a magnifying glass

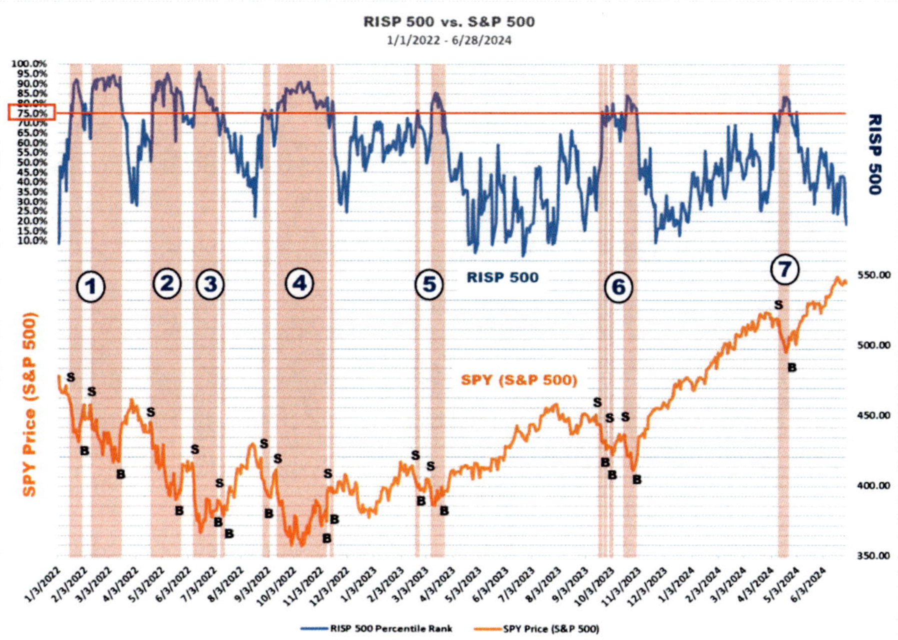

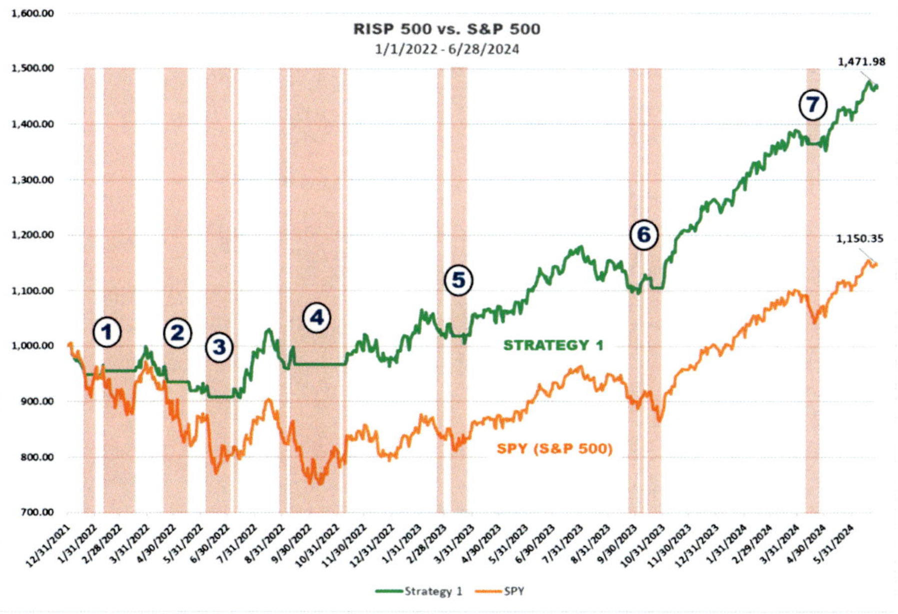

Let's analyze what happened with the 7 major market turning points for safety since live trading started on 01/01/2022. This covers the worst part of the 2022 bear market and is the best sample to let you visualize and understand how the RISP 500™ has guided our live trading out of trouble. See tables below with the details of the live trading showing the daily measurements of the RISP 500™, every buy and sell trade of the SPY ETF, the trailing stop levels, and the cycle number. Remember that for **Strategy 1**, we rotate only between SPY and Cash. Dates given are approximate.

① - First Quarter of the 2022 Bear Market: After a great year of 2021 for the S&P 500 with +26.89% return, emerging from the 2020 Coronavirus Crash, it started the year on a negative tone. Since day 1, the market went downhill and has not recovered that peak until January 19, 2024! Imagine a Buy & Hold passive index investor throwing 746 days in the trash bin.

From January 12th to March 18th, the market made 3 major waves of descent (red) with 2 bear market rallies (green) in between. The average of the RISP 500™ percentile rank during the period was 76.7% with maximum at 94.2%, indicating the seriousness of the trouble.

② - Second Quarter of the 2022 Bear Market (First Half): From March 18th to May 27th, the new rally lasted only two weeks and the market took on the descent again. The average of the RISP 500™ percentile rank during the period was 70.5% with maximum at 95.4%, suggesting that the bear market might be losing some steam, but only slightly.

③ - Second Quarter of the 2022 Bear Market (Second Half): From May 27th to July 13th, the market was mostly on the way down, with just brief moments of retracement. The average of the RISP 500™ percentile rank during the period was 78.5% with maximum at 96.0%, suggesting that the bear market was gaining strength again and that the end of the bear market might not be too far away.

Between ③ and ④ - Third Quarter of the 2022 Bear Market: From July 13th to about September 1st, the bear market rally was pretty awesome during this interregnum. The average of the RISP 500™ percentile rank during the period was 54.4% with maximum at 76.6%, suggesting that the retracement wasn't too strong. In other words, the bear market wasn't over just yet.

④ - Fourth Quarter of the 2022 Bear Market: The market confirmed the rally was short-lived. Again! But the end shouldn't be too far away though. The period from September 1st to November 17th turned out to be the last leg of the 2022 bear market. The bottom was finally reached on October 12th. But we weren't out of the woods yet. The RISP 500™ only left the danger zone for our chosen RPT level of 75% definitively after November 17th. During this period, the average of the RISP 500™ percentile rank during the period was 70.5% with maximum at 90.7%.

Between ④ and ⑤ - First Quarter of the 2023 Recovery: The first recovery rally started from November 17th and lasted 111 days, ending on March 8th, 2023. During this period, the average of the RISP 500™ percentile rank during the period was 58.2% with maximum at 76.5%. It wasn't a firm indication that the bear market was definitely over. If you look at the chart of the S&P 500, you will see that the market was mostly moving rangebound and the stats of the RISP 500™ percentile rank already reflected the weakness of the first wave of recovery.

⑤ - The Month of March of the 2023 Recovery: Understandably, the rally lost strength and the short period between March 9th and March 23rd saw the market go down again. It didn't last long (just a couple of weeks) and it was really the final attempt by bears to pull the market down.

Between ⑤ and ⑥ - Second and Third Quarters of the 2023 Recovery: The second recovery rally started on March 24th and unlike the first, it grew with strength and lasted 180 days, ending on September 20th. It really took us out of the bear market but still far from a total recovery, which would only occur much later in early 2024. During this period, the average of the RISP 500™ percentile rank during the period was 33.6% with maximum at 67.9%, attesting the strength of the recovery ascent of the market.

⑥ - The Month of October of the 2023 Recovery: A hiccup on the recovery path took place between September 21st and October 30th. It pushed the market down for 5 weeks. During this period, the average of the RISP 500™ percentile rank during the period was 74.0% with maximum at 60.9%. From these numbers, you can see it wasn't too bad and not enough to derail the recovery process of the S&P 500.

Between ⑥ and ⑦ - Fourth Quarter of 2023 and First Quarter of 2024 of the Recovery: The third leg of the recovery starting from October 31st lasted 163 days, ending on April 11th, 2024. This time, the strength of the recovery was good and produced an awesome climb in stock prices. During this period, the average of the RISP 500™ percentile rank during the period was 40.7% with maximum at 74.6%. Thanks to the final leg of this recovery rally, the S&P 500 finally recovered its last peak on December 31st, 2019. On January 19th, 2024, those who held the index through the entire bear market could finally breathe a sigh of relief.

⑦ - The Month of April 2024: On April 12th, another hiccup of just 10 days shook the market again. It wasn't really able to do much damage to the bull market that was already evident by then.

Post ⑦ - 2024 and Beyond: The market kept moving higher on an ascending trajectory. Here we ended the detailed analysis.

5. How about trade frequency? We totally understand that the vast majority of investors aren't traders and don't want to be making trades too frequently. Even for professional traders, it would always be best not to place too many trades. Cost of execution and commissions can quickly add up. So, how about 1 to 3 trades a month, on average? This would be more than reasonable, right? In reality, it would really depend on the market. Days with volatile market would require more trades than days with a calm market, but since the former are much more numerous than the latter, trade frequency will be quite low under the SMIGRM framework. For you to have a better idea about this, we show the number of trades for each of the 8 strategies in the table below. We show the RPTs used for each strategy. Note that from 2008 to 2021, the results came from back-testing and from 2022 to 2024, the results came from live trading. At the bottom of the table, we calculated the average of all full years of data (i.e., excluded the years 2008 and 2024 for all strategies, except Strategies 5 and 8, which we excluded the years 2008-2011 and 2024).

TRADING FREQUENCY: NUMBER OF TRADES PER YEAR

Year		Strategy 1 SPY / Cash	Strategy 2 QQQ / Cash	Strategy 3 SSO / Cash	Strategy 4 QLD / Cash	Strategy 5 SVXY / Cash	Strategy 6 SSO / SPY / GLD	Strategy 7 QLD / QQQ / GLD	Strategy 8 VIXM / SPY / SVXY
	RPT >	75%	75%	75%	75%	75%	70%/90%	70%/90%	70%/96%
2008*	BT	15	15	15	15		49	49	
2009	BT	9	9	9	9		39	39	
2010	BT	10	10	10	10		16	16	
2011	BT	10	10	10	10	2	50	50	4
2012	BT	3	3	3	3	3	21	21	7
2013	BT	13	13	13	13	13	31	31	25
2014	BT	15	15	15	15	15	40	40	38
2015	BT	15	15	15	15	15	55	55	40
2016	BT	9	9	9	9	9	39	39	22
2017	BT	5	5	5	5	5	11	11	10
2018	BT	14	14	14	14	14	52	52	44
2019	BT	15	15	15	15	15	37	37	34
2020	BT	13	13	13	13	13	42	42	33
2021	BT	12	12	12	12	12	30	30	24
2022	LT	18	17	15	16	14	53	53	29
2023	LT	9	8	8	8	8	22	22	16
2024*	LT	2	2	2	2	2	6	6	4
Average Per Year (2009-2023)		11	11	11	11	11	36	36	27

* From 29 Apr 2008 to 01 Jul 2024

Note from the table above that the average number of trades for Strategies 1 through 5 (2-risk level strategies with Cash as the safe asset) was 11 trades per year, or **less than 1 trade per month**. The average number of trades for Strategies 6 and 7 (3-risk level strategies) was 36 trades per year, or **3 trades per month**. The average number of trades for Strategy 8 (3-risk level strategy) was 27 trades per year, or **less than 3 trades per month**. Note that it varies from year to year. That is because the market behaved differently every year. As mentioned earlier, trade frequency will depend on the year's volatility. It will also depend on the chosen RPT. The higher the RPT, less trades will be necessary.

6. Have we found a crystal ball? Is that how the story ends, meaning we have found the holy grail of investing, so we can now sit back and relax, let our investments run on autopilot for the rest of our lives and watch profits pile up? Well, no. We did create a very powerful tool, at least in our humble opinion. But we know that the market is constantly changing. The economy at large is changing. New geopolitical and geo-economic forces are redefining the status quo. We are currently living through a major technological revolution with A.I. and other new technologies. Climate change and potential pandemics (antibiotics-resistant bacteria, etc.) are threatening to further change life on Earth itself. Social unrest is growing with income and wealth inequality. All these things will reflect on the stock market. That is why we must be constantly evolving with the market. There are no guarantees that what has worked for us up to now will still work tomorrow or 5 years from now. That is why we are constantly testing and back-testing our strategies and new strategies all the time. We are also studying new incoming data for what might be changing and affecting our strategies' performance. You want to be smart and be able to evolve rapidly to always be a step ahead of the market.

Now, compare all this work with those static balanced portfolios of stocks and bonds or those all-weather portfolios with fixed allocations that do not respond to a changing environment. A pie chart showing allocation to multiple asset classes on a piece of marketing material may look beautiful on paper but after all you have learned from this book, do you still believe they would be any effective going forward? We bet you will not want to get back to those types of investing or just doing "buy & hold" for the long-run with no regard to the market ever again.

If you appreciate our work and our performance results, you don't need to face this brave new world alone. Join us. Follow us on social media, learn new things every day, and become a better and better investor every day together with us.

CHAPTER 7

7. Leverage the Power of the RISP 500™ for Yourself

How to Use the RISP 500™ for Your Own Strategies

(Or Get Inspired by Our Ideas)

How can the RISP 500™ take your existing strategies to the next level? Many of you already have your own investing methods, trading strategies, and portfolios you are managing. Would the RISP 500™ help you outperform your current self? We believe it certainly will. Here are some ways the RISP 500™ can help you enhance your own strategies:

- **Early warning system to protect your portfolios from harm** – at the very least, you can simply use the daily RISP 500™ as an early warning signal to alert you of higher risks detected in the stock market so that you can take protective actions early and preemptively in your investment portfolios. Call it a "Crash Detector" if you like, but this is an active risk management system protecting your wealth. Averting dangerous drawdowns is defense creating the best conditions for offense to shine: you boost your returns as a result, and that's awesome. If you are a professional wealth manager, you will look like a superhero to your clients, doing what is best for them, protecting their money from harm and outperforming your peers and competitors.

What about the Value at Risk? Would it be equivalent? Absolutely not! VAR was not created to guide investments or explore risk environments. The VAR will alert investors that their potential loss amount reached (or is approaching) a limit they had previously set. What essentially causes VAR to change are basically two things: size of the position in risky assets and their volatilities. Assuming the amount of the investment hasn't changed, what can trigger a VAR limit breach is the market volatility that might have increased. Most people use historical, realized volatility, usually one calculated over the last 5 or 10 trading days (on the short end) or monthly, annual, or longer. As a result, this would only trigger a protective action with some delay, after an initial loss has already been realized, which may be sizeable. In contrast, the RISP 500™ barely uses historical or actual volatility in its model. It does rely on real-time VIX information, extracted from implied volatilities priced in options from live trading, which will signal trouble much faster than actual, realized, or historical volatility. For this reason, you can't use VAR to explore different risk/volatility conditions like we do with the RISP 500™. Not even the VIX!

- **Maximization of win-loss odds for Day Traders** – By knowing the actual level of risks in the market, day traders will be more able to confidently execute their strategies during the day. If the RISP 500™ is indicating a low-risk environment for the stock market, day traders will know that odds favor buying early in the day to sell later in the day, and vice-versa. If day traders want an even more accurate measure of risk, they may want to subscribe for the All Day Long Real-Time RISP 500™.

We have not yet simulated or tested day trading by the time of this writing but we do have plans to do so in the future.

- **Timing tool for both short-term trading and long-term investing** - The RISP 500™ can help you determine the best time to execute your market entry and exit, regardless of your investment horizon. You can use it in conjunction with your technical analysis tools. Timing the markets is always a complicated area for most investors and we get that. Timing has also been treated more like an art than science, including technical analysis, or just regarded as pure luck. Not anymore! With the RISP 500™, we are adding a little bit of science to market timing.

- **Perfect and easy for DIYers ("Do It Yourself-ers")** – If you like to manage your own investments getting data from multiple sources (e.g. VIX Futures, VRP, etc.) to make decisions, you can benefit from the test-proven RISP 500™ as we do the heavy-lifting for you for a small fee. You will get the daily guidance you need to navigate the stock market.

The above-listed are benefits that the RISP 500™ can add to your existing investment strategies, methods, and portfolio management services. If you want to add new strategies to explore untapped profit opportunities that open up a new world of possibilities for you because of RISP 500™, you may want to consider some of our ideas as well.

RISP 500™: Get Inspired by Our Ideas to Create Your Own Strategies

If you want to create your own strategies or just have fresh ideas to add to your existing strategies to fully explore the power of the RISP 500™ to take your investment to the next level, all you have to do is take these three steps:

3 STEPS
TO OUTPERFORMANCE

❶ **DEFINE STRATEGY**
- Choose the number of **risk levels**
- Select **best assets for each risk level**
- Choose **RPT(s)**

❷ **MEASURE RISK DAILY**
- Read the RISP 500™ Percentile

❸ **TAKE ACTION**
- Follow the strategy investing in the assets (risky/safe) defined above and the RISP 500™ to explore each risk level

And that's all there is! As soon as you start, you will realize how easy it is and all you need is just a couple of minutes a day for it on your way to outperformance.

You can start implementing SMIGRM right away with all you have read up to this point. You already know the concepts of RISP 500™ Percentile Rank and RPT.

If you want a quick refresher of these concepts and tips to feel more confident before you start, we prepared a quick summary for you below.

3 STEPS TO OUTPERFORMANCE

(STEP 1 of 3) DEFINE STRATEGY: In the first step, you must define the parameters for your desired strategy. It can be separated into 4 smaller steps:

1-a) Choose the Number of Risk Levels

It's up to you how many risk levels you want in your SMIGRM system. The minimum and the simplest is two levels (risky/safe). You can choose three risk levels (low risk/medium risk/high risk, for example) or four risk levels (very low risk/low risk/high risk/extremely high risk, for example). See diagrams for two and four risk levels below, for example:

THE RISP 500™ ASSET-RISK STRATEGY MATRIX

Level of Risk (2)	Directional Asset	Leverage	Volatility
HIGH	CASH	NO	VXIM (LONG VOL)
LOW	SPY (S&P 500)	SSO (S&P x2)	SVXY (SHORT VOL)

RISP 500™ ▶ (points to the arrow between HIGH and LOW)

Conservative Investor (brackets the Directional Asset column)

Moderate Investor (brackets Directional Asset through Leverage)

Aggressive Investor (brackets Directional Asset through Volatility)

* NOTE: This asset selection is only an **example**. Asset selection must be customized for each investor according to risk-return profile, risk tolerance, and goals.

THE RISP 500™ ASSET-RISK STRATEGY MATRIX

Level of Risk (4)	Directional Asset	Leverage	Volatility
EXTREMELY HIGH	CASH	NO	VXIM (LONG VOL)
MODERATELY HIGH	IEF, IYR (BONDS, RE)	NO	NO
MODERATELY LOW	SPY (S&P 500)	SSO (S&P x2)	NO
EXTREMELY LOW	QQQ (NASDAQ 100)	QLD (NASDAQ x2)	SVXY (SHORT VOL)

RISP 500™ ▶ (points to the arrow at MODERATELY HIGH)

Conservative Investor (brackets the Directional Asset column)

Moderate Investor (brackets Directional Asset through Leverage)

Aggressive Investor (brackets Directional Asset through Volatility)

NOTE: This asset selection is only an **example**. Asset selection must be customized for each investor according to risk-return profile, risk tolerance, and goals.

Note that a higher number of risk levels doesn't necessarily mean better results. It really depends on the quality of your execution. Adding more granularity to the system will add more complexity with a better required quality of execution but may potentially offer investors greater returns. In the next mini-step, assets for each risk level must be selected carefully to match the risk levels and keeping in mind the investors' risk-return profiles.

1-b) Select the Best Assets for Each Risk Level

Take a second look at our 8 strategies for inspiration: they were designed in a way that helps investors achieve a wide spectrum of risk-return profiles. Investors can substitute our chosen assets for their own preferred assets. As we said, they could choose individual stocks, but they don't need to (see below). Can investors choose the Dow Jones

Industrial index or the Russell 1000 or 3000 indexes instead? The answer is yes, absolutely!

Like stocks, ETFs are available for trading from the comfort of your home on the brokerage firm's internet platforms. All you need is a phone/computer with an internet connection and a brokerage account. An ETF trades like a stock and in most American brokerage firms, you may even trade them for zero commission.

Note: You also do **not** need to use the exact same particular ETFs we used for our tests. For example, we used SPY to track the S&P 500® index. But you can use any other ETF available in the market that serves the same purpose. There are many of them available in the market at the time of this writing, such as SPY, VOO, IVV, and SPLG. Any one of them works just fine. We chose the SPY because we traded it for as long as we can remember and it's the most liquid, easy to execute trades. We also like SPLG for its low reference price, making it easier to invest small amounts. But, again, they all work just the same. We do not endorse any specific ETF in particular.

What about Leveraged and Volatility ETFs?

We do and the reason is simple. We invest in a risky asset like the SSO and the QLD only on days we know the risk is low (as measured by the RISP 500™), which is when the probability for the S&P 500® to close those days in red is low. The SSO is a leveraged ETF that tracks 2x the daily returns of the S&P 500®. The QLD is a leveraged ETF that tracks 2x the daily returns of the Nasdaq 100. Both ETFs are much riskier than the unleveraged original indices they track. On days the S&P 500® returns +1%, the SSO will return +2%; but on days the S&P 500® returns -1%, the SSO will return -2%. It's a double-edged sword and cuts both ways. Without a reliable risk-measuring tool like the RISP 500™, it would be just too perilous to take on such risky assets blindly, in our opinion.

Normally, we wouldn't ever invest in leveraged ETFs because of the high risk; however, with a tool like the RISP 500™ to measure the risk and guide us, we are now empowered to confidently take that risk!

Volatility ETFs, recommended only to advanced investors who understand options and volatility, are more advanced, but equally benefit from the knowledge of the risk measured by the RISP 500™. High risk and high volatility in the stock market benefit those holding ETFs that track long positions in volatility such as the VXIM. This ETF tracks the middle section of the VIX Futures curve. On the other hand, low risk and low volatility in the stock market benefit those holding ETFs that track short positions in volatility such as the SVXY. This ETF tracks the inverse of the two front contracts of the VIX Futures. If this paragraph sounds Greek to you, you should NOT invest in these ETFs. You can still achieve decent returns without ever entering the world of derivatives. Or you can learn from us! At the end of the book, you will find information about our courses and mentorship programs.

To use high risk or high complexity instruments with the RISP 500™, it's also strongly recommended to perform back-testing studies before trading them live. If you want us to perform the studies for you for the assets you selected, feel free to contact us by email. We offer this service.

How about Individual Stocks?

We don't believe we need individual stocks because index ETFs alone can produce an ample spectrum of risk-return profiles ranging all the way from conservative to aggressive. Besides, investing in individual stocks isn't really practical for everyday investors from all walks of life. To succeed in consistently picking winning stocks requires not only a lot of specific industry expertise and knowledge of corporate finance, it also requires a tremendous amount of time to perform the fundamental analyses. Honestly, it's not really feasible for most people. Index funds also have the advantage of being well-diversified, though the S&P 500® and Nasdaq are heavily concentrated in large cap stocks and tech stocks. But there is a reason: innovation and capital are driving the American economy! But what if you are a stock investor who picks stocks for your portfolio – can you use the RISP 500™? Yes, absolutely! SMIGRM is a method and RISP 500™ is a tool. As we said, you don't need to select an index like we did to harness of the power of SMIGRM and the RISP 500™ to protect your portfolio of individual stocks expertly picked by you.

With a tool like the RISP 500™ designed to let you know how risky the market is at any moment in time, you may want to exploit the risk-reward feature of each risk level to maximize the reward it can afford you, if your bet is correct. The idea is rather simple:

Level of Risk		Win-Loss Odds		Assets that should perform best
LOW	→	Favorable to Investor	→	Riskiest Assets (directional), Short Volatility Assets
HIGH	→	Unfavorable to Investor	→	Safest Assets (directional), Long Volatility Assets

But whatever assets you decide to select, bear in mind that they **must**:

i) **Match the corresponding risk level** - Remember that riskier assets perform better when risks are low and vice-versa. If not sure, ask us to run back-test studies for you on your selected assets.

ii) **Be compatible with your own risk tolerance level** – Don't choose a risky asset only for its potential return; consider its risk. Look at past maximum drawdowns to make sure you have stomach for losses if it happens again with your money on the line.

1-c) Choose RPT(s)

Next, you will need to define the RPT(s) for your strategy. The number of RPTs will depend on the number of risk levels chosen. If you chose two risk levels, you only need one RPT to distinguish what level of risk is considered High and what is considered Low. But if you have chosen four risk levels for your strategy, you would need to define three RPTs.

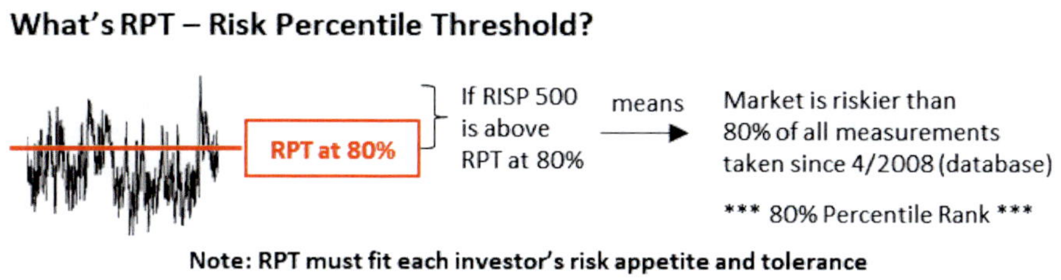

Remember the concept of percentile? A quick refresher: if you took an exam and scored better than 80% of the class, your score is at the 80th percentile. It means that in the universe of scores in your class, your score is higher than 80% of all scores.

Similarly, if the RISP 500™ measured the risk today in the 85th Percentile, it means that today's risk is higher than 85% of all previous measurements in the database (data since April 29, 2008).

Conservative investors should consider lower RPTs. For example, let's say this investor — we'll call her Rebecca — chose an RPT at 70%. This means that Rebecca is willing to hold risky assets only when the risk measured is within the 70% lowest risks measured in the past (data goes back to April 29, 2008). In other words, Rebecca wants to avoid the 30% highest risks in history*. A lower RPT will trigger more often to take Rebecca to safety, averting risks she is unwilling to take. On the other hand, aggressive investors, who seek risks and tolerate them well, may use a higher RPT. For example, this other investor — we'll call him Nathan — chose an RPT at 90%. Nathan is willing only to avoid risks greater than the top 10% of all the risks ever measured in history* (* data goes back to April 29, 2008).

Keep in mind that:

(i) Two-risk level systems require one RPT.
(ii) Three-risk level systems require two RPTs.
(iii) Four-risk level systems require three RPTs.
(iv) And so on and so forth.

Investors should always select RPT that is appropriate to their own personal risk tolerance level and appetite for return. Although Back-Testing may suggest higher RPTs had resulted in greater returns during the 14-year test period, remember that the future may not repeat the past exactly. Will the stock market grow with the same intensity for the next 50 years as it did for the last 50? Maybe yes, maybe no. You should select a RPT level that reflects who you are as an investor.

Variable RPT? It's possible. RPT levels can be changed from time to time. There is no requirement to keep them fixed. In principle, you can make it dependent on other variables, such as the type of market you believe we are in (e.g., bullish, bearish, volatile, hard to decipher, etc.). You can also change RPT based on your results and experience. If after a while, you analyze your own performance with SMIGRM and believe you can improve by changing RPT, you certainly can. You may also want to test different RPT levels before making a decision as well. Again, RISP 500™ is a tool, so you can use it as you find it most useful for you. We suggest not to change RPT too often as to lose control, though. If you are a methodical investor and know what you are doing, the RISP 500™ is your tool to use as you please.

One final word of caution if you are setting up an aggressive strategy: make sure to start small testing out the waters first. If you need help or want us to perform back-testing for your chosen assets and RPTs, send us an email.

Create Your Asset-Risk Strategy Matrix

	Level of Risk (3)	Based on S&P 500	Based on Nasdaq 100	Based on Volatility
	EXTREME	GLD	GLD	**VIXM**
RISP 500™ at 95% percentile				
	ELEVATED	**SPY**	**QQQ**	SPY
RISP 500™ at 70% percentile				
	LOW	SSO	QLD	**SVXY**
		STRATEGY	STRATEGY	STRATEGY

Now that you completed STEP 1 (congratulations!), you can summarize your chosen number of risk levels, your chosen assets, and your chosen RPT(s) in your very own Asset-Risk Strategy Matrix!

(STEP 2 of 3) MEASURE RISK DAILY: Now you can get started with your investing! Subscribe to receive the daily RISP 500™ newsletter and use it to implement your SMIGRM strategies as laid out by your Asset Risk Strategy Matrix.

If you are an individual, non-professional investor, you may want to subscribe to the RISP 500™ published once a day or 3x a day. For busy people looking for solid investing without spending more than a couple of minutes a day just to open the daily email, read the RISP 500™ information, and execute a trade (if necessary, generally less than 2x a week, often not even that), it's sufficient. For professional investors, who need an edge over their competitor funds or advisors, these folks may want to subscribe for the All Day Long Real Time RISP 500™. Professional investors are watching the markets all day, every day and can use the continuous RISP 500™ information to extract maximum value from their investing.

(STEP 3 of 3) TAKE ACTION: Take action as necessary with RISP 500™ as your guide. Follow your strategies defined in the Asset Risk Strategy Matrix. Unless you are subscribing to All Day Long Real Time RISP 500™, we suggest setting up a stop loss order to your positions with your brokerage platform to protect against potential intraday's sudden moves. This is because after the RISP 500™ measured the risk, the market is still open and adverse movements may still occur until the next measurement is made the next day.

What is the best time to execute trades? This is a long discussion. We publish the RISP 500™ early in the day but unless you subscribe to the premium All Day Long Real-Time RISP 500™, we believe you should execute your trade as soon as you read the RISP 500™ measurement.

TIP: Don't know where to start? Over time, by reading the RISP 500™ every day and seeing the market, you will have a better sense of which RPT to choose. But for first-timers, we understand it may be hard to decide. Although every investor has a different risk-return profile, we may suggest starting with a RPT like in the low 70s if you are more on the conservative side of the spectrum and 85-95% if you are on the aggressive side. Moderates can choose anywhere in between 70% and 85%. It is just a suggestion where to start. Make adjustments as you get more experienced with the tool.

IN CONCLUSION

So, You Don't Know Where the Market Is Heading Next?

When I first learned how life insurance companies worked, I had a moment of clarity and inspiration. I was intrigued how life insurers could take on so much risk because payouts of death benefits were so much greater than the premiums collected. I wondered how life insurers ultimately priced mortality risk. They do it using actuarial science, which I will comment below, but the important lesson for me was the following. Life insurers don't know how long you and I, or any particular person, will live. They have no clue on an individual basis but they do know on a collective basis. They know the average life expectancy of all 20-year-olds, all 30-year-olds, males, females, etc. living today and the dispersion around the averages. This is where all this is so interesting, in my view. To mitigate the risk, life insurers need only to sell life insurance to a sufficiently large number of people, in all age groups, genders, races, etc. – the more diverse the better - so that they will make money in the long run. They are statistically protected from running out of money to pay death benefits and still make a profit.

Life insurance is based on Actuarial Science. According to Wikipedia, here is the definition:

---

*"**Actuarial science** is the discipline that applies **mathematical and statistical methods to assess risk** in insurance, pension, finance, investment and other industries and professions. More generally, actuaries **apply rigorous mathematics to model matters of uncertainty** and life expectancy." (Wikipedia)*

Isn't this exactly what SMIGRM is all about?

Now think about the very purpose of the RISP 500™ project. Is it a crystal ball that can predict where the stock market is heading next? No, that was never the purpose. Will the RISP 500™ assure you to make money every single day always getting the direction of the market right? Again, no. But the purpose is, just like life insurers operating in a world of uncertainty, that the RISP 500™ was designed to give you a positive edge that will accumulate a series of small and large victories (e.g., averting major crashes), which statistically over the long run, should deliver solid and tangible results for you or your clients.

So, no problem if you don't know where the stock market is heading next. We don't know either and we don't care because we measure risks and apply the concepts of SMIGM, including the trio Statistical Edge + Asymmetrical Payoff + Law of Large Numbers, all conveniently baked into the RISP 500™ tool. Investors trying to predict where the market is moving next with methods that are deterministic and trying to be crystal balls (forecasting, price targets, etc.) might be just chasing impossible dreams.

Crystal ball? Meh, we really don't need it to be successful. All we need is an edge that is statistically favorable to get magnified over time.

SPECIAL

Sharing Lessons from My Own Journey

As you know, I learned the most during successive market crashes. I can confidently say that every time they occurred, they gave me the opportunity to really make quantum leaps in terms of knowledge and experience. So much is exposed that the amount of learning can be staggering following a significant market crash. Let me share quickly just a few lessons learned from a long list that are not too complex to explain here, just so you can have a general idea. Often, we don't necessarily find answers to our questions, but we start asking new questions. Actually, more specific questions on deeper issues. That is a sign of learning progress, I hope!

Lesson #1: Shortcomings of traditional tools: VAR - One such issue I faced early in my career, when the 1999 Brazilian currency maxi-devaluation hit had to do with the crisis data. Before the crisis, the data didn't include anything near what we were about to experience. Sure, we had the Mexican, Russian, and the Asian crises reflected in our data, but they could not have predicted a much larger crisis hitting my own market right to its core. But after the crisis, we have got another problem. Things calmed down significantly and markets were back to normal again. However, our data now contains a crisis that was not likely to occur anytime soon. So, what is the big deal? The problem is that at the bank, we used VAR (Value at Risk) to control our risks. And VAR is derived from realized volatility in the historical database. A high volatility will increase your VAR, and in turn, impose a smaller trading limit to the traders. During the crisis, this was very helpful, but after the crisis, your data became "contaminated" with very high volatilities that were unlikely to occur any time soon. That was the first time I realized the limitations and the weaknesses of the VAR. So, to keep our traders operating normally, we had to judgmentally ignore the crisis data. But was it the right thing to do? Or the best? After all, the crisis did happen. By manually removing data we were subjectively altering it and this is not good.

In fact, this problem becomes a no problem for SMIGRM. Unlike VAR, RISP 500™ stratifies risks. It won't matter if a risk reading is too high or too low; it will get incorporated in the database and have its own percentile rank. If we had SMIGRM back then, it would have saved us a lot of headaches.

Lesson #2: Shortcomings of traditional tools: Technical Analysis - At first sight, technical analysis seemed pretty logical. It made sense to me. RSI, MACD, oscillators, moving averages, patterns, etc. And easy to use too, so I thought, because there weren't any complicated rules. In practice though, it turned out anything but. I really struggled to use the tool to make decisions taking risk positions in the markets. I soon realized that despite differences in terms of results, none of the indicators seemed to work more than 50-60% of the time, at best. I doubted myself many times, believing that it must be my fault because probably I wasn’t using the tool correctly. I tested different parameters with different cutoff levels. I changed the time interval many times too. I tried combining multiple indicators to make final decisions. Still, I wasn't doing much better. That is when I started to doubt the tool itself. After all, I have never seen any strong proof that would convince me unequivocally that technical analysis worked. I have heard anecdotal evidence and stories from others but I suspected they may have been just biased. An engineer by education, I'm naturally skeptical and require proof for everything. Not only did I never find the proof I wanted but I heard other traders voice similar concerns. But technical analysis was the only tool we had for market timing. I had no choice but to keep using it the best I could. In normal market conditions, it wasn't a big deal. But when hit by a very volatile market, any small problem gets magnified many times over. Small losses can quickly become big losses. My savior this time was... the stop loss! I executed stops mercilessly without ever thinking twice. That saved my desk from losing big. If losing money is never fun, imagine losing someone else's money! But by doing so, I unintentionally learned a very valuable lesson: #3 below.

Lesson #3: Cut losses quickly; don't let it grow and forget about rescuing a defeat -You see, I was always cutting my losses quickly before giving them a chance to snowball. Of course, sometimes I felt like a fool seeing the market go up right after I stopped out. But I learned never to cry over spilled milk because you can't go back in time. But stopping losses early - in the aggregate of 100, 200 trades, or more - was actually saving me from much larger troubles.

Lesson #4: The best solution for the unexpected - Another lesson learned was how to keep my mind sharp and clear of distractions and fear when the storm hits. It's a real challenge and we all have our own limits and fears. After all, we are all humans, and we are emotional beings. Under threat, our limbic system fires up and our rational brain tends to shut down clouding judgment. One of the best ways to deal with stressful situations like these in the middle of a market crash is to have a plan carefully prepared beforehand when our mind is at its sharpest and at ease. After all, the best time to fix the roof is when the sun is shining. If you were prepared, if and when the storm hits, you will know exactly what to do. Of course, you are not a robot and you will keep an open mind in case anything totally unexpected happens to reassess the situation but you can also prepare a plan to deal with the unexpected. Just a side note: realize that SMIGRM naturally resolves this problem too. This is because by measuring risks with the RISP 500™, you will know exactly what to do if risks go up to the extreme. With SMIGRM, you won't need to debate, wonder, doubt yourself, or struggle to decide what to do under such pressure.

Lesson #5: It's impossible to account for everything that moves markets - Lastly, another example of a lesson learned took place during the 2020 Coronavirus Crash. It really felt like the crash came from nowhere. By the time the world celebrated the New Year, there were reports of a newly emerging disease spreading in Asia, but we got used to these reports and it really did not get us too concerned. After all, there were repeated outbreaks of flu in Asia in past decades (e.g., SARS and MERS) and all had been more or less contained in Asia. But when Covid-19 went global, panic hit the markets hard. In February and March 2020, the S&P 500 dropped 35% in just a few weeks. For months, disinformation and political interference muddled the waters. It became clear the economy was going to be a casualty along with hundreds of thousands of people dying around the world. If you read the news at the time, few were anywhere near optimistic about the short-term future. However, the S&P 500 was climbing again. By May or so, I received a text from a friend in London talking about how we were out of good investment options. I replied to her that I was bullish on the U.S. stock market. How come if fundamentals were so bleak and uncertainty was the only certainty at the time, she asked. I couldn't really pinpoint a fundamental reason why but by then I already had a tool we called Outperform, which was the working algorithm that preceded the RISP 500™. For reasons that were unknown to me at the time, Outperform has guided me back to the market, while most were still shocked by the spectacular tumble the market had suffered just a few weeks earlier. Later I found out some of the reasons for the market's behavior. The federal government had injected record amounts of liquidity in the system by an unprecedented large QE (Quantitative Easing aka printing money) and sending "economy stimulus" checks to people and especially businesses affected by the pandemic. Some of this excessive liquidity found its way to the stock market, inflating a bubble there; some went to the housing market, inflating another bubble there, and so on; creating conditions for the emergence of the 2022 Everything Bubble and inflation that followed right after! But I didn't know exactly what was fueling the market at the time because like everyone else, I was looking at the economy's fundamentals and they didn't look good. But I returned to the market guided by (and thanks to) Outperform, the predecessor of RISP 500™, early to catch the rebound of the market while most investors were still on the sidelines.

With a tool like the RISP 500™, I didn't really need to know everything that was going on out there. The lesson here is that there are way too many variables that can affect stock prices. It's virtually impossible to know them all or factor them all in our models. In fundamental analysis, we try to cover the most relevant and direct factors that influence prices. But we don't see so many other indirect factors that are invisible or just neglected, which may lead to wrong conclusions. And there is always the randomness of the entire system, which no one can predict. After all, we live in a probabilistic world.

In summary, the tools we use will in a certain way determine the outcome of what we do, just like a good knife performing a better cut than a bad knife. A tool made for a deterministic world will naturally do poorly in a probabilistic world. After learning valuable lessons, we should rethink our tools and make improvements to them so they can help us achieve what we want more efficiently. That is what tools are for, in the first place. If still not working satisfactorily, try new tools.

Lesson #6: Never invest when you don't know what's really going on - Another lesson I learned was that whenever you are not sure, not feeling confident, just don't do it. Stay away from risk when you are not sure about what is really going on for the market to behave in a particular way. Wait until things get clear again.

In addition, never ever invest any money in anything you don't 100% understand and dominate. Just buying dips blindly without knowing exactly why works only until the market reverses. Don't get greedy just because others are panicking. Yes, I don't agree with this famous Warren Buffett quote, unless you know exactly what you are doing and getting yourself into, aware of the consequences of being wrong.

Lesson #7: Savvy warriors know when to wait to fight another day - There is no shame in waiting out for the storm to pass. Plus, you really don't need to catch every movement in the market to be successful. You can be like surfers patiently searching for the perfect wave to ride. You can also adopt sniper tactics: attack only when you have a clear view on the target, then shoot and quickly disappear. Why? The longer you are holding risk positions in the market, the more exposed you are to adverse market movements (ironically a long-term buy & hold passive investor thinks they were investing conservatively but they were the most exposed to market risks: 100% of the time!). You really don't have to chase every market movement to be successful. Remember, opportunities to make money in the stock market are like buses. If you missed one, there is another one coming, right behind. Also, a savvy warrior can always fight another day.

These lessons and others discussed in the book helped me throughout my career. I started very humbly knowing very little about finance and markets but I have learned a little bit every day. Sometimes I paid a hefty price but what I have learned was invaluable for the rest of my life. In all, my journey has been highly enjoyable and fulfilling. For you, regardless of the current stage of your investor career, beginner or pro, I'm sure you will find your journey quite enjoyable too. There is always so much to learn every day. Keep your mind open to new ideas and keep an eye on what new technologies may mean for your investments. Change always brings risks but also great opportunities. I hope the lessons I have learned can help you and at least inspire you a bit. I wish you the best of luck in your own journey! -- Happy investing! 😊

JUST IN… LAST MINUTE ADDITION!

The August 2024 Market Rout: How did SMIGRM fare?

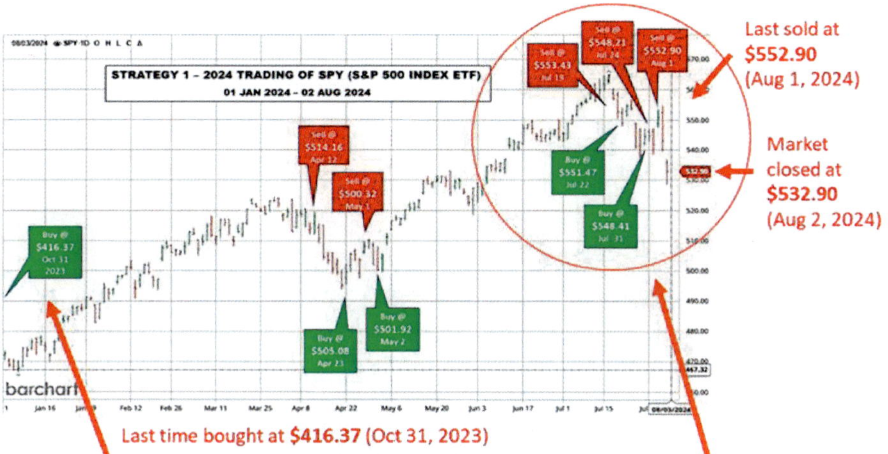

Date	RISP 500 value	Percentile Rank	RISK ON/OFF	Strategy 1 - ST-2L-SP500 (Based on S&P 500) Trade action	Trade price	SPY Close	Stop level	Stopped? YES/NO	Cycle #	Day's Return	YTD Return	LTD Return
11/9/2023	97.1	51.5%	On		-	433.84	424.13	No	27	-0.78%	17.78%	15.18%
11/8/2023	91.9	42.9%	On		-	437.25	423.82	No	27	0.07%	18.71%	16.09%
11/7/2023	93.8	45.8%	On		-	436.93	422.62	No	27	0.28%	18.62%	16.00%
11/6/2023	94.6	47.2%	On		-	435.69	421.65	No	27	0.23%	18.28%	15.68%
11/3/2023	91.3	41.4%	On		-	434.69	417.84	No	27	0.91%	18.01%	15.41%
11/2/2023	96.5	50.1%	On		-	430.76	409.98	No	27	1.92%	16.94%	14.37%
11/1/2023	104.1	62.8%	On		-	422.66	405.65	No	27	1.07%	14.74%	12.22%
10/31/2023	109.1	70.2%	On	Buy	416.37	418.2	403.88	No	27	0.44%	13.53%	11.03%
10/30/2023	114.7	77.4%	OFF		-	415.59	398.36		26	0.00%	13.04%	10.55%
10/27/2023	116.3	79.0%	OFF		-	410.68	400.17		26	0.00%	13.04%	10.55%

Date	RISP 500 value	Percentile Rank	RISK ON/OFF	Strategy 1 - ST-2L-SP500 (Based on S&P 500) Trade action	Trade price	SPY Close	Stop level	Stopped? YES/NO	Cycle #	Day's Return	YTD Return	LTD Return
8/2/2024	127.8	91.4%	OFF		-	532.9	534.29		31	0.00%	18.41%	58.48%
8/1/2024	115.2	77.8%	OFF	Sell	552.90	543.01	534.29		31	0.38%	18.41%	58.48%
7/31/2024	112.2	74.3%	On	Buy	548.41	550.81	531.96	No	31	0.44%	17.97%	57.88%
7/30/2024	113.4	75.7%	OFF		-	542	528.42		30	0.00%	17.45%	57.19%
7/29/2024	114.1	76.7%	OFF		-	544.76	528.11		30	0.00%	17.45%	57.19%
7/26/2024	115.6	78.0%	OFF		-	544.44	522.26		30	0.00%	17.45%	57.19%
7/25/2024	122.8	85.7%	OFF		-	538.41	538.01		30	0.00%	17.45%	57.19%
7/24/2024	114.9	77.5%	OFF	Sell	548.21	541.23	538.01		30	-1.01%	17.45%	57.19%
7/23/2024	103.1	61.6%	On		-	553.78	538.01	No	30	-0.16%	18.65%	58.79%
7/22/2024	109.2	70.2%	On	Buy	551.47	554.65	534.93	No	30	0.58%	18.83%	59.04%
7/19/2024	115.8	78.3%	OFF	Sell	553.43	548.99	547.91		29	0.14%	18.15%	58.13%
7/18/2024	96.7	50.4%	On		-	552.66	547.91	No	29	-0.77%	17.99%	57.91%
7/17/2024	93.3	44.9%	On		-	556.94	547.91	No	29	-1.40%	18.90%	59.13%
7/16/2024	90.7	40.2%	On		-	564.86	544.68	No	29	0.59%	20.59%	61.39%
7/15/2024	90.7	40.4%	On		-	561.53	543.19	No	29	0.28%	19.88%	60.44%
7/12/2024	81.5	23.6%	On		-	559.99	544.48	No	29	0.63%	19.55%	60.00%
7/11/2024	93.1	44.6%	On		-	556.48	544.48	No	29	-0.86%	18.80%	59.00%
7/10/2024	84.7	29.3%	On		-	561.32	539.15	No	29	0.99%	19.84%	60.38%
7/9/2024	85.4	30.7%	On		-	555.82	538.62	No	29	0.10%	18.66%	58.81%
7/8/2024	87.9	35.1%	On		-	555.28	538.00	No	29	0.12%	18.55%	58.65%

The book had already been sent for final formatting and publishing when the July-August 2024 global market rout caused a strong selloff of stocks plunging the S&P 500 and Nasdaq indexes. Since we believe that this event is very relevant to the subject, we decided to include this short final addition in the book. It illustrates how the RISP 500™ guided us to avoid the worse of the plunge keeping our investments safe and outperforming in the long run, which is exactly the very purpose of SMIGRM.

A few days before, the percentile rank of RISP 500™ had already detected higher risks building up in the market. We sought safety as a result. Strategies 1 thru 5 (at 75% RPT) rotated to cash and Strategies 6 thru 8 stated to deleverage. In the early days, the market was still sending somewhat mixed signs, which is normal and were picked up by the algorithm. This triggered us to start trading again to avoid a potential dangerous downturn in formation. Note that I haven't said a word about what caused the rout or discussed the markets. Even if we were totally unaware of what is going on in the world, lost in an isolated island on vacation, but only with access to RISP 500™, we could still be able to pull this off, achieving the same results.

As you can see from the image above, for Strategy 1, we were holding the risk asset SPY since October 31, 2023, when we bought at $416.37. We sold on April 17, 2024 for $514.16 and after a few trades, we bought back at $501.92. We held the SPY again for months, gaining the upside again, just like we did previously. Then the rout started in mid to late July and we ultimately sold for $552.90.

The SPY plunged and closed at $532.90 the next day, Friday, August 2, 2024. The story continues, of course, but now we must conclude the writing of this book for good. 😊 Thank you!

FAQ

I find it hard to believe: How could some strategies of SMIGRM outperform the S&P 500® by so much?

Answer: We understand the skepticism. If we hadn't tested it, audited the data, and performed live trading ourselves, we wouldn't have believed it either. Avoiding costly drawdowns and the absurd time-wasting caused by the gain-loss asymmetry pays off in the long run because avoided losses will have long-lasting effects. Avoided losses are gains when compared with a benchmark, and compounding effects cause the gap to snowball over time.

In addition, leveraged strategies benefit even more from SMIGRM. The compounding effect of gains and avoided losses snowball even faster for leveraged strategies.

How do I know RISP 500™ will work for me? Do you offer guarantees?

Answer: While there is no such thing as guarantees in the investment world, we strive to make the RISP 500™ the best tool to navigate a probabilistic world. The RISP 500™ is already helping many managers successfully navigate turbulent markets and unless your investment philosophy is from out of this world, we trust you will benefit from it too. In fact, Risk Scientific LLC runs the subscription programs and offers a free trial period. You are free to cancel anytime if not entirely satisfied.

If this is so good, why don't you keep it a secret and make all the money for yourselves?

Answer: We believe there is more in life than money. We want to revolutionize risk management and aid investors, especially those who

DIY, and also assist wealth managers in helping their clients. Besides, Risk Scientific LLC is a risk management solutions firm. Remember, this is not a crystal ball or a guaranteed payout. We believe in challenging the status quo of the risk management world.

From the author: After I turned 55, I know laws of biology won't let me reverse the clock inside. So I figured that it was time to give back and share with others what I have learned and benefitted from. I started writing books and will continue to do so. I'm certainly not the know-it-all man -- I still live to learn every single day -- but any contribution I can give others to help improve or even change their lives for the better, even if it's just to avoid making the same mistakes I made, would already be more than fulfilling for me.

Why do you invest in leveraged strategies? Is it possible to outperform the S&P 500® only with Strategies 1 and 2 without any leverage?

Answer: Yes! You really don't need to use any strategy involving leverage to be successful. For example, Strategies 1 and 2, based on a simple SPY or Cash and QQQ or Cash pairs of assets, don't involve any leverage and can help you be successful in the long run. Leverage is a two-edged sword and can really hurt investors. We would have never used any leveraged strategy if we have not had the RISP 500™ guiding us. In fact, RISP 500™ helped us avoid the edge of the sword that can hurt us. In other words, knowing when to get rid of the leveraged ETF (when risks are high) and when to hold it (when risks are low) made all the difference for us, as reflected in our performance results over time. A leveraged strategy with the guidance of RISP 500™ would allow investors to achieve higher returns or a faster return on their money. But non-leveraged strategies like Strategy 1 and 2 or similar strategies are excellent choices for those who don't want any leverage.

I already have and love my methods and my own strategies.

Answer: Great! We believe adding RISP 500™ to your toolbox to work with them will help you be even more successful. SMIGRM may work on its own but it can also work in tandem with any other methods and strategies, helping them perform better! Remember, we will never tell you what to do. You are always the decision maker. RISP 500™ is another tool that provides you valuable information about the risks in the market. We believe risk is an important piece of the puzzle to help you visualize the investment landscape to make decisions.

I am a passive index investor. I'm investing in the simplest way possible with a buy and hold for the long run. I just want to build my retirement nest egg over time. How can SMIGRM help me?

Answer: We personally love passive investing because we are not stock pickers but we also believe passive investing by itself is only a halfway solution. In other words, there is a lot of room to improve and we can seriously improve it! We are confident that SMIGRM is the exact missing piece for passive investing. This is because SMIGRM will help investors avoid the serious corrections and dangerous crashes that will make them waste valuable years catching up after a significant market downturn. In the first chapter of the book, we discussed extensively how SMIGRM is the missing piece for passive investors to be successful in the long run. Remember, the best way to climb out of a hole is by never falling in it in the first place. The main challenge in long-term investing is that a few market crashes are almost guaranteed to be encountered at some point. For a very reasonable cost, you can avoid the most serious ones and leave more money in your own pocket for your retirement.

Here is a perfect analogy for stocks held for a long time. Imagine you are on the beach and watching the waves coming to shore. The waves come and go. In this case, we can pretend that the coming wave is the stock price going up and bringing you profits. But soon, the same wave turned back to the ocean, taking with it your profits. Before you sell and realize your profits, while you are still holding the stock, every profit you gained is unrealized. They can go away just as easily. They are not real profits. They are just numbers on a computer. They would only become real profits in your pocket when you actually sell the stocks for cash, realizing the profits. So this is what happens for investors holding assets for the long run: waves come with profits and waves go away with them. And the cycle repeats over and over like waves on the beach. The catch: from time to time, especially after riding a long bull market, you want to lock your profits in. You don't want the next receding wave to take them back to the ocean. Do you want to know when will be the best times to lock them in? The RISP 500™ will provide that answer.

I am a professional stock picker and I love building my own portfolio of stocks. I have been successful doing so. How can SMIGRM help me?

Answer: Great! You should always do what you do best and we cherish you for your success. We tested and showed strategies involving index ETFs (Strategies 1 through 8) because they are easy to trade, liquid, and represent the overall market universe well with the most relevant stocks in highly diversified portfolios. However, we could have picked individual stocks or a portfolio of stocks too. We don't know your portfolio to know exactly how successful you would be with SMIGRM but we strongly believe the guidance of RISP 500™ will help you outperform your current investments without it. The market timing information per se will help you protect your portfolio when needed and ride the rallies when the stock market is on a bullish mode. You may want to introduce Beta to test it with RISP 500™ to find the right adjustments to fit your portfolio. This is just an idea, a suggestion, but we have not done that test ourselves.

I am a day trader / swing trader. Can SMIGRM help me?

Answer: It absolutely can. We suggest subscribing to the All Day Long Real-Time RISP 500™ if you are a day trader or a swing trader. It will give you minute by minute updates about risks measured in real-time. As you become familiar with the RISP 500™ tool, you will know how to create setpoints (or RPTs) for entry and exit to/from the market for each of the assets you trade, executing your own trading tactics. In other words, you will be able to fine-tune market timing decisions with it in tandem with any other trading tools and methods you currently have.

I have avoided investing in stocks all my life. I tried it once and hated the experience. Should I keep avoiding it? Can SMIGRM help with my fears? I'm super-conservative; I only want to have a decent retirement.

Answer: We completely understand you. The most prudent thing to do after a bad experience is to avoid it. We believe that what happened to you happens to everyone, ourselves included. Nobody likes to lose money and we have been there ourselves, too. We also believe that probably the problem you encountered was not having the right tools. This wasn't your fault. If you think about it, traditional methods like fundamental analysis and technical analysis help you with many things but aren't great tools to help you deal with losses. Even traditional risk management often helped *after* losses had already happened. As I said, we have been there too and losing scared the hell out of us. That is exactly why we developed the SMIGRM method. The primary goal of SMIGRM is to help detect dangerous downturns early, still in their process of formation. This way, every early loss will be cut small. We totally understand that the first *sine qua non* condition to long-term successful investing is survival in the game. Therefore, SMIGRM was developed with the goal to improve long-term survival odds front and center and firmly built in.

We believe you should not avoid the stock market for fear if you now have the right tool to deal with your worst enemies: wrong timing, market crashes and losses resulting from them. Traditionally, the U.S. stock market has been a must have for people building retirement nest eggs. This is because of its long-term returns helping people build on their retirement savings. With the right tool helping to avoid the negative side of it, you can more confidently explore the positive side of it.

I'm a busy person and I normally don't have time to make my own investments or even to strategize or plan them. Can SMIGRM help someone like me?

Answer: Actually, the subscription model and the nature of SMIGRM are perfect for busy investors, who don't have time to study, manage or even plan their investments. With the RISP 500™ subscription model, all you need is less than 5 minutes a day. We believe most people, even the busiest ones, can afford 5 minutes a day to care for their own finances, can't they? All they need to do is open their email and see the RISP 500™ percentile rank number once a day. Just one number and it will tell you whether you need to do one trade or not. If you do, you can just log in to your brokerage account and give the order to execute the trade online. That's it. It won't take more than 5 minutes for the entire daily routine. Most of the days, however, there is no trade to execute at all; so it's just the time to open one email. You won't even need to formulate a new investment strategy or make a financial plan. If you want, you can simply follow one or more of our 8 strategies that best fit your goals and risk tolerance. It's that easy if you are too busy to make elaborate plans.

Are you licensed investment advisors?

Answer: Nope. The authors are not licensed and don't offer any investment advice nor sell any securities. Risk Scientific LLC is a risk management solutions and financial education firm.

Do you recommend DIY or working with a financial advisor? Can RISP 500™ replace my advisor?

Answer: This is entirely up to you to decide. We cannot offer a recommendation one way or another. If you are working with financial advisors, SMIGRM can be your best ally to help you make sure that your advisors:

a) are really good professionals. Like in any services field, quality varies widely.
b) are putting your best interests first (fiduciary relationship).
c) are obtaining the best results possible for the amount of risk taken for your money.

Great advisors are worth every dollar of their fees. Unfortunately, not everyone is, just like in any profession. With SMIGRM, you will be able to make that distinction by comparison. You can simply follow the RISP 500™ for a small portion of your portfolio and over time compare its results with the results your advisors are obtaining for you. You can also share this book with them. Some advisors may show some resistance because they are not very versed with the VIX world, options, volatility, and derivatives, which is okay. If they read the book, they will learn and make a powerful addition to their toolbox. The SMIGRM has also been designed to be a great tool for financial advisors or wealth managers to use to help their clients.

What is the best trade execution time after reading the daily RISP 500™?

Answer: While there is not an exact answer, we understand it is a very valid question. We recommend executing trades right after you read the daily RISP 500™, if there is an action to take. Remember that there won't be any action to take in most days. The reason is that RISP 500™ is an instant snapshot of the risks in the market at the moment it is measured. It changes with the market and time, especially during volatile market days. It's like taking your body temperature to decide whether you should take medication for fever. If you measured 102° F (38.9° C), for example, you may want to take it right away, not wait an hour or two later. It's the exact same principle here.

Can RISP 500™ predict future stock prices? What about predicting the same day or the next day?

Answer: SMIGRM is not about making any kind of future projection or forecasting future values or prices. SMIGRM is about measuring risks at the present time, which is much more reliable than any forecast, even if it's just for 1 day. Having said that, a high RISP 500™ percentile rank is associated with a higher probability for the stock market to go down and a low RISP 500™ percentile rank is associated with a higher probability for the stock market to go up. But a probability is only a probability, not a certainty. Otherwise, it would be a crystal ball but it is not. Therefore, it's perfectly possible and even normal to have a day in which the market is rallying while the RISP 500™ percentile rank is high. Nevertheless, over a long period of time, statistically, such days should be rare. We live in a probabilistic world and we should treat it as such.

I'm undecided about what RPT to choose; can you help?

Answer: You can start testing a RPT and over time make changes as appropriate to fit not only your personal risk tolerance but also your goals and needs. We can make a suggestion for the starting RPT according to your return-risk profile:

- Conservative investor: 70%
- Moderate investor: 75% or 80%
- Aggressive investor: 85% or 90%

Watch your performance results and the market behavior. Over time, you will have a better sensibility to make adjustments to your RPT. You can test further by adjusting notches higher or lower accordingly.

May I use RPT my way? For example: Fast Exit, Faster Reentry?

Answer: Yes. SMIGRM is a method and the RISP 500™ is a tool. As such, you have the power to use it any way you like or customize it for your own needs and goals. Yes, you can get creative! We have seen users who use different RPTs such as a low RPT to rotate to safety quickly when risks rise and a higher RPT to signal a return to risk assets faster when risks fall. Again, it's your tool and you have every right to be creative! Please share your experience and success stories with us! We would love to hear from you. E-mail us at admin@risp500.com.

Is RISP 500™ only for traders?

Answer: No, any investor who wants results and more return with less risks can benefit from SMIGRM and the guidance of the RISP 500™ tool. SMIGRM is all about maximizing RoMaD, which in other words, is all about making sure you are getting the most reward possible for the risks you are taking.

Why don't you sell trading signals in a subscription?

Answer: We know that there are others using similar models selling subscriptions for trading signals. The problem with trading signals is that there is little room for customization and creativity. The investment assets have been pre-selected for you. You basically follow what they are doing trying to replicate their results. It also treats everyone the same, regardless of their risk tolerance. What we do through Risk Scientific LLC is very different. It's a different vision and concept. Our purpose is to deliver a risk management tool with a set of concepts (the pillars described in chapter 1) consolidated in a method we called SMIGRM. As a tool, it gives users a wide spectrum of possibilities, many of which not even we have envisioned before. Many of you already have your own preferred strategies so the addition of the RISP 500™ tool will only improve what you already do. If you don't have a preferred existing strategy, you can replicate one of ours (Strategies 1 through 8) or get inspired to create your own. Let your creativity fly! Test your ideas seeing how they work with RISP 500™. Make adjustments as necessary. You may well obtain even better results than ours!

What is the role of Risk Scientific LLC?

Answer: Risk Scientific LLC, based in Wyoming, is the risk management solutions company in charge of running the algorithm that powers the RISP 500™. It provides customized solutions to wealth management firms and investment professionals.

Do you offer a free trial period?

Answer: Yes, the subscription programs are managed by Risk Scientific LLC and it offers a free trial period.

Do I need to subscribe for the All Day Long Real-Time RISP 500™?

Answer: It depends on your needs and goals. Generally, however, individual investors don't need All Day Long Real-Time RISP 500™. Note that all performance results shown in this book for both back-testing and live trading have been obtained with reading the RISP 500™ once a day only and taking action, when necessary, also once a day. This was done with the explicit purpose of proving that measuring the risk once a day is perfectly sufficient to produce excellent results. Most investors, who aren't professional wealth managers, simply don't have the time to be watching screens and trading all day. However, professional wealth managers looking for an edge to outperform their competition and professional traders, especially day traders, swing traders, option traders, and those who manage large accounts with sizeable amounts at risk, should seriously consider subscribing the All Day Long Real-Time RISP 500™.

What if I don't subscribe to RISP 500™? Is it possible to DIY with some of the indicators the algorithm reads?

Answer: It depends on your goals. If you just want to invest passively for the long run very inexpensively, more concerned about capital preservation, can afford to lose money, and have no ambitious goals, you may DIY with some of the indicators we described in The Science Behind the RISP 500™ Algorithm chapter in the book. As you know, our algorithm takes in at least 15 variables to produce the RISP 500™. Anything less will probably not produce the same results. Risk Scientific LLC will offer affordable options for those concerned about cost but realize that losses from corrections and crashes can quickly and easily cost you a LOT more!

Can you summarize why SMIGRM is beating mainstream traditional methods?

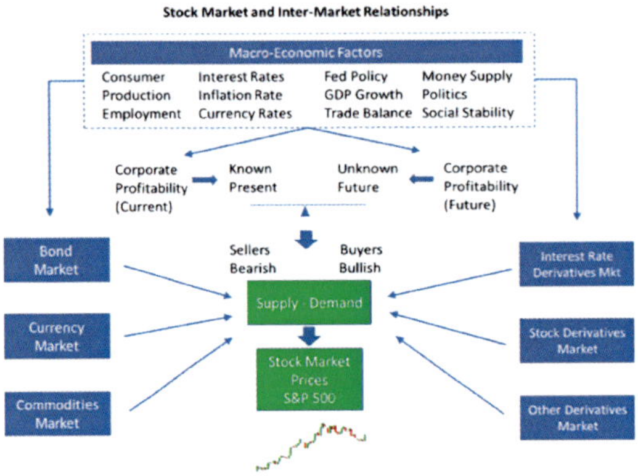

Answer: If you have invested in the past and used a few different methods to guide your investment decisions, you would have already realized that it's totally impossible to factor in everything that may affect stock prices. As you can see in the diagram, the number of factors that can influence stock prices is gigantic and no model or method can capture them all. SMIGRM is no exception but here is the ace in the hole: the RISP 500™ algorithm captures the information closest to the action – at the supply and demand for stocks and for hedge. This is where information from all sources are most consolidated. This is also where buy and sell decisions by the collective of all market participants, big and small, are taking real action, betting on their convictions with real money on the table. After all, what ultimately moves prices are supply and demand.

In addition, risk is rarely at the center of mainstream methods, even though taking risk is what really gives the investor the possibility of earning a return. But they are more concerned about a company's profitability and the economy than risk. Thus, these methods treat the investment world as deterministic, while in fact, it is probabilistic.

SMIGRM, on the other hand, incorporates the concept of Risk Context-Dependent Dynamic Asset Allocation and the trio Statistical Edge + Asymmetrical Payoff + Law of Large Numbers, all built inside the model framework. In layman's terms, the relative risk measured at every moment (the RISP 500™ Percentile Rank) provides a proxy for the odds for the market at that moment. If the risk is greater than your chosen RPT, it means that the odds for the market to end up the day lower is greater than the odds for it to end up higher, given your own risk tolerance. If you play this game every day, **only taking risk when the odds favor you**, after a long period of time, your statistical edge should pay off beautifully for you.

Remember Roger Federer's 4% win rate edge? That is SMIGRM in essence.

FAQ for Wealth Managers

I'm a manager based outside the United States and I never invested in American stocks. Why should I?

Answer: The U.S. stock market has had an enviable performance record and it's home to the largest and most influential companies in the world. With the RISP 500™ now you can easily and confidently invest in the U.S. even if you have never bought a single American stock before. Think of your clients. They deserve the best. Diversify your investments.

Are you going to execute trades for my firm and manage my clients' funds?

Answer: No, not even if you sign up the Full Trading Desk package. We will send you timely information for you to execute the trades in your firm. We help control your risks and P/L and will prepare daily reports but we never touch your money.

Are you licensed investment advisors or wealth managers?

Answer: Although we are retired professional traders with many years of battlefield experience in large trading floors at international banks, Risk Scientific LLC is a risk management solutions company. We are not an investment firm nor an investment adviser. The RISP 500™ is a risk management tool designed to help investors and wealth managers protect their clients' money first and foremost. Our goal is also to empower managers and investors with tools that can actually give them an edge over their competitors and deliver outstanding results to their clients.

What is the cost of your services? Do you offer a free trial?

Answer: Yes! We do offer a free trial period. The cost of services depends on the needs of each client. We work on customized pricing because our services are 100% customized to each client. Contact us by email at **VIPclientservice@risp500.com** to discuss how we can help!

Photo: iStock by Getty Images

SPECIAL

Next Developments for the RISP 500™

The Future is Right Upon Us

Risk Scientific LLC is definitely embracing the adoption of **Artificial Intelligence (Generative AI) with Machine Learning (Deep Learning)** for the continuous development of the RISP 500™ project. When it was first started many years ago, such technologies were still at their infancy, so everything was built everything "manually". As you know, we are constantly mining data and testing many strategies (way more than the 8 strategies shown in this book) on a live trading mode and back-testing too. In time, we will share with our students new strategies that pass minimum quality tests and which we believe can help investors gain an edge in the markets.

GPT-4o is already helping us with data collection, processing, dataset filtration, visualization, and drawing insights from datasets. It is also helping us do some cross-validation to assess the model's performance across different datasets (different assets, time periods, etc.) and parameter optimization. It's way faster and more accurate than previous LLMs (Large Language Models). But this is just the beginning and the tip of the iceberg; we are fully committed to evolve with the new and exciting world of new technologies. We are all about evolution and progress, challenging the status quo. These are the next steps we are planning to incorporate in our routine in the coming future:

- Use **GPT-4o's VSL** (Visual to Language model) to read and interpret all types of charts for us and integrate it with our existing analytic tools and models for data analysis.

- Test, refine, and implement **Machine Learning** algorithms to pair with the RISP 500™ model algorithm and help it improve and expand its current capabilities and reach. The learning process involves statistical models to identify patterns and relationships within the data that we may have missed earlier.

- Test analytics techniques or approaches for **Generative AI** and **Deep Learning**'s data learning capabilities to help us test new hypotheses and identify trends with its predictive analytics in time series data.

- In addition to new technologies, as said earlier, we are also testing multiple strategies to explore the application of the RISP 500™. Here are some of the main initiatives we are currently working on (at the time of this writing):

    - Testing **Variable RPTs** in response to contextual variables and potential market indicators to maximize RoMaD.

    - Testing **strategies to better explore sideways markets** (volatile and not volatile) with no clear trend. Under the guidance of the RISP 500™, options strategies such as strangles, straddles, spreads, iron condors, boxes, etc. can deliver great results when the market is moving sideways. Making money in no trend markets helps neutralizing any whipsaw effect in RISP 500™ signaling and improve the overall investment performance.

We Provide 100% Customized Services to Funds and Wealth Management Firms

Are you ready to take your investment management business to the next level with the RISP 500™?

We are here to help you all the way to outperformance. Your clients deserve only the very best, never forget that. You want the best tools you can possibly land your hands on to deliver the best investing performance results possible. As our client, you deserve the best too, so we strive to deliver the best service possible to you if you sign up with us.

We designed 5 levels of services 100% customizable to meet your unique needs. Send us a message so that we start answering your questions and establish a relationship. We offer a free trial period so you have the opportunity to experience what it is like to receive the RISP 500™ measured every day in your mailbox. This is information you can start acting upon and make money even during the trial period.

5 LEVELS OF SERVICES 100% CUSTOMIZED FOR WEALTH MANAGEMENT FIRMS

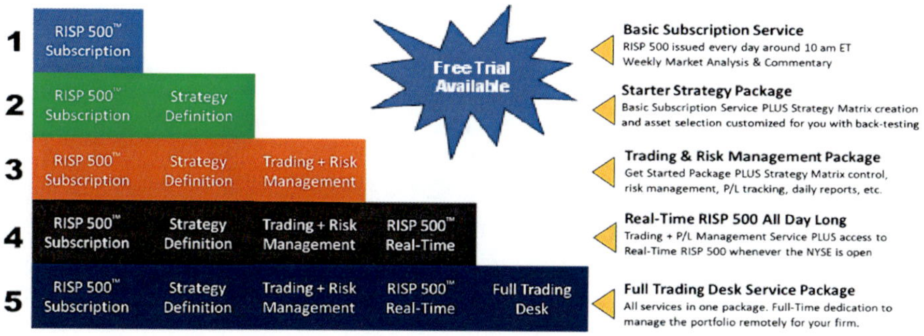

E-Mail: VIPclientservice@risp500.com

www.RISP500.com

Performance Acceleration Mentorship Coaching Programs

We understand that everyone has a different learning style, has a unique blend of needs and goals, and may be at a different point on the learning curve. For this reason, we are offering mentorship coaching programs to help those who want a more personalized experience and one-on-one coaching environment in a small community of like-minded learners on the same journey to outperformance. Mentorship is focused on implementation and goals based.

For more information, be sure to sign up for our free newsletter to be informed of new programs and other educational resources on our website: www.engineering-finance.com.

Customized Services to Financial Advisors, Professional Investors, Wealth Management Firms and Fund Managers

Risk Scientific LLC, owner of RISP 500™, offers special services to financial advisors, professional investors, wealth management firms, and fund managers. Contact us by email: VIPclientservice@risp500.com.

Final Words of Gratitude

I hope I was able to meet your expectations when you set out to read this book. Writing the book took me months, but I hope I was able to deliver real value to you. I also hope you will be able to make good use of what you learned here to transform your life, if you are an investor, or the life of your clients, if you are a wealth manager.

I would like to offer my words of gratitude for your trust. After "speaking" so much, now I wish to hear what you have to say. I only ask you to leave me your honest assessment as feedback to help me improve myself as an author and communicator. I truly value what you think! I would very much appreciate an honest review on Amazon:

https://www.Amazon.com/review/create-review?&asin=1960691104

Your input will guide my next steps to create better content, make changes, improve, and better help everyone.

Thank you! 😊

Sidney Shauy, MBA

Made in United States
North Haven, CT
22 October 2024

59324183R00131